BOW LAKE

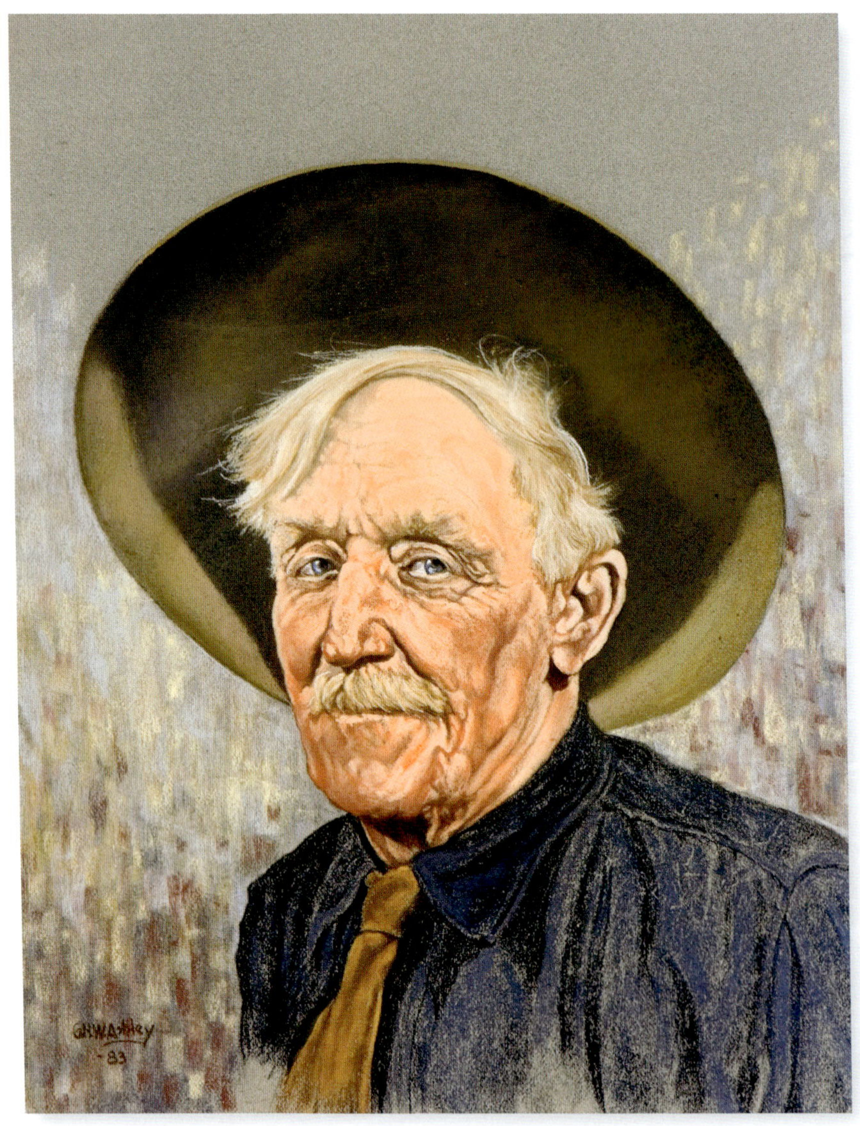

G.H.W. (Herb) Ashley, *Jimmy Simpson,* 1983. Pastel, 65.0 x 50.0 cm. Collection of the Whyte Museum of the Canadian Rockies.

BOW LAKE

Wellspring of Art

JANE LYTTON GOOCH

PREFACE BY ROBERT SANDFORD

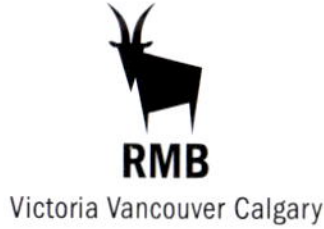

Victoria Vancouver Calgary

Rocky Mountain Books
www.rmbooks.com

Library and Archives Canada Cataloguing in Publication

Gooch, Jane Lytton
Bow Lake : wellspring of art / Jane Lytton Gooch.

Includes bibliographical references and index.
ISBN 978-1-926855-05-9

1. Bow Lake (Alta.)—In art. 2. Landscape painting, Canadian—Alberta—Bow Lake. I. Title.

ND1352.C36G66 2010 758'.1712332 C2010-902815-5

Front cover image: Alice Saltiel-Marshall, *Crowfoot Mountain through the Looking Glass.*
Back cover image: G.H.W. (Herb) Ashley, *Jimmy Simpson.* Collection of the Whyte Museum of the Canadian Rockies.

Printed in Canada

Rocky Mountain Books acknowledges the financial support for its publishing program from the Government of Canada through the Canada Book Fund (CBF), Canada Council for the Arts, and the province of British Columbia through the British Columbia Arts Council and the Book Publishing Tax Credit.

Canada Council for the Arts Conseil des Arts du Canada

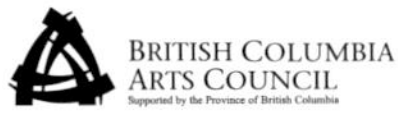

This book was produced using FSC-certified, acid-free paper, processed chlorine free and printed with vegetable-based inks.

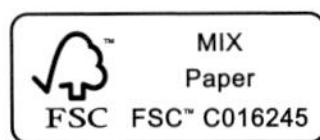

Acknowledgements

Many people have given me moral support and practical assistance from the beginning to the end of this project. My family and friends have offered encouragement, making discreet inquiries about progress on writing the manuscript. My husband, Bryan, has answered bibliographical questions, discovered websites with Bow Lake paintings and proofread the final draft. My son Arthur has provided valuable computer expertise, and his younger brother, Robert, has hiked the trails around Bow Lake with me on many occasions.

The idea for a book on the art of Bow Lake came from the artist Max Elliott. Following the publication of my volume *Artists of the Rockies: Inspiration of Lake O'Hara*, Max envisioned a similar book about Bow Lake. In April 2004 she brought me, Lee O'Donnell, innkeeper of Num-Ti-Jah at the time, and Roy Andersen, a Banff photographer, together for a memorable meeting, sitting in the spring sunshine outside Num-Ti-Jah Lodge surrounded by piles of lingering snow. The combined efforts of Lee and Max, with the support of the lodge owner, Tim Whyte, have resulted in a significant collection of art at Num-Ti-Jah. Roy photographed many of these paintings in the lodge's collection for the book, and other paintings as well, and he is always ready to help when additional photographs are needed, sometimes travelling many miles.

Quyen Hoang of the Glenbow Museum has provided much valuable assistance over the years by locating paintings in the vast collection and arranging for photography. She was also immensely helpful in sending me the list of works in the Simpson Collection. Steve Waite of the Glenbow promptly sorted out some final details with respect to documentation, and Lia Melemenis coordinated the digital images. Paula Swann at the Leighton Centre has graciously given me copyright permission, and Pamela Clark of the Art Gallery of Alberta has facilitated the reproduction of A.C. Leighton's untitled image of Bow Lake. Lena Goon and Elizabeth Kundert-Cameron in the Archives of the Whyte Museum have been outstanding in their willingness to find materials and answer my numerous questions. In the photography department at the Whyte, D.L. Cameron and Craig Richards have provided many digital images, and in the art department, Lindsay Maynard, Deserae Komar and Michale Lang have been very helpful. The account of the Panabakers' expedition up the Bow River is possible because their daughter, Frances Schwenger, made their journal entries available to me. The University of British Columbia's Rare Books and Special Collections department gave me access to some crucial sources for my research, and Dominique Yupangco of the English Department at UBC and Henry He of True Colours generously provided technical assistance.

Bob Sandford's continued support of my research is evident in his willingness to write another fine preface, despite the demands of his own writing. Without question, this book would not have been possible without the co-operation and enthusiastic support of the owners of paintings, the holders of copyright and especially the artists who enrich our lives with their images of the alpine landscape.

Finally, my thanks go to Don Gorman of Rocky Mountain Books for guiding me patiently and cheerfully through the publication process.

Dedication

"To all who treasure the mountains"

Contents

Map 8

Preface 9

Introduction 15

Plates & Commentary 74

Notes 182

List of Artists 185

Bibliography 187

Index 190

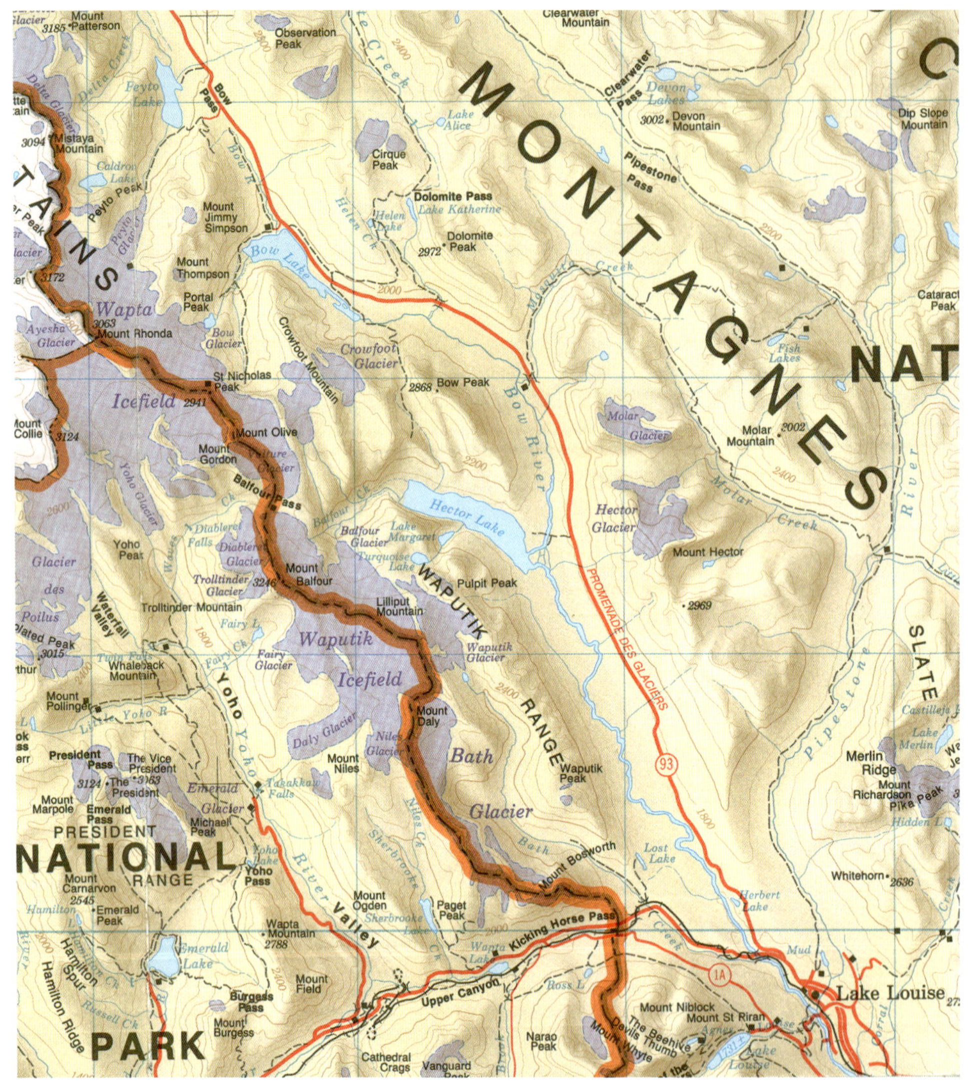

Map based on portion of Banff, Kootenay and Yoho national parks, *Atlas of Canada*, MCR 220 (Ottawa: Department of Energy, Mines & Resources, 1985), reproduced with permission.

Preface

THIS IS JANE GOOCH'S THIRD BOOK celebrating paintings of specific landscapes that have drawn her back again and again to her beloved Canadian Rockies. As with her earlier volumes, on Lake O'Hara and Mount Assiniboine, this book is comprised of selected works of art created by painters over the past five generations who possessed an uncommon ability to capture the aesthetic drama and sense of place that have made the main ranges of the Rocky Mountains a famous place to live in and visit. This volume, however, differs from the previous two in a fundamental way.

Lake O'Hara and Mount Assiniboine are wilderness shrines, places of extraordinary natural power that are divorced from the rest of the West by their remoteness and the degree of protection they enjoy. Visitation to these places is carefully managed. Because one has to make a ritual or actual sacrifice to go there, the spiritual quality of the experience is heightened. While Bow Lake is every bit as beautiful in its own way as Lake O'Hara or Mount Assiniboine, it has the distinction of being not only a readily accessible natural feature in a famous national park and World Heritage Site, but also the headwaters of one the most heavily used rivers in the Canadian West. That the Bow, the stream that has its origins at Bow Lake, is also under silent threat adds greater poignancy to the works of art Gooch has selected to portray the lake's spectacular nature and changing character.

While a casual, one-time visitor may not notice, the paintings Gooch has selected clearly demonstrate that the Bow Glacier, which provides the water to fill the lake and sustains the flow of the river, has been quietly disappearing for more than a century. Thus, for the more than one million Canadians who live downstream from Bow Lake, this fascinating assemblage of images is more than a compendium of some of our nation's art treasures. These paintings are telling us something vitally important about what is happening to our world. They illustrate the progression of the landscape change that has been happening on a massive scale in the mountain West over the last one hundred years. The rate of this change poses a challenge not just for the people who live in the Bow River basin but for art itself.

In this book Gooch homes in on essential questions concerning the transience and preciousness of earthly beauty. Collectively these images mark a point at which art and history become indistinguishable, for the one is completely embedded in the other. These images force us to ask what art will mean in the context of history as our glaciers disappear and the snowpack and snowcover that have created them are diminished. One wonders how we will relate to the images we grew up with as a nation when they no longer represent the place where we live. What will these paintings mean to us when the world they portray no longer exists?

If, in the future, we discover that an irrevocable increase in CO_2 has in fact altered the nature and function of our planet's atmosphere and put an end to nature as we know it, what will this knowledge mean to our sense of place? If we have changed the very nature of the world in which we live, what does that mean for the relevance of history, natural or otherwise? How will that realization influence our historical connection to the world as expressed by our art? How will the structure and function of our economic systems change? How will the meaning and value of our political institutions as they are presently ordered be affected?

Jane Gooch knows the power of mountain places and knows how water in all its forms contributes to that power. The landscapes pictured in each of the paintings she has selected were all fashioned by ice. It could not be otherwise at Bow Lake. In the last million years the place we now know as Bow Lake was shaped by no fewer than four major glacial periods and perhaps as many as 20 minor glacial advances. It was this ice that gave the peaks in many of the paintings in this book their sharp relief.

At the end of the last ice age, the Bow Glacier was two kilometres, or about a mile, deep and extended all the way to where Calgary is today. The paintings in this book are testimony to the glacier's past and present glory and to its decline. There is an enormous valley between the lake and the glacier headwall that only very recently was filled with ice. To borrow from the poet Earle Birney, the receding glacier has created a valley so big the moon could be rolled in it. Those who have walked to the ever-farther glacier will have observed that the distance between today's lake and the ice is foreshortened in almost all contemporary paintings.

The meltwaters of the Bow Glacier and the nearby Crowfoot Glacier are more than just an aesthetic attraction. They are crucial to the flow of the Bow River. In low-flow years, glacial melt in the upper reaches of the Bow Valley, including Lake Louise, supplies just over 10 per cent of the summer flows of the Bow at Banff. But in drought years, up to half of the late-summer flow of this river is produced by glacial melt along the Great Divide of the Rockies. We know from the paintings, however, that the Bow Glacier and the icefield from which it flows are receding at startling rates. Though we act as though we were the first to discover this, the fact of rapid glacial recession has been obvious for a very long time. It is interesting to note that it was an artist and not a scientist who made this discovery.

Jimmy Simpson was an early packer and horse guide who came to the Rockies in the last decade of the 19th century. I can say from meeting him before he died that he was a real character. In 1920 Simpson applied to the Parks Branch for the lease of five acres on the shores of Bow Lake, one of his favourite camping sites. Parks officials notified him that he could only be granted a lease with the proviso that $5,000 worth of improvements be made to the site. Using the stunted trees of the high altitude of Bow Lake, Simpson designed and built an octagonal structure, the Ram Pasture, with sides no wider that ten feet. Windows and doors required for finishing the interior were hauled in by horse from the CPR line at Lake Louise. As Gooch explains, years later when the Banff–Jasper highway was completed past Bow Lake, Simpson constructed the much larger Num-Ti-Jah Lodge, named after the Stoney word for pine marten, an animal Simpson had trapped abundantly during his early years in the fur trade.

The first cabins were not completed until 1922, and it wasn't until a year later that Simpson was able to entertain his first paying guests, an expedition of mountaineers bound for the Columbia Icefield.

Simpson predicted, however, that it wouldn't be long before the automobile would change the Rockies forever. He also foretold that the Bow Glacier was about to disappear. He was right on both counts.

As Jane Gooch points out, Jimmy Simpson, besides being a famous hunter, was a fine watercolourist who had a good eye for local landscape. He painted widely in the Rockies, as is evidenced by the presence of his work in Gooch's earlier book on Mount Assiniboine. His interest in art also attracted other painters to Bow Lake. Painting, Simpson would have been the first to tell you, teaches one to see with penetrating intent. It is not surprising that nearly 60 years ago Simpson had already observed the rapid recession of the Bow Glacier.

In an interview with Peter and Catharine Whyte on March 30, 1952, Simpson gave the glacier 50 to 100 years before it melted over the horizon. He predicted that other glaciers along the Divide would also melt and that Lake Louise and Bow Lake would become sinkholes. He foresaw that, as a result of the glacial melt, the prairies would have trouble with water supply.

Simpson and the Whytes concluded that they lived in the best of times and that they wouldn't want to be around to witness the kind of West that would exist after the glaciers disappeared. Unfortunately perhaps for us, however, we are around and are witnessing the changes Simpson saw coming.

Over the lifetimes of the artists whose work is presented in this book, one-quarter of the glacial mass in the Western cordillera has disappeared. Scientists recently released research findings that demonstrate that as many as 300 glaciers disappeared in the Canadian Rockies between 1920 and 2005. Climbing routes on the icefield that forms Bow Lake are now changing faster than guidebooks can keep up. Many climbers are also observing dramatic changes in the amount of rockfall on many routes as higher temperatures melt the ice that holds broken rock to the mountainsides.

Preliminary scientific analyses suggest that at rates of melt that have occurred over the past four decades, the Bow Glacier may disappear completely within about 50 years. The nearby Crowfoot Glacier, featured in many of the paintings Gooch has selected, may disappear decades sooner.

The science also corroborates Simpson's prediction about the effect of glacier melt on the prairies' water supply. The Bow River is 657 kilometres long. From its headwaters at Bow Lake to its confluence with the Oldman to form the South Saskatchewan River, it drains some 25,000 square kilometres, or about 4 per cent of Alberta's total land area. But although the Bow amounts to only 3 per cent of the water that flows on the surface of the province, its water serves an astounding 33 per cent of the province's population. In a way, the stunning beauty of the Bow's headwaters is somewhat misleading. From the moment the river leaves Banff National Park, every last drop of the water in it has been fully allocated to human ends.

Protecting the headwaters of the river in Banff National Park was a wise thing to have done, and not just for reasons of aesthetics. What is good for art is also good for nature. If a national park model of careful upper watershed management could be expanded outward from the Bow's protected headwaters and applied downstream as well, the West of the future could be a very different place. Not only would a more reliable water supply be assured, but the national park example could become a foundation for a truly sustainable Western Canadian society.

Until that dream is realized, however, we can only hope that the perceptual leadership provided by artists will encourage in society what history and science have not been able to elicit: the larger desire to prevent the landscapes of the mountain West that inspired a century of great art from disappearing before our very eyes.

With this book, Jane Gooch makes it clear that as long as Bow Glacier exists and Bow Lake still has water in it, artists will be painting it and in so doing will continue their timeless task of teaching the rest of us the meaning and value of place. Therein resides our hope.

Robert William Sandford
Canmore, Alberta
October 2010

Introduction

First European Explorer to Visit Bow Lake (1858)

Dr. James Hector

The recorded history of Bow Lake begins with the journal of Dr. James Hector, a member of the expedition organized by Captain John Palliser to explore British North America west of Lake Superior. Hector was given the responsibility for searching the Rocky Mountains to see if a pass suitable for transportation could be found through this formidable barrier. On Wednesday, September 8, 1858,[1] Hector and his companions left a Stoney camp near the base of Mount Hector and set out to follow the Bow River north to its source, hoping eventually to find the North Saskatchewan River and a pass leading across the Continental Divide to the west. A few days earlier, a Stoney hunter had discovered Hector's men, exhausted and starving, camped near the confluence of Bath Creek and the Bow River, east of Kicking Horse Pass. The hunter invited them to join the Stoneys about ten kilometres to the northwest, beside a small lake with a view of Mount Hector. When Hector's party arrived at the native encampment, the Stoney women welcomed them hospitably:

> Immediately on our arrival at camp, which was in a pretty, secluded spot, by the side of a mossy lake, the [native women] took the whole management of our affairs – unpacked the horses, put up the tent, lined it beautifully with pine foliage, lighted a fire, and cut wood into most conveniently sized billets, and piled them ready to hand. They then set about cooking us all sorts of Indian delicacies – moose nose and entrails, boiled blood and roast kidneys, &c.[2]

In the evening, the brother of Captain Palliser's guide came into camp and offered Hector some valuable advice: following the Bow River north to its source and down into the next valley would lead to Hector's goal, the North Saskatchewan River. The explorers would pass through valleys of ice dominated by spectacular peaks, on a trail made difficult by fallen timber and muskeg; the route also offered little game beyond white goats, which were inedible.[3]

Hector showed considerable courage in his willingness to continue explorations despite recent hardships. Hector and his men struggled to ascend the gorge of the Kicking Horse River on a perilous ledge so narrow that the laden horses scarcely had room to travel; one horse had to be rescued after tumbling off the trail and coming to rest on a tree projecting at a right angle from the cliff. The march to the eastern slopes of the mountains was necessary, though, to find game to feed his starving men. Before embarking on the trek along the canyon walls, Hector had been incapacitated for two days as a result of being kicked in the chest by his horse; the name given to the pass commemorates this almost fatal blow. Even though in pain and weak from lack of food, Hector successfully led his men over Kicking Horse Pass to an area of good pasture and better hunting. Nimrod, the Stoney guide, had just managed to track and shoot a moose, and Hector's men were enjoying the first full meal in many days when they were invited to join the Stoney camp. For Hector, famine was followed by fire when his tent burst into flames during the night. Undaunted by these misfortunes, he still set out to follow the Bow, hoping that a supply of dried moose meat would carry them through. Upon his departure, the Stoneys entrusted Hector with the care of an orphaned boy so that he could be reunited with other members of the band camping on the Kootenay Plains near the North Saskatchewan River.

Shortly after taking leave of the friendly Stoneys, Hector and his party experienced a severe snowstorm; the weather was so cold that they made winter camp that night in the valley of Hector Lake, with Goat Mountain (now Bow Peak) to the northwest. The next day, Thursday, September

9, on a trail with fewer trees and more open space, the men were able to travel easily. They covered 24 kilometres, crossing Bow Pass and descending to Mistaya Lake to camp. Hector, in his scientific fashion, provides the first recorded observations of the beauty of Bow Lake on the way to the pass:

> An hour's ride brought us to where Bow River dilates to form a narrow lake, the water of which was of a bright green colour. Two miles further we reached a second and larger lake, being two miles long and one broad. Along its western shore the mountains rise precipitously, except at one point where a narrow valley allows a short glacier to reach water's edge, being fed from the perpetual ice and snow that mantle the mountains in that direction. We kept along the east shore of the lake till it was terminated by an open prairie with a considerable slope, the surface of which is mossy, with many springs, from which the first waters of the Bow River rise. Ascending this prairie slope, we reached some open spruce woods, which clothe the valley, and halted just before the valley begins to descend to the north-west in lat. 51° 40' N. The altitude at this point is about 6,350 feet above the sea, being much higher than the height of land either at the Vermilion or Kicking Horse passes.[4]

Hector's description notes significant features of this landscape that carry on to inspire later explorers and artists: the lake's vibrant colour; the contrast between the spectacular cliffs to the west and the meadows to the east; and the glacier, later known as the Crowfoot Glacier, that extends to the water's edge. In addition, high on the pass leading north to a paradise for hunters and climbers, Hector remarks on the spring that is one of the sources of the Bow. All of the elements of alpine beauty are present – peaks, glaciers, lakes and meadows.

Hector and his men enjoyed the magnificent view from Bow Summit; they could see north for about 25 miles along a river valley with mountains jutting in from either side. On this high pass, the water separated, flowing into the great drainage systems of the North and South Saskatchewan rivers. Travelling about a mile along Bow Pass, the explorers came to a steep trail that led down to the "Little Fork," the Mistaya River. The men followed the river to Mistaya Lake, surrounded by trees with a glacier on the west side reaching almost to the water. On September 10, they passed the Waterfowl Lakes and, crossing to the left side of the valley, cut their way through fallen timber until they found the Howse River, just a short distance above where it joins the North Saskatchewan.[5] Here, Hector notes in his journal, they found "a very distinct trail,"[6] undoubtedly the path travelled by the Kootenays and David Thompson over the Howse Pass.[7] When the trail disappeared, Hector followed a tributary from the west that took them through a heavily forested area to Glacier Lake.[8] After a series of adventures while exploring the Lyell Glacier (in moccasins), climbing a mountain and skirting a forest fire caused by his men's carelessness, Hector decided to return to Fort Edmonton by way of Kootenay Plains.

Exploring North from Laggan Along the Bow River (1882–1893)

Tom Wilson

Twenty-four years later, in 1882, Howse Pass was under consideration as a possible route for the Canadian Pacific Railway (CPR). Major A.B. Rogers, intent on following Hector's path and surveying the pass, took his packer and personal assistant, Tom Wilson, into the swamps and burnt timber of the Bow River valley north of Laggan (Lake Louise). The tough Major Rogers lasted only two days before retreating, but before he left he promised Wilson a $50 reward to continue over Howse Pass and meet him on the Columbia River to the west. Wilson fulfilled his part of the bargain, but only after a 13-day struggle in which he was short of food and faced with the formidable obstacles of high water and fallen timber.[9]

The CPR line eventually went over Kicking Horse Pass instead, but Wilson's exploration north along the Bow would prove invaluable in 1887 when he started his own business. Wilson's first trip as a guide and outfitter included H.W. Calverley and Arthur Brearley, two Englishmen who wished to hunt for big game, a sport advertised by the CPR. Their exact route is unknown, but to find game they would have left the noise and burnt timber along the railway. The men probably went north, perhaps to the Kootenay Plains on the North Saskatchewan River. In the end, they returned over Howse Pass, where they encountered the same terrible conditions of Wilson's trip in 1882 that provided his $50 reward. Eventually, the horses could go no further, and consequently Wilson walked down the Blaeberry River to Moberly with his clients, returning later with hired men to chop a trail for the horses.[10]

Wilson's knowledge of the mountains along the railway increased through his work packing supplies for surveyors J.J. McArthur and W.S. Drewry, who, from 1889 until 1893, mapped the peaks close to the CPR mainline with a technique that involved taking photographs from mountain summits.[11] These photographs, an integral part of the Dominion Topographic Survey, helped to advertise the mountaineering challenges in the Canadian Rockies. Wilson's role was primarily to provide transportation and a comfortable camp at the mountain's base, but on occasion he would help carry the heavy photographic equipment up the mountain.[12] Wilson's work on the Topographic Survey gave him the knowledge to advise Philip Abbot and other climbers from the Appalachian Club.

Mount Hector: Lofty Summit North of Laggan (1895)

Abbot, Fay and Thompson

In his account of climbing Mount Hector in 1895, Philip Abbot notes Wilson's earlier experience climbing to 10,400 feet with the Canadian surveyors, and, further, the outfitter's assurance that the mountain could be climbed. Not only did Wilson offer the challenge of a first ascent of Mount Hector, but he could also describe the view west across the valley to an unexplored icefield, accessible by way of a col at the foot of a high peak, Mount Balfour.[13] These exciting prospects were offered to Abbot and two other members of the Appalachian Club, Dr. Charles Fay and Charles S. Thompson. In mid-summer 1895, laden with rucksacks, they enthusiastically left the railway station at Laggan on foot, with Wilson as their guide and a porter called Hiland who carried "an enormous and shapeless pack composed of the tin things and all the other articles which the rest of us refused to touch."[14]

At the beginning of his description of the climb in *Appalachia*, Abbot summarizes the club's two main accomplishments: for the first time, members had reached a summit without a climbing guide, and, in their struggle to reach the base of Hector, they had conquered great natural obstacles. The trail north of Laggan was developing the reputation of a hell that must be endured in order to reach the paradise of mountains, glaciers and lakes that lay beyond. The mountaineers' boyish eagerness faded after they spent over three hours in the burnt forest without shade, struggling over fallen timber and using their ice-axes for balance. Every 30 minutes they stopped to rest. When they finally left the blackened timber behind and moved onto easier terrain, mosquitoes assaulted them. They did not reach their camping place until 9 p.m. on that hot summer's night. And despite their fatigue, sleep was impossible because they had to cover all their exposed flesh, except the ends of their noses, to protect themselves from the mosquitoes that hovered noisily like "whole orchestras, shrill with rage."[15]

By the time Abbot was roused by Professor Fay at 3 a.m., his initial enthusiasm at Laggan, only a day earlier, seems to have fully evaporated in "the depressing chill of the dying night; the half-warmed and wholly unappetizing breakfast; the silence, not to say crustiness, of the other members of the party; [and] the unconfessed half-wish for some decent excuse for not starting at all...."[16] The climb itself encouraged the three men. They made steady progress up the limestone cliffs, snow fields and talus slopes until they could see over the edge of the southern buttress, where they were astonished to find a glacier sloping up to the peak of Mount Hector. The distant view of the mountain from the Laggan station had not prepared them for the surprise of the great glacier to the northwest. They climbed over the snow and reached the summit cautiously but without difficulty.

The view from Hector's peak was a revelation. The isolated position of the mountain and the elevation, at over 11,000 feet, suddenly rewarded them with a stunning prospect: "one unbroken wilderness of ice and snow and crag, an ocean without shores whose waves were mountain ranges."[17] Abbot marvelled at the magnificent panorama; on the west alone, the view stretched for 80 miles to the Selkirks. The western prospect also included their next challenge – Mount Balfour, a high peak rising from the Waputik Icefield on the Continental Divide and, like Hector, offering a panoramic view because of its isolation.

The descent from Hector's summit involved a tricky traverse of a gully where a misstep would have meant sliding down a chute and over a 1,000-foot precipice. The three climbers moved carefully, as Abbot humorously comments, "like the villains in a melodrama about to commit a crime."[18] Once past the gully and a bergschrund lower down, they could move quickly, occasionally sliding playfully down the soft snow patches. They reached their camp on the Bow River in time for a dinner of fresh trout. Wilson had waited anxiously for their return, and before hurrying away to Laggan, he gave them instructions on where to ford the Bow to establish a camp in preparation for their attempt on Balfour the next morning. Without their guide, crossing the swiftly running river proved too much for the tired climbers, and they abandoned their attempt. Abbot concludes with prophetic irony by saying that the sight of Mount Balfour from the summit of Hector haunts him, enticing him to return. The following summer, lured by the challenges of climbing, Abbot tragically fell from Mount Lefroy, becoming the first mountaineering fatality in the Canadian Rockies.

Through the Eyes of an Explorer, Mountaineer, Writer and Photographer (1895)

Walter Wilcox

Walter Wilcox explored the mountains and lakes near Lake Louise in 1894 with Samuel Allen. The pair had just completed the first ascent of Mount Temple when Dr. Charles Fay met them at the Lake Louise Chalet. Their achievement at Mount Temple prompted Fay to suggest that the Appalachian Club use the chalet as a base for its summer camp in 1895.[19] That summer, shortly after experienced mountaineers Abbot, Fay and Thompson successfully reached the summit of Mount Hector, Tom Wilson outfitted Wilcox to travel north of Lake Louise along the Bow. Wilson used his past experience to promote the wonderful region north of Laggan, saying that "few, if any, tourists"[20] had visited the Bow Lakes and the source of the Bow River. This intrigued Wilcox, who, despite having just returned from a gruelling 51-mile circuit of Mount Assiniboine early in August, was eager to take advantage of the remaining days of summer exploration. Just nine days after returning from Assiniboine, the energetic Wilcox ventured into the wilderness once more on August 14, with Bill Peyto as his guide and accompanied by Harry Lang and five horses.

Wilcox's endurance was second only to his appreciation of the natural beauty in the Rockies. Despite the hardships of trail life, his charming descriptions of his mountain travels entice the reader to follow. His original volume, *Camping in the Canadian Rockies* (1896), was so successful that Wilcox revised and enlarged it in *The Rockies of Canada* (1900) as his explorations increased. His text is illustrated with his own photographs, as he believed that pictures give a much better idea of the landscape than words. However, taking good photographs involved much labour in transporting the heavy camera, and much patience in waiting for just the right weather or for smoke from forest fires to dissipate.[21] Wilcox, through his sensitive, detailed descriptions and his stunning images, captivates the reader. His chapter on the Bow Lakes is the most appealing and most complete description of the area in the early accounts. Similar to the first mountaineers who ventured north of Laggan, Wilcox is drawn into the wilderness by his joy of exploring unknown territory and his hope of first ascents. He does not only concentrate, however, on the thrill of conquering high peaks, but also focuses on the beauty at lower elevations: meadows filled with wildflowers and lakes reflecting the surrounding mountains.

Wilcox begins his account of the Bow Lakes by placing them in the larger geographical context of the Waputehk (Waputik) Range, a Stoney name that means white goat.[22] For centuries, storms from the west produced heavy snow on the mountain ranges extending north from Kicking Horse Pass, resulting in vast icefields surrounding the high peaks along the Continental Divide. At various locations, above Hector, Bow and Peyto lakes for example, the glaciers project tongues of ice down into the valleys. To reach those lakes with the spectacular views of glaciers and peaks, the explorers first had to endure the same torturous trail north of Laggan that the Mount Hector climbers had struggled through just a few weeks earlier. Tom Wilson had guided the Hector trio on foot, encumbered with 30-pound packs, but they still made much better progress than this group of Peyto's accompanied by horses that required a good deal of chopping through fallen trees. Wilcox, usually enthusiastic, cannot find any redeeming features in this part of the journey:

> The less said about the first eleven or twelve miles the better. It is nothing but a continuous burnt forest where much of the timber has fallen and become inextricably crossed, and where the trail, when most needed, invariably disappears under a pile of logs. Though I had had two men cutting out the trail for several days, it required two days' march to reach the first Bow Lake, only a little more than ten miles in a straight line from Laggan.[23]

The trail followed an old tote road some of the time before disappearing into the burnt forest. This tote road may have dated from 1884 when James Ross, the head of construction for the CPR, initiated a survey of Howse Pass because the Kicking Horse route looked too difficult.[24] The tote path was now derelict, its previous existence evident only in some remnants of corduroy road and collapsed bridges. Camps for the men constructing the road were also apparent in the debris left behind: wooden boxes, tin cans and rusty stoves. The first camp of Wilcox and his two companions was found at the base of Mount Hector near the first, or lower, Bow Lake (now called Hector Lake), which had a view west to the ice sheet falling over the precipice down to the water, with Mount Balfour above. Most early accounts report excellent fishing in Hector Lake and Wilcox confirms that his party "caught all the trout that [they] could eat."[25]

Unlike Abbot and the other Appalachian Club members, who had been unsuccessful in finding a suitable place to ford the Bow River and reach the western shore of Hector Lake, Peyto and Wilcox were able to cross by both riding bareback on Peyto's horse. After a difficult walk of four miles to

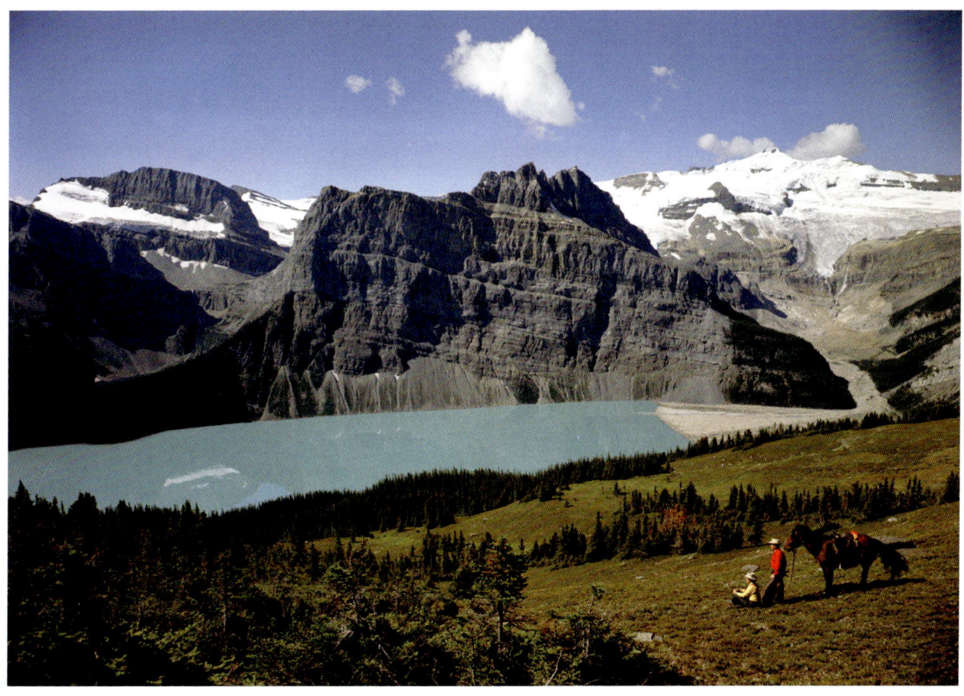

Nicholas Morant, Photograph of Hector Lake and Balfour Glacier, c.1961 (includes Willie Morant and Jimmy Simpson Jr.). Whyte Museum of the Canadian Rockies (v500/a5/z-47). Lake Margaret across Hector Lake in the cirque on the left; Mount Balfour's peak (3246 m) rising out of the glacier level with the lowest clouds.

the northern end of the lake, they found a gravel delta and a valley leading to a glacier descending from the Waputik icefield. From the glacier, they could see Mount Balfour covered with snow and ice, 5,000 feet above them. Wilcox describes the spectacular fingers of ice reaching down to the lake:

> The glaciers showed the lines of flow very clearly. Six converging streams of ice united to form the part on our right, while that on the left descended steeply and made a fine ice cascade. A waterfall poured gracefully over a dark precipice on the opposite side of the valley, and added a little life and motion to the dazzling expanse of snow.[26]

After exploring in the vicinity of Hector Lake, Peyto led the pack train to the Upper Bow Lake, or Cold Water Lake as Wilcox called it. The valley rises about 800 feet between the lower and the upper lakes. The Bow River at this point flows around the base of a partly isolated peak that is called Goat Mountain on Dawson's map of 1886 but which we now know as Bow Peak. Once past this prominent landmark, the two smaller lakes connected to Upper Bow Lake come into view. Here, one can see the striking Crowfoot Glacier:

> The approach to the Cold Water or Upper Bow Lake is full of interest. The trail leads out of a stunted wood into open moors, diversified by rock ridges and dry meadows in alternation. Above this comparatively level place a precipitous mountain stands on the west and shows a very fine escarpment which rises over three thousand feet from the valley. One of these glaciers, characteristic of that range, clings to the less precipitous parts of the cliff and descends in a three-pronged mass, resembling in outline the claws of an eagle. Soon after the open country is reached, the Cold Water Lake appears in the distance. In shape, size, and situation, it bears a striking resemblance to the Lower Bow Lake, but while the latter is comparatively uninteresting, the upper lake is one of the noblest and most beautiful of all those so far discovered in the Canadian Rockies.[27]

The trail to the upper lake passes through woods some distance from the water in order to avoid the swamps and muskeg caused by springs and streams running over moss. Muskeg here and on the trail below Hector Lake is the bane of a pack train's existence; a man can cross safely but a heavily laden horse will break through the surface vegetation and become mired in the mud, eventually unable to move. From a distance, the appearance of muskeg is deceptive, looking like a meadow of grass and reeds. On a subsequent trip over the same trail in July 1896, Wilcox describes how four horses had to be rescued from the bog, but not before their supplies were seriously depleted when half of the sugar, the tea and coffee, and most of the baking powder were dissolved.[28] This loss was significant because they were on a more ambitious expedition of 60 days, on which Wilcox, accompanied by Tom Lusk, Fred Stephens and Arthur Arnold, discovered a route to the Athabasca drainage system over Wilcox Pass.

On Wilcox's first visit to Bow Lake, Peyto led the pack train through the shallow water by the shore to find better footing on the gravel. The group set up camp about one-half mile from the upper end of the lake, near the stream that flows from Bow Pass. Peyto caught a five-pound trout just by fishing from the shore, and Wilcox predicts that Bow Lake, almost unknown to fishermen, would produce fish of considerable weight. In a later edition of *The Rockies of Canada* (1909), Wilcox reports on the excellent fishing in the Bow Lakes. The party of General Fred Pearson and Captain Dickerson, for example, caught just over 60 pounds of trout between September 13 and 18, 1898.[29]

From the men's camp on Bow Lake, the Bow Glacier was visible to the west, enticing them to explore the gorge that had an immense boulder wedged between its sides acting as a natural bridge. They climbed to the lower edge of the glacier, "a thin knife-edge on level ground,"[30] about one-half mile wide. Wilcox does not mention a waterfall, which suggests that the ice extended over the cliff where the Bow Falls are today. After the horrible trails approaching the Bow Lakes, Wilcox describes, in contrast, their departure to the northwest over undulating moors to a pass appearing more like a garden:

> ... a broad and meadowy lane leads nearly to the pass. The pass itself is a delightful region sixty-seven hundred feet above sea level. The broad valley slopes upwards in grand sweeps to the mountains east and west, and insensibly downward to the valleys north and south. Some very old spruces grow in scattered clumps or singly throughout pleasant meadows where myriads of mountain flowers make a bright colouring. Rivulets come from melting snows on the higher slopes or else burst from the ground in sparkling pools. One of those springs poured forth a constant stream of air bubbles, like a mineral spring. The trees are symmetrical, especially those that grow in the open, and the place resembles a carefully tended park rather than a bit of wilderness.[31]

The natural beauty of flowers, springs and trees is enhanced by the spectacular view from Bow Pass along a narrow valley, the Bear (or Mistaya) Creek, almost 60 miles to the northwest. Here, looking a thousand feet immediately below, the explorers could see the brilliant blue waters of Peyto Lake, which are fed by a glacier falling from the great Wapta snowfield to the west.

Attempt on Mount Balfour from the Upper Bow Valley (1897)

Collie, Dixon, Thompson, Baker, Fay, Sarbach and Peyto

After reaching the summit of Mount Hector in 1895, Abbot, Fay and Thompson could see Mount Balfour rising majestically from the Waputik icefield, just to the west beyond Hector Lake. However, their hopes to approach the peak by ascending the glacier above Hector Lake were thwarted by high water in the Bow River. Abbot vowed to return to Balfour, but as noted earlier he lost his life in a fall from Mount Lefroy on August 3, 1896.

To honour Abbot's memory, the Appalachian Club organized an international expedition of accomplished climbers to attempt Lefroy a year later on the same day. The party included two British climbers from the Alpine Club, J. Norman Collie and Harold B. Dixon, and a Swiss guide, Peter Sarbach. They made the first ascent of Lefroy from Lake Louise by climbing an icy chute known as the Death Trap. The view from the summit offered many unclimbed peaks for adventurous mountaineers, including two mountains that were prominent because of their unsurpassed height: Mount Assiniboine to the southeast and Mount Balfour to the north. Collie notes that their interest focused on Balfour because they planned to climb it in just a few days.[32] After a first ascent of Mount Victoria on August 5 by Collie, Fay, Michael and Sarbach, a larger expedition of nine climbers set out from Lake Louise to conquer Mount Balfour. Guide Bill Peyto had gone ahead over the trail of fallen trees and swamp with two men and most of the horses, expecting the climbers to catch up.

Four members of the expedition, Collie, Dixon, Thompson and Fay, have published accounts of this inauspicious trip; their tales focus on a number of misadventures, not the least of which was climbing the wrong mountain. The first problem occurred on the day of their departure, August 7, 1897, when they lost the trail through the muskeg north of Laggan, misled by upright stakes connected to the earlier railway survey.[33] Charles Thompson, a member of the Appalachian Club, has given us a lively account of the climbers' struggle to lead two horses through the swamp as the light faded:

> Just before dusk we came to open ground, a series of bogs or muskeags, old lake beds filled by ages of decomposing vegetation, moist and trembling beneath our tread, but during daylight tolerably safe. Across these muskeags there was no path, at best a stake or two – quite invisible when twilight came – working a way to the farther margin and the renewed trail. With increasing darkness our affairs grew steadily worse. We stumbled constantly through pools of shallow water; the horses floundered behind, often knee-deep in muck, at times stubbornly refusing to move. Then the end came. I stood with one horse upon a tussock of marsh grass, encircled by water, not daring to move. Somewhere before me Collie was calling for aid to Baker and Michael, saying that his horse was mired. Dixon was nursing a lame knee upon the dry root of a neighboring evergreen. Out in the Stygian blackness I heard Noyes splashing indefinitely to and fro. Fay and Parker, lightly loaded, had hastened

> on some time before, hoping thereby to find the camp and to send Peyto to our assistance. The would-be mountain climbers were undeniably prisoners in the swamp with dawn five hours away.[34]

Resigned to their fate, the climbers were astonished to hear a dog barking. After twenty minutes of silence, Peyto came into view to lead them to camp, leaving the horses and luggage to be extricated in daylight.

The next day was Sunday, and Peyto wisely gave his clients a day of relaxation, which they spent, according to Dixon, "in idleness at the Lower Bow Lake, bathing, fishing and photographing."[35] The decision to approach Balfour from Bow Lake instead of Hector Lake was wrong, as Collie admits in his 1903 narrative.[36] Charles Fay, who had seen Balfour from the summit of Mount Hector, later explained that the Americans' topographical knowledge was overruled by the greater climbing experience of their British companions, Collie and Dixon.[37] A steady march on the rainy Monday morning took them on a good trail around a spur of the Waputik Range (Bow Peak) and under the northern base of Mount Hector. Then, at about 2 p.m., the rain stopped and the mist rose to reveal a large meadow before them full of flowers freshly washed by the rain. Thompson describes the striking scenery of Bow Lake and Bow Pass:

> Beyond this great sweep of meadow up the valley lay the blue waters of the Upper Bow Lake, half hidden behind a forest of evergreens and sparkling in the afternoon wind. At its farther edge a snow-capped rock peak, still cloud encircled, stood side by side with another sweep of meadow land studded with clumps of trees, rising gently to the north. The warmth and brilliancy of a summer sun illuminated that harmony of green and blue, of gray and purest white. Heretofore I had seen the Canadian Rockies in their severest majesty, a majesty not untouched with grim desolation, with decay and death. Here they were softly beautiful, glowing with life.[38]

From their camp at the northern end of the lake where it bends to the west, the climbers could see the Bow Glacier extending from the Wapta Icefield, a region they hoped to be the first to explore. Early on Tuesday, August 10, they set out to climb Bow Glacier. The first obstacle was the tree-covered terminal moraine that extended the width of the gorge below the glacier. Dividing into two groups, Thompson and two companions climbed beside a gully that had been eroded by the stream from the glacier; they recognized the natural bridge created by an immense boulder that Wilcox had earlier described.[39] The other members of the group went up and over the moraine, where they crossed over the stones left by the retreating ice and stepped onto the lower part of the glacier below the first icefall:[40] the cliff now famous for Bow Falls. Crossing to the left, they scrambled up a steep lateral moraine with some difficulty because of the slippery mud and rolling stones. This brought them above the lower icefall and level with a terrace of ice between the lower and upper icefalls, the present location of Iceberg Lake. After some deliberation, they decided that the best route was directly over the glacier and up the icefall.

Two parties set out, led by Collie and Sarbach. They did not encounter problems until about halfway, when the crevasses became increasingly more dangerous. Thompson describes their search for a path through the maze of icy chasms as "a most thrilling and exciting hour" where to overcome the worst of the crevasses "Collie cut us down into the blue depths, and led us magnificently up an almost vertical ice face on the farther side."[41] Sarbach's party took a more conservative route to the right, finally overcoming the dangers of the icefalls by climbing up at the base of Portal Peak. Both groups reached the great icefield at the same time, so both could claim honours for being the first to set foot in this unexplored region. Thompson describes the scene before them:

> A rock-rimmed level ice-plain rising on the south into an almost perfect dome of white, and falling ever so slightly on the north toward two openings in the basin, the source of other great glaciers.… the only visible mountain that could possibly be Balfour was a sharp peak on the southern rim continuous with the snow dome.[42]

The climbers eagerly hurried toward the peak, reaching its base where a V-shaped opening in the escarpment, which they named Vulture Col, allowed them a splendid view of glaciers descending to Hector Lake. They made an easy ascent to the right of the col, reaching the summit at 12:50 p.m., only to discover that the peak was not Balfour at all. Balfour was four miles away, too far for them to attempt. They christened the mountain that they had climbed Aberdeen after the Governor General, the Earl of Aberdeen, but another mountain near Lake Louise already bore that name, and, as a result, the peak was subsequently called Gordon, to honour the family name of the Governor General, Sir John Campbell Hamilton Gordon. The climbers also named a mountain to the northeast Mount Olive because of the greenish colour of rocks near the peak. They happily spent an hour taking photographs and admiring distant summits, especially Mount Forbes, which seemed to them to be almost

14,000 feet. Thompson even mentions that they sketched the amazing panorama, creating possibly the first artistic representations of this landscape.

The Americans decided to cross a snow ridge to a second summit, a snow dome slightly higher. Without ropes, all successfully jumped a snow-covered crevasse, until the last man; the snow gave way as Thompson tried to cross and he fell 60 feet into the crevasse. Wedged, with his head downward, he was only able to move his left arm. Collie, Dixon and Sarbach were on the first summit of Mount Gordon when they noticed the American climbers waving wildly in the distance.[43] Sarbach suddenly realized that he could only discern four shapes instead of five, so he raced to the rescue, followed by the British climbers.

Thompson could not be seen, but his cries for help urged them to hurry because, although unhurt, he was in a most uncomfortable position upside down. Thompson's four American companions were caught on the other side of the crevasse and could do nothing until rescued with a rope.[44] Collie and Dixon both provide detailed accounts of a miraculous rescue, but from different physical perspectives: Collie was lowered into the crevasse and Dixon remained on the surface. Thompson, who gives us lively and detailed descriptions of the trials of the swamp and the excitement of climbing the icefield, does not allude to the terror of his fall or his gratitude for his rescue. In his account, Thompson is simply silent on the details of his nearly fatal accident.

Collie, the lightest climber and unmarried, was lowered into the perpendicular crack in the ice securely attached to two ropes. When he descended into the gloom, almost to the end of the rope, Collie himself became jammed between the icy walls, only able to move his arms. Collie's feet could almost touch Thompson's, but Thompson could not see his rescuer because his head was downward and covered with snow. Despite their perilous situation at this point, Collie reports an incredibly civilized conversation in which Thompson acknowledges all responsibility for his predicament and Collie promises, without any concrete ideas on how to effect this miracle, a quick rescue. Collie then called up for another rope and threw one end of it in the direction of Thompson's left hand. Thompson was able to catch the rope, but he was too weak to hold on.

The resourceful Collie then did something amazing: holding his hands over his head, he made a noose and lassoed the only part of Thompson's anatomy still visible, his left arm. Then came moments of incredible anxiety as those on the surface cautiously increased the tension on the rope.

Collie could not help because he was unable to reach Thompson; if Thompson were to faint, the rescue would be impossible. By incredible good luck, the rope held. Thompson was pulled up until he was beside Collie, who somehow managed to tie a jamming knot above Thompson's right elbow. Then Collie watched as his companion was raised quickly out of sight. Now, however, Collie himself was in great danger. If the knot on Thompson's arm gave way, his falling body could land right on Collie. Fortunately, Collie's courageous rescue was successful.

The only difficulty, Dixon reports, arose when Thompson was within six feet of the surface but could not be raised to safety because the rope was cutting into the snow. Bracing an ice axe under the rope, they pushed the axe forward until the rope was free. They then raised Thompson another three feet, close enough for Sarbach to grab his collar and haul him out. Soon after, Collie was raised from the icy twilight, wet and nearly frozen like Thompson. Collie and Thompson were each roped to a dry companion before descending quickly to restore their bodies' warmth. Dixon, Collie and Fay[45] remark on Thompson's amazing escape from death and injury, but Thompson's only reference to the accident is a humorous note, as reported by Collie, that scientific exploration 60 feet below the ice, upside down, was not only dangerous but also not of any significance.

The next day, the climbers returned to their camp near Hector Lake, hoping to set out the following morning, August 12, for their original objective, Mount Balfour. Low cloud and fresh snow at higher elevations prevented their attempt on the summit, but they found consolation in climbing the escarpment above the head of the lake, where they had a magnificent view similar to the one Wilcox observed two years earlier:

> Below were the three white ribbons of the glacier; beyond them on the opposite wall of the valley beneath Mt. Gordon was a waterfall of perhaps five hundred feet, dropping in one clear pale brown leap from higher to lower glacier.[46]

Once over the top of the escarpment, they could see Balfour shrouded in cloud about a mile away. As the cloud showed no sign of lifting, the climbers decided to descend to Hector Lake by way of two smaller lakes that Thompson, Fay and Abbot had seen from the summit of Mount Hector in 1895. The lower one had been named Lake Margaret by the 1895 explorers, but now these men were the first to visit the upper, called Turquoise Lake by George Baker, another member of the Appalachian Club. From the edge of the bowl containing Turquoise Lake, Thompson describes a stunning scene:

> On one side, precipice-girt, overshadowed by Pulpit Peak, were the light blue waters of Turquoise Lake; on the other, at the base of a perpendicular wall, forest-encircled, were the dark blue waters of Lake Margaret. Beyond the forest were the light green waters of the Lower Bow Lake. No more remarkable grouping of lacustrine color can be found in all this region, perhaps in all the world.[47]

The Gateway to a Climber's Paradise (1897)

Collie, Baker, Sarbach and Peyto

After the successful ascent of Mount Gordon and the exploration of the great icefield on the Continental Divide, Collie and Baker, accompanied by Sarbach, abandoned their plan to go south to Assiniboine next. Instead, they were inspired to head north of Laggan once again to seek the mountain they assumed was Murchison, which they had seen to the northwest from the summit of Mount Gordon. Only a few days after the weather had defeated their attempt on Balfour, Wilson outfitted the explorers and they set out from Laggan on August 17, 1897, with Peyto again as the guide, L. Richardson as packer and C. Black as cook.[48]

For the second time in ten days, they toiled through the confused jumble of fallen trees on the trail just north of Laggan; they often walked on logs two feet from the ground and sometimes as high as ten feet. The intense heat and swarms of mosquitoes added to their discomfort, but this time Peyto made certain they were not marooned in the swamp. After three days, the open country and magnificent scenery around Bow Lake were ample compensation for their earlier trials. Collie comments that the views of forest and meadows, lakes, glaciers and snowy peaks will reward anyone willing to undertake the journey. In addition, he promises good fishing, claiming that trout over 30 pounds have been caught.[49] While less detailed, Collie's description of the Bow Lake region is similar to those provided by Hector and Wilcox before him: Bow Lake is the perfect camping spot, a place of rest in the midst of stunning beauty.

Collie's party then spent a day at the head of the Bow Valley. They climbed a 9,000-foot mountain southwest of Bow Pass in order to gain spectacular views of the Bow Valley to the south, and over Peyto Lake, along the Mistaya Valley, to the north. Bow Pass was the gateway to a climber's paradise of unexplored peaks. Just over a week later, on August 29, from the side of Mount Freshfield (named by Collie after Douglas Freshfield of the Alpine Club), Collie was inspired by the sight of a magnificent peak that he believed must be either Mount Brown or Mount Hooker, the legendary summits thought to be 16,000 and 15,700 feet. He decided to return the next year to explore the vast, unknown region further.[50]

The Summer of 1898

Laggan Station

On the station platform at Laggan on July 30, 1898, Tom Wilson met six members of the Appalachian Club and Dr. J. Norman Collie; all of the men required outfitting for one of three different expeditions.[51] Collie was waiting for the arrival of his two companions, Stutfield and Woolley, before leaving with their guide Bill Peyto the next day, bound for climbing challenges in the vicinity of the North Saskatchewan River. Four of the Appalachian Club members, Rev. Harry P. Nichols, Rev. Charles L. Noyes, Charles S. Thompson and George M. Weed, were to be guided by Ralph Edwards with a similar objective. However, if the river proved too far for the two weeks of holiday allowed Thompson, they were content to go to the Bow Valley and explore the Waputik peaks and glaciers further. Professor Charles E. Fay and Rest F. Curtis had a definite goal, the first ascent of Mount Balfour. Wilson provided them with a third man on the rope, Bob Campbell, a young schoolteacher from Banff.

The Summer of 1898: North to Discover the Columbia Icefield

Collie, Stutfield, Woolley and Peyto

To avoid the muskeg along the Bow River that had caused such grief for Collie and his companions the previous summer, Peyto led the pack train up the Pipestone River to Pipestone Pass, then over to the Siffleur Valley, eventually reaching the Kootenay Plains on the North Saskatchewan River. Their explorations then took them north, where they were the first to climb Mount Athabasca and record seeing the vast Columbia Icefield stretching to the west.[52] This amazing expedition concluded by travelling south over Bow Pass and camping beside Bow Lake. In the early morning of September 5, the intrepid climbers set off for more adventure, despite the fact that a dog had devoured their last loaf of bread.[53] Collie led his companions along the same route he had followed the previous summer in the ascent of Mount Gordon: along the north side of the lake, past the gorge with the natural bridge and, with some tricky crossings of ice bridges, over the Bow Glacier. Eighteen inches of fresh powder had fallen over loose shale, causing the climbers to move carefully toward the summit which Collie named Thompson Peak after Charles Thompson, the man he had rescued from the crevasse on Mount Gordon the summer before.

Rain had cleared the air of smoke; as a result, the climbers enjoyed the most impressive views during the entire trip. Mountains stretched away in all directions: Mount Assiniboine was visible in the south, along with Mount Temple closer to Lake Louise; Mount Sir Donald in the Selkirks could be seen 70 miles away to the west; and north they could recognize peaks from their recent explorations – Forbes, Lyell and Murchison. This panorama was a fitting conclusion to a remarkable expedition. After a few more days camping and fishing they returned to Laggan on the hellish trail through burnt timber. Woolley, who had gone ahead to take photographs, became hopelessly lost. Collie and Stutfield, also ahead of the pack train, missed the trail. Mountaineers who had accomplished such daring feats on the heights ended up finding their way back to civilization by following the sound of a locomotive whistle.[54]

The Summer of 1898: Another Attempt to Climb Mount Balfour

Fay, Curtis and Campbell

Mount Balfour, at 10,735 feet (3,272 metres), dominates the Waputik Range, stretching from Mount Daly near Laggan northwest to Howse Peak. Ralph Edwards had accompanied Professor Habel on his expedition in July 1897 to see if Balfour could be climbed on the western side, from the Yoho Valley, but such an approach seemed impossible. Edwards, in his account of this attempt in *The Trail to the Charmed Land*, describes the formidable reputation surrounding Balfour, encouraging other climbers to take up the challenge.[55]

Charles Fay had seen the great mountain from the summit of Mount Hector in 1895, and despite his lack of success when his British and American expedition approached from the northwest in 1897, he was inspired to try again. This time, he travelled along the Waputik Icefield from the opposite direction, starting in the Sherbrooke Valley.[56] Fay, Curtis and Campbell walked for miles over the soft snow, until eventually the stout Curtis was sinking in so far that he sent the other two on without him. Fay and Campbell reached the northern arête of Balfour when a curious accident caused them to retreat: Fay dropped his ice axe. Although the axe was easily retrieved, Campbell anxiously reminded his companion that he had a family in Banff. At that moment, Fay looked at his watch and realized that it was 5:30 p.m. on August 3. Only two years earlier on the same day, at precisely the same time, Abbot had fatally fallen from Mount Lefroy. Fay thought it wise to consider such an omen seriously and Balfour had again defeated its challengers.

The Summer of 1898: First Ascent of Mount Balfour

Nichols, Noyes, Thompson, Weed and Edwards

The third mountaineering expedition that began in Laggan at the end of July was ostensibly seeking summits in the region of the North Saskatchewan River. However, as events transpired, the four Appalachian Club members found themselves at Bow Lake with an opportunity to extend explorations of the great icefield above Bow Glacier. Then right at the end of their trip, they had a chance to climb Mount Balfour by ascending the glacier above Hector Lake. Ralph Edwards guided his clients on the perfect expedition. Without mishap, he led them over an unknown pass, the Dolomite, into the Bow Valley, an accomplishment almost equal to the subsequent first ascent of Mount Balfour.[57]

Instead of following the Siffleur River to the valley of the North Saskatchewan, as Collie's party did just a few days earlier, Edwards ventured into uncharted territory by following Dolomite Creek south from its junction with the Siffleur. As the group travelled along the valley bottom, they discovered Isabella Lake and later passed under the eastern flank of Observation Peak, which Noyes, Thompson and Nichols climbed to discover a fine view of Peyto Lake across the Bow Valley.[58] With great patience and skill, Edwards managed to lead the pack horses over the scree slope blocking the ascent to Dolomite Pass. He gave strict instructions to everyone to allow the horses to find their own way over the unstable slabs of rock without any of the usual words of encouragement.[59] Once over this high pass, at 7,858 feet (2,395 metres), where there were no trees and not a single stick of wood for a fire, they descended to Katherine Lake, named after Nichols' daughter, which was also treacherous for the heavily laden horses as they had to jump from a two-foot cliff onto a steep slope below.[60]

Again the horses performed admirably under Edwards' watchful eye and before long the pack train had passed Helen Lake, named after another of Nichols' daughters, and crossed the alpine meadows leading to the ridge overlooking Crowfoot Glacier and Bow Lake. On the afternoon of August 6, the group camped beside Bow Lake "at the old spot in the angle of the northern shore."[61]

Now that the climbers had fortuitously found the Bow Valley, after crossing a previously unexplored pass, they were ready to follow their alternate plan to explore the vast Waputik snowfield. They decided to approach this largely unknown region by climbing the glaciers descending to the three lakes – Hector, Bow and Peyto – below the eastern escarpment. On the first day, August 7, they travelled west along the shore of Bow Lake and followed the same route up the Bow Glacier as Noyes and Thompson had taken the previous summer. From a rock outcropping 1,000 feet above the snowfield, they could see the highest peak rising out of the snow to the north, named Mount Baker by Collie to honour George Baker of the Appalachian Club. Then the mountaineers turned their attention to the southwest, to Mount Collie, and set out on a two-hour trek in intense heat over the softening snow. The route to the summit became increasingly dangerous when their feet began sinking alarmingly close to snow-covered crevasses. As they felt their way past the unseen dangers, their progress was so slow that by 4 p.m. they decided to abandon the climb and return to their camp beside Bow Lake.

The next morning, refreshed and ready for more adventure, the men moved their tents up to Bow Pass, a plateau of such charm and natural beauty that it provided a marked contrast to the setting of the day before. The view from the pass was spectacular:

> If the traveler will trend to the left as he threads his way among the open spaces between these cedar groves, so as to come out on the edge of this plateau at its north western corner, he will be greeted with one of the most magnificent surprises that the manifold resources of mountain scenery can achieve. This is Point Lookout. Abreast of here, the plain drops down suddenly in steep, densely wooded ridges and gorges to the blue waters of Peyto's Lake, shaped like a bended arm.[62]

Noyes and his companions ascended the glacier at the head of Peyto Lake without difficulty. A diagonal traverse over the ice took them behind the northern lateral moraine to a delightful blue lake, now called Cauldron Lake, which they had seen from Observation Peak. Noyes enthusiastically extols the beauty of the northern end of the icefield with its magnificent curving glaciers, water lying in emerald pools and the musical sounds of running streams: "All these singing waters set the ice a-ringing, and, instead of a domain frozen into silence and death that one might expect, the glacier is vocal and resonant …"[63] The high peaks of Baker and Portal guard this northern entrance to the great icefield. Between mounts Baker and Olive lies the uniquely shaped Mount Rhondda, identified by Edwards[64] and described by Noyes, with "a snow arête [that] sweeps round in a wide spiral curve of even grade from crown to base, a white winding stair, that fairly beckons the climber to improve its offered access."[65] But the climbers' goal was now the irresistible Mount Balfour. They set out in the direction of Mount Gordon and Vulture Col, but, unlike the previous summer, the snow was melting quickly, forcing them to feel for the hidden crevasses once past the top of Bow Glacier. On reaching Vulture Col, with its enticing view of Mount Balfour, they were unable to find a way down to Hector Lake and camp as they had planned. Instead they were forced to retrace their steps over the dangerous snowfield and camp beside Bow Lake.

Noyes, Thompson and Nichols were expecting a cold, bleak night without blankets or tents because they had arranged to meet their guide, Edwards, his cook, Wilfred Beatty, and Weed, whose eyes were inflamed, at Hector Lake. As the wet and tired men returned along the lakeshore of Bow Lake in the darkness, they were astonished to see the outline of a tent against a flickering fire. They could not guess who had made camp, but it turned out that Weed was sitting by the fire keeping Beatty company, because the cook had exhausted himself through overwork and was too unwell to travel. When Edwards joined them the next day, they moved the entire camp to the southern end of Hector Lake. During a day of rest and good fishing, they also established a small camp on the western side of the lake, near the outlet of Lake Margaret, in preparation for an early start to attempt Balfour the next morning. Finally, Thompson, who had seen Mount Balfour from the summit of Mount Hector in 1895, was in the most advantageous spot to launch an assault on the notorious mountain.

At 4 a.m., the four climbers, Thompson, Noyes, Nichols and Weed (whose eyes had improved), began the ascent to the Waputik Icefield, past Lake Margaret and up a rock precipice to the bowl containing Turquoise Lake. Nichols was so entranced by this beautiful lake in its magnificent alpine landscape that he decided to rest his injured back and spend the day there. His three comrades found climbing the glacier above Turquoise Lake to be dangerous in the warm conditions, with snow bridges over the crevasses weakened through melting. Once on the snowfield above, though, they were rewarded with a splendid view of Balfour. Crossing the Continental Divide to the south of the mountain, they were delighted to find more stable snow on Balfour's western face, allowing easier access to the final ridge and the summit. After four hours of climbing, Noyes, Thompson and Weed had conquered Balfour at last. Noyes describes their exhilaration standing on the great peak rising from the Waputik Icefield:

> Suppose it is really a bit of the coping of the continent, lifted toward eleven thousand feet, thinned down till it is no more than the fine edge of a wedge protruding through slopes of snow that cling to its sides high as the steepness will allow, flanked beyond stupendous gorges on either hand by a wilderness of mountains reaching everywhere to the sky-line, rising in great steps along an untrodden way to an untouched peak – that is what the final climb in the capture of Balfour meant for us.[66]

The first ascent of Mount Balfour was the crowning achievement of two weeks of alpine adventure in perfect weather. The members of the Appalachian Club had explored the Dolomite Valley, bringing them to three large lakes lying against the eastern wall of the Continental Divide – Hector, Bow and Peyto. From each lake, they used the glaciers draped over this eastern escarpment as gateways to the vast snowfields extending along North America's backbone. The expedition faced just one more of nature's challenges before returning to Laggan: the fallen trees in the burnt forest. Nevertheless, even that misery was soon forgotten with the happy memories of their adventures.

Joining "Tom Wilson's Gang" (1898)

Jimmy Simpson

Jimmy Simpson would one day build Num-Ti-Jah Lodge near his favourite camping spot at the head of Bow Lake. In his reminiscences, conveyed through letters to his friend Dr. J. Monroe Thorington, Simpson says that at the age of 21 he began his career in the outfitting and guiding business by joining "Tom Wilson's gang in 1898."[67] Simpson's first assignment was the hellish task of building a trail north of Laggan. The CPR was trying to encourage climbers to travel to the Rockies, and Lake Louise was a popular destination with its comfortable chalet. However, when mountaineers journeyed north to a land of unclimbed peaks, their pack trains had to pass through a forest of blackened tree trunks with a tangle of fallen timber that was, in the words of Noyes, "a misery to justify profanity if not suicide."[68] To overcome the bad reputation of this stretch along the Bow River, the CPR gave Wilson a contract to cut a trail through the infernal region. Simpson was put in charge of two assistants, Frank McNichol and Jim Tabuteau, and the three men proved equal to the strenuous task of chopping through hundreds of logs, work that was complicated by having to ford the swiftly flowing Bow River numerous times.[69] When Collie returned with Stutfield and Woolley in 1902, he noted that a good trail existed for the first five or six miles, but the muskeg was worse because of the increased number of pack trains taking climbers and explorers north.[70]

Simpson and his crew continued to construct a trail past Hector Lake and around Bow Lake when one day the whole panorama of snow-covered peaks, hanging glaciers and alpine meadows surrounding a beautiful lake came into view. The scene captivated Simpson. When the three men camped at the usual spot, the north end of the lake near the stream flowing from Bow Pass, Simpson vowed that one day he could construct a shack on that location.[71] He never gave up his dream, even though decades would pass before he could fully realize it. Bill Beach, one of Simpson's clients from New York, remarks, in a letter dated June 7, 1921, that news about Jimmy starting a cabin at Bow Lake is most welcome.[72] This octagonal cabin, the Ram Pasture, still stands beside the Num-Ti-Jah Lodge, which was started in 1937 when Simpson was 60 years old.[73]

After building the trail to Bow Lake, Simpson was given the job of cook for two groups of tourists in the summer of 1898. The first trip was to Emerald Lake with some Philadelphians, including Mary Schäffer, who would become an influential supporter of Jimmy's.[74] The second involved guiding a Canadian historian, Agnes Laut, and her companion, Miss Brunstermann, to Moraine Lake, Emerald Lake and north of Laggan through the muskeg to Hector Lake.[75] In October 1899, Wilson gave Simpson a chance to expand his duties to include the role of hunting guide as well as cook, while Ralph Edwards guided the Englishmen Parker and Twyford north of Lake Louise to the area around Wilcox Pass in search of bighorn sheep.[76] Then, in the summer of 1900, Simpson had his first experience as a member of a climbing expedition while working as cook for a group that included three Swiss guides, a Montreal artist and the infamous Walling brothers from Chicago. Although unsuccessful in climbing Mount Assiniboine, they did get close to the summit. Jimmy, however, remembered the expedition as a fiasco because on their return to Banff, the brothers thought they were lost and "killed a saddle horse for meat within fifty yards of a lumber road."[77]

Amazing Accomplishments Climbing in the Canadian Rockies (1902)

Outram, Kaufmann, Ballard and Simpson

In 1902, Simpson went to work for his hero Bill Peyto, who had established his own outfitting business in Banff. Peyto had been successful in guiding James Outram to Assiniboine at the end of the climbing season in 1901, allowing Outram to make the first ascent of this great mountain before the weather changed. The next summer, Outram looked for mountaineering challenges in the region of the North Saskatchewan River. He again asked for Peyto's help, but this time to seek the lofty summits of Columbia, Forbes, Freshfield, Bryce, Lyell and any others that might be possible should the opportunity arise.[78] Outram's ambition and enthusiasm were boundless. On his 1902 trip of 54 days, Outram, with his CPR guide Christian Kaufmann, accomplished eight first ascents of mountains higher than 10,000 feet, including mounts Columbia, Lyell and Bryce. He later joined forces with Professor Norman Collie for two more, one of which was Mount Forbes.[79]

Peyto was called back to Banff as the Outram expedition reached the North Saskatchewan River, and, as a result, Peyto put Simpson in charge. Jimmy's assistant packer and cook was Fred Ballard, who was also his partner in a winter trapline the two men ran between Bow Lake and the mouth of the Mistaya River. Before Outram's expedition left in July, Simpson and Ballard were sent some weeks earlier to clear fallen trees from the trail between Bow Lake and the Mistaya's mouth; while chopping through in excess of 300 trees, they also had the opportunity to choose possible sites for future trapping cabins.[80] Simpson and Ballard's ability to guide the pack train through difficult terrain, particularly the fording of swollen rivers, was the foundation of Outram's tremendous success. Outram praises both men in his account of the expedition in *In the Heart of the Canadian Rockies*. Simpson's memory of Outram, however, is less positive because Outram would not allow him to participate in the first ascent of Mount Columbia, although Jimmy exacted his revenge later by refusing to carry scientific equipment to the summit of Mount Lyell.[81] The next summer, when working as the packer for A.O. Wheeler and his crew doing the Dominion Topographic Survey, Jimmy had his chance to complete first ascents when he helped carry heavy equipment to the summits of Mount Niblock, near Lake Louise and Cirque Peak, overlooking his favourite camping spot at Bow Lake.[82]

Despite Simpson's reservation about Outram's egotism, the accomplishments of the expedition in terms of exploration and first ascents were outstanding. Outram describes his journeys of discovery in his charming book, offering details about the trails, camp life, significant features of the terrain and earlier mountaineering triumphs in the region between 1895 and 1901. His chapter called "The Valley of the Upper Bow" is a delightful account of the trail from Laggan to Bow Pass, well known as the gateway to the mouth of the Mistaya for climbing expeditions, and beyond to Wilcox Pass for hunters of bighorn sheep and mountain goats:

> The weather was perfect as we slowly wound our way along the old trail, probably largely the same as that taken by Dr. Hector in 1858, when the first white man sought the sources of the Bow. Behind us rose the well-known peaks beyond Laggan, Mts. Victoria, Lefroy and Temple grandly prominent. To the right, a fire-swept desolate expanse extends to the south-eastern spur of Mt. Hector and gradually leads the eye to the sharp, fortress-like apex of that peak, the dominating mountain of the Upper Bow. On the left, wooded slopes merge in the rugged escarpments of Mt. Daly and its neighbours, till, in the distance, the palisades are broken by a sudden gorge, where the vast ice-fields of the Waputik sweep down to Hector Lake, and on the farther side a wooded spur juts into the valley, culminating in Bow Peak and folding the shining waters in its close embrace.[83]

Underfoot, the trail to the usual camp about a mile below the south end of Hector Lake was almost impossible. Heavy snow combined with a late spring caused the pack horses to sink into the mud, but with great effort all were successfully rescued. By early afternoon, the men reached their first camp. After dining on rainbow trout, Outram had a chance to explore the shores of Hector Lake, which he had first seen in the summer of 1901 when he crossed Balfour Pass from the Yoho Valley.[84]

The next day, the men followed the trail winding north around Bow Peak. A spectacular view met their eyes:

> Beyond [Bow Peak's] long rampart, where the valley narrows to nearly half its former width, a strikingly fine series of hanging-glaciers appears on the dark, lofty cliffs that bound the Waputik snow-fields, and a tremendous cornice is conspicuous upon the summit of their southern outpost. At their base the glacier-green waters of Bow Lake gleam brilliantly below the moraine and stretch away to the north for about two miles, then, curving round the buttresses that push their way far into the angle, they sweep towards their source at the end of the Bow Glacier.[85]

The pack train took the usual path to avoid the spongy ground, over the gravel in the shallow water at the lakeshore, and the men set up their tents in Jimmy's perfect spot, just across the creek at the northern end of Bow Lake. Outram spent the afternoon exploring the gorge that Wilcox also described, with its natural bridge and eroded walls, funnelling the torrent of glacial runoff down to the gravel flats before meandering to the lake. Outram concludes his chapter on the upper Bow Valley by describing the stunning view from his tent door – the same scene that captivates artists today: the shores of Bow Lake bounded by the precipitous cliffs of Crowfoot Mountain, with the great Bow Glacier shining in the west, and, in dramatic contrast, the gentle slopes of forest and meadow to the east.

First Artist at Bow Lake (1907)

Mary Schäffer

For years, Mary Schäffer helped her husband, Dr. Charles Schäffer, with his botanical work on wildflowers in the Canadian Rockies, first by drying and pressing specimens and later by taking photographs and creating precise watercolour illustrations.[86] When Mary was in her early thirties, her husband died (1903) and she made the bold decision to finish his work. She sought the help of Stewardson Brown to write detailed analyses of the flowers, and, in return, his name would appear as the author on the cover of the volume. To complete the collection of specimens, Mary needed to venture farther afield than the areas close to the railway, so she turned to Tom Wilson for the name of someone who could help her to learn how to travel comfortably in the wilderness.[87] Wilson suggested Billy Warren, a man who eventually became Mary's trusted guide, sympathetic companion and, years later, her second husband.

After the successful publication of the botanical work in 1907, illustrated with Mary's photographs and 30 full-colour plates of her watercolour sketches, Mary was free to follow her other ambitions. Having read all the accounts by early explorers – Hector, Wilcox, Coleman, Collie and Outram – she courageously decided that two women, Mary and her companion Mollie Adams, could fare just as well in the wilderness as men. Mary's dream of exploring unknown territory had blossomed in 1903, when she had the good fortune to meet Sir James Hector at Glacier House and hear his account of being kicked by a horse more than four decades earlier.[88] The events of 1903 – the unfortunate death of Mary's husband and Hector's visit – combined to direct Mary on a new path. Her commitment to completing Charles' work was the immediate incentive for her to learn about wilderness travel, but once *Alpine Flora of the Canadian Rocky Mountains* was published, she could indulge in the pure joy of exploration.

On June 20, 1907, the two intrepid women left Laggan on a four-month trek into the unknown with their guide Billy Warren and assistant Sid Unwin. Ostensibly, their goal was to reach the sources of the North Saskatchewan and Athabasca rivers, but the real objective was simply exploration in the untamed wilderness.[89] The first two days were spent on the trail north of Laggan, proving how inhospitable the wilds can be. After negotiating the fallen trees by jumping over and chopping through them, they camped in mud. The second day greeted the explorers with low cloud and hail. One hundred yards from camp, a horse with 200 pounds of flour and bacon sank almost out of sight in the muskeg and could only be saved by cutting the pack ropes. That evening, they reached the favourite campground near Hector Lake, which Mary Schäffer called Bow Park.[90]

The explorers began their third day on the trail basking in sunshine. After the pack train travelled past Hector Lake and Bow Peak, they paused for a photograph of Crowfoot Glacier. Half an hour later, the horses were splashing through slush in the shallows of Bow Lake on their way to the meadow leading up to Bow Pass. Mary Schäffer describes the wonderful scene before her:

> Never have I seen the lake look more beautiful than on that fair morning in June. It was as blue as the sky could make it, the ice reflected the most vivid emerald green; in the distance a fine glacier swept to the lake-shore, whose every crevasse was a brilliant blue line; the bleak grey mountains towered above, at our feet the bright spring flowers bloomed in the green grass, and overall hung the deep blue sky. Around us hovered the peace which only the beauty and silence of the hills could portray.[91]

She notes the flowers in bloom in the meadows, the first after the snow melts: snow lilies, spring beauties and yellow violets. The snow or glacier lily is illustrated in *Alpine Flora* with a watercolour sketch.[92]

Excursion to Bow Lake and Wapta Icefield (1910)

Alpine Club of Canada

During the Alpine Club of Canada's general mountaineering camp at Consolation Lake in 1910, Jimmy Simpson helped to provide an efficient pony service from the Moraine Lake road to the lake.[93] After the camp, the ACC offered its guests a six-day excursion up the Bow River valley to Bow Lake by pony. Among those who participated were Dr. Thomas G. Longstaff, the famous British mountaineer, his sister Miss Katherine Longstaff and Miss Mary Vaux, who in 1925, as Mary Vaux Walcott, would publish *North American Wild Flowers* with life-size watercolour sketches of flora from the Bow Lake area, including the Alberta primrose (plate 274), snow willow (plate 277) and purple mountain violet (plate 181). The horses on this trip were probably under Jimmy Simpson's guidance, because a year earlier, at the 1909 O'Hara camp, A.O. Wheeler, the ACC director, had appointed him as assistant to the outfitters, the Otto Brothers, with a responsibility for horse transport.[94] After attending the O'Hara camp, two English guests, on a subsequent expedition to the Yoho Valley, remarked on how the club's Master of the Horse, Jimmy Simpson, followed at the end of the pack train making "a most entertaining and instructive companion. His control over the animals struck [us] as wonderful. When one of them went wrong he rated it, either by its individual name or by names (also used in England) of more general and forcible application; and the offender always returned promptly to the trail."[95]

From Bow Lake, the club members and their guests set out on foot, carrying only the necessities on their backs, and climbed the Bow Glacier to the vast snowfield above. By passing between Mount Gordon on one side and St. Nicholas Peak and Mount Olive on the other, they came to Vulture Col. They crossed the col and descended to Balfour Pass, then trekked west to the Yoho Glacier, where they were met by another string of horses. The trip was perfect, except for low clouds on the crossing from Bow Lake to the Yoho Valley.[96] Byron Harmon, a founding member of the ACC and the club's first official photographer, produced some wonderful images to illustrate the account of the trip in the *Canadian Alpine Journal*, one of which shows the Bow Glacier flowing right over the cliff of the present Bow Falls, down to the boulders below.

Artistic Legacy of Bow Lake

Simpson and Rungius

By 1910, Jimmy Simpson had established himself as an outfitter and guide. He had provided reliable horse transport for A.O. Wheeler's ACC camps and, some years earlier, had guided Outram and Kaufmann to some of the great unclimbed peaks north of Bow Lake. His outfitting experiences ranged from acting as hunting guide for Parker and Twyford on Jimmy's first expedition to find big game in October 1899,[97] to collecting butterflies with Mrs. Mary de la Beach-Nichol in the summers of 1904, 1905 and 1907.[98] On the last trip with the "butterfly lady," Simpson travelled up the north fork of the North Saskatchewan River to Wilcox Pass. On their return, they happened to cross wilderness paths with Mary Schäffer, who records the highest praise for Jimmy in her *Old Indian Trails*. As a tribute to the man who cleared old trails, making them passable for later explorers, Schäffer suggests that the west branch of the north fork of the North Saskatchewan (now the Alexandra River) be named after the Stoney nickname given to Jimmy as a compliment to his speed in the wilderness: Nashan-esen, meaning "wolverine-go-quick."[99]

Simpson's success, along with his survival, depended on his knowledge of the terrain and the habits of wild animals. In his own words, Jimmy summed up the necessity of awareness: "If you listen, the wilderness teaches you. If you don't, it can kill you."[100] His summer guiding and his winter trapline in the Mistaya Valley allowed him to use his wilderness experience to make a living. Over time, Jimmy's energy and vitality led him to explore new interests to enhance his outfitting business. With his love of the natural world, it seems logical that he would join a society dedicated to the study and conservation of North America's big game: the New York Zoological Society, which founded the Bronx Zoo. Perhaps he was looking for more clients among the society's membership, or possibly Jimmy saw an opportunity to send live animals, particularly bighorn sheep and goats, to the zoo.[101] In any case, the society's *Bulletin* proved to be the catalyst for bringing Carl Rungius, a wildlife artist based in New York, to the wilds of the Canadian Rockies.

The cover of the January 1910 *Bulletin* was a reproduction of the painting *Wary Game*, which Rungius had completed after participating in a scientific expedition to study mountain sheep in the Yukon in 1904. The New York Zoological Society had acquired the canvas and published the image of this elusive species in its natural habitat.[102] In the painting, six Dall sheep have stopped on a steep rocky slope well above treeline; sensing danger, they have focused their attention beyond the frame of the painting to the right, perhaps on an approaching hunter. Jimmy admired Rungius' skill in portraying the tension of the animals and the artist's willingness to undergo the rigours of climbing in such inhospitable terrain. Here was a man whom Jimmy would like to meet.

Jimmy wrote a letter to Rungius offering free outfitting and guiding services so that the artist could learn more about the wild animals in their natural environment. As Jimmy rather bluntly put it in his reminiscences decades later, he told Rungius "to come west and get real game and develop his

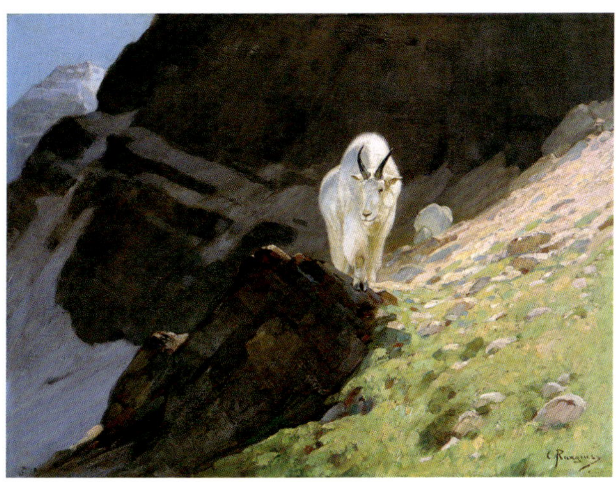

CARL RUNGIUS. *The Old Billy,* 1911. Oil on canvas, 76.7 x 102.2 cm
Collection of Glenbow Museum

talent."[103] Rungius initially refused the generous suggestion, but his wife, Louise, believed Jimmy's letter revealed a sincere interest in promoting Rungius' wildlife art. Eventually, she persuaded her husband to reconsider the offer. Jimmy was able to arrange free passes on the CPR and in August 1910 Carl and Louise Rungius arrived in Banff. Jimmy first took the artist to the Ptarmigan Valley for some sketching. Then, in late August, the pack train headed north along the Bow toward the usual camping spot at Bow Lake.[104] Once over Bow Pass, they followed the Mistaya Valley in search of big game. Rungius describes his first successful hunt in the Canadian Rockies:

> We had camped on the Waterfowl Lakes, on Bear Creek, and as we were packing to go on I spotted a bunch of goats on Pyramid Peak (now Mount Yefren). I wanted to try for one, so we unpacked, crossed the stream and started climbing the east face of the peak. It wasn't as difficult as it seemed from a casual look at the mountainside, but still it was quite a climb. We came out on the last green, a little above the goats. The bunch had drifted down to the Howard Glacier, but one fine billy had remained within easy gun-shot and I bagged him without difficulty. It was my first goat – in fact I had never seen a live one before – and I was delighted, for I was as anxious to get goat as sheep.[105]

The next winter these sketches became the foundation for a painting called *The Old Billy*, which Rungius sent to Jimmy in return for his outfitting and guiding. Jimmy was so pleased with the gift that he hung the painting over his fireplace.[106]

For the next decade, Rungius returned almost every fall to go hunting, but Jimmy did not think it necessary to accompany him as guide. The artist had demonstrated some years earlier, on his hunting trips in Wyoming, that he was self-sufficient in the wilderness and skilled at tracking game. Instead, Jimmy supplied the outfit and Rungius paid for the food, a cook and the help of Harry Lang, one of Jimmy's packers.[107] Until 1920, in return for the use of the horses and equipment, the artist gave Jimmy a painting after each fall hunting trip.[108] Over the years, these works by Carl Rungius became the foundation for an outstanding art collection that would, one day, be in the Glenbow Museum.

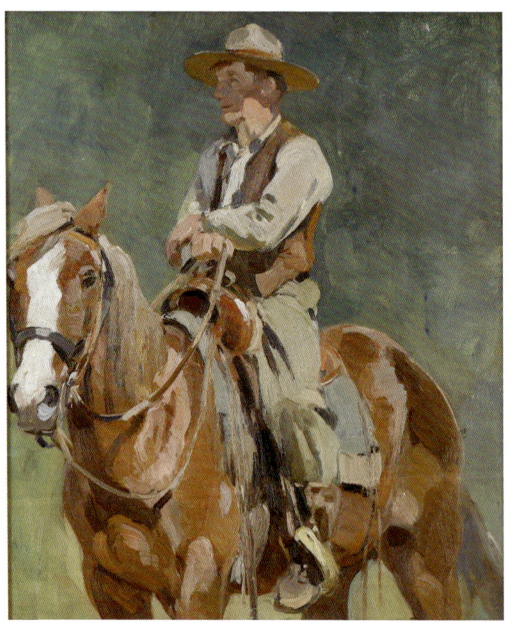

Carl Rungius. Preliminary Sketch for *The Mountaineer*, c.1920. Oil on canvas, 44.2 x 37.4 cm. Collection of Glenbow Museum. Jimmy Simpson was the model for this sketch, the basis of a popular painting (see note 106).

Building an Art Collection: Wildlife and Landscape

Jimmy Simpson

The Jimmy Simpson Collection in the Glenbow Museum consists of 28 paintings, ten of which are by Carl Rungius – largely images of big game. Nine paintings in the collection are of birds by the English artist Archibald Thorburn, and three landscapes and one image of mountain sheep are by Jimmy himself. There are also two watercolours by Charles Russell, the renowned painter of the American West, and two bird paintings by Louis Agassiz Fuertes, an American artist. Finally, one oil of a pack train coming to a stream is by Philip Goodwin, a friend of Carl Rungius. A similar painting by Rungius is in the collection, suggesting that both works were inspired on a pack trip the two artists took together.[109] In a letter to Jimmy on December 4, 1911, Goodwin speaks of a hunting trip the previous summer with Rungius. The letter is humorously illustrated with drawings, including one called "A Picture without Words" in which a hunter has just missed a goat standing calmly on a ridge. In the letter, Goodwin also reports that a watercolour of his representing a pack train at the Bow Divide is being shown in the New York exhibition of the Salmagundi Club, an association for artists to which Rungius also belonged.[110]

Jimmy's correspondence reveals frequent requests from individuals, and even the Smithsonian, for natural history specimens, including skulls, horns, live animals, birds' eggs and birds' skins. In a series of letters, in the spring of 1921, the artist Louis Agassiz Fuertes asks Jimmy to find some mule deer horns, with a normal shape but large and strong, to use as a model for drawing. Jimmy's generous response included, as well, an offer of sheep horns. In return, Fuertes suggests that he would like to give Jimmy a painting of a bird of his choice. In April, Fuertes was delighted to receive a large sheep head with horns curling in front of the eyes. Then in May, just as Fuertes sent the requested blue jay on its flight to become part of Jimmy's art collection, he received the horns of an elk and a mule deer.[111] At some other time, Fuertes gave Jimmy another painting of birds, possibly of Canada geese, in return for guiding services near Lake Louise.[112]

In March 1920, Jimmy received a letter from another collector of bird paintings, Philip E. Dennison, asking about the cost of a Thorburn work and even offering to buy the painting of the snipe if Jimmy would part with it.[113] Jimmy's art collection in his Banff home at that time was becoming well known. Later the same year, Jimmy sent some ptarmigan skins to Thorburn and requested the price of more paintings.[114] Subsequently, Jimmy paid £31.10s for six small paintings (generally about 15.2 × 22.9 cm) of game birds.[115] The Thorburn sketches are all done in gouache on tinted paper. Only one, *Prairie Chicken*, is undated. Two, *Goldfinches* and *White-Tailed Ptarmigan*, were painted in 1909, and six, *Red Grouse*, *Mallard*, *Wilson's Snipe*, *Ring-Necked Pheasant*, *Blackcock* and *Woodcock*, date from 1912.

When Joseph McAleenan, a client from New York who dealt in diamonds, first visited Jimmy's house in Banff in 1915, he was surprised to discover Jimmy's interest in literature, music and art, considering the fact that Jimmy had spent much of his life in the wilderness:

> An upright piano stood against the east wall. Pelts of bear, cat and wolf covered the floor and hung over comfortable chairs. There was the latest Victrola, with records of Caruso, Kubelik and other great artists. On the walls hung paintings of landscapes and animals, typical of the owner's taste. Here, appearing at their best, were the works of Carl Rungius, a friend of Simpson's, a splendid library of books, the titles of which paid eloquent tribute to their owner ...[116]

After Jimmy married Williamina (Billie) Ross Reid on January 31, 1916, in Calgary, the couple went on the CPR to Montreal and then to New York, where they planned to spend two months seeing the city and visiting with clients. On February 6, the newlyweds registered at the Belmont Hotel, the guests of the McAleenans.[117] Jimmy was able to spend many afternoons in Rungius' studio learning about painting and actually watching the creation of one or two paintings that the artist owed him in return for outfitting. When the Salmagundi Club held art exhibitions, Jimmy went with Rungius and McAleenan. At one exhibition, McAleenan bought Albert Groll's oil painting *Arizona Desert* and, knowing the guide's fondness for art, presented it to Jimmy.[118] The canvas travelled back to Banff with the Simpsons and became part of their collection, eventually finding its way into the Glenbow as well.

One of the highlights of Jimmy's stay in New York was going to the Folsom Galleries to see an exhibition of the work of western artist Charlie Russell. Fortunately, Jimmy met the artist and the artist's wife at the show, and Russell invited him to visit his studio. Before leaving the exhibition, Jimmy paid $75 for a watercolour called *The Mankiller*. Then, a week later, in Russell's studio, he commissioned a painting of his saddle horse, *Bucking Bronco*, which also became part of his growing art collection. Russell's sense of humour appealed to Jimmy and he vividly remembered how the artist could carry on a conversation without even looking at his hands, which were effortlessly creating plasticine shapes of a buffalo and a mountain sheep.[119]

In October 1922, an artist named Allan Brooks wrote to Jimmy hoping that he might see Jimmy's renowned collection of paintings. Jimmy had previously owned some works by Brooks, but they had been stolen. Nevertheless, Jimmy felt that Banff would be a good market for Brooks and offered to act as his agent by arranging with Mr. Noble, a Banff shopkeeper, to sell the artist's watercolours. The business arrangement turned out to be successful, and Brooks subsequently sent four more paintings to Banff. Jimmy kept in touch with the artist, and more than twenty years later, in 1944, they exchanged watercolour paintings of scenes outside their respective windows. Brooks, in his letter accompanying the gift to Jimmy, explains the technique for his illustration work, probably in response to a question from Jimmy, who was looking for ways to develop his own technique.[120] Jimmy's correspondence with Brooks serves to confirm his genuine interest in collecting art, promoting the work of artists and improving his own artistic talent.

On Tour

Jimmy Simpson's Collection

In a move to give his art collection more publicity, Jimmy generously offered to loan it to the Calgary Stampede in 1928, in return for dogwood and honeysuckle plants.[121] Carl Rungius, whose work was well represented in the collection, approved of Jimmy's offer, and the artist even suggested that he clean his pictures a little before they were sent off to Calgary.[122] After the Stampede, a friend of Jimmy's, Lars Haukaness, an artist who taught at the Provincial Institute of Technology and Art in Calgary (now the Alberta College of Art and Design), asked to display the collection at the Institute as well.[123] The collection's permanent home was in the Simpson home in Banff, but when the initial construction of Num-Ti-Jah Lodge was completed in 1940, Jimmy had a splendid location to display the paintings.[124] At that point, the entire collection moved with Jimmy to the lodge each spring, returning to Banff with him in the winter.[125]

Jimmy was not only concerned with preserving his valuable paintings, but he also wanted to honour the artistic achievement of his good friend Carl Rungius. During the summer of Rungius' last visit to Banff, in 1957, the Banff School of Fine Arts put on an exhibition which included the eight Rungius works that Jimmy owned, as well as 16 other paintings from Simpson's collection. After the show at the Banff School, Eric Harvie, a philanthropist and art collector from Calgary, persuaded Jimmy to allow his paintings to go on exhibit at the Calgary Allied Arts Centre and then in the fall of 1957 to the offices of the Glenbow Foundation.

Jimmy's paintings found their way back to Banff by November, but Harvie recognized their value and wanted to add them to the collection of western art he had started a few years earlier for the Glenbow Foundation. In 1954, Harvie had already purchased Rungius' personal collection in Banff, as well as the artist's summer home and studio, the Paintbox. While Jimmy bargained with the collector over the sale price, 23 paintings, including works by Goodwin, Fuertes, Thorburn, Groll, Russell and Rungius, were loaned to Harvie for safekeeping in the spring of 1958, but it was more than a year later, the summer of 1959, when Jimmy finally agreed to a price of $15,800 for the collection on loan.[126] Eventually, the art and artifacts owned by Harvie and his Glenbow Foundation became the basis for the collection in the Glenbow Museum. In a letter to Thorington on January 23, 1969, Jimmy remembers having discussions with Rungius and various government officials in Banff about the future home of his collection; he rejected the idea of keeping the paintings in Banff, because of his concerns about their security, and he dismissed the suggestion that they be sent to Ottawa, because he feared that politicians would take the paintings home.[127] Jimmy's collected art works, often acquired over the years in exchange for services rendered, are now safely housed in the Glenbow Museum as the Simpson Collection, a tribute to Jimmy as a patron of the arts.

The Aspiring Artist

Jimmy Simpson

While Jimmy was negotiating the sale of his paintings in 1958, the Glenbow Foundation purchased one of his watercolours for its collection of Alberta artists.[128] Jimmy's posterity as an artist, as well as a guide and outfitter, was now assured. His friendships with artists and an enduring interest in

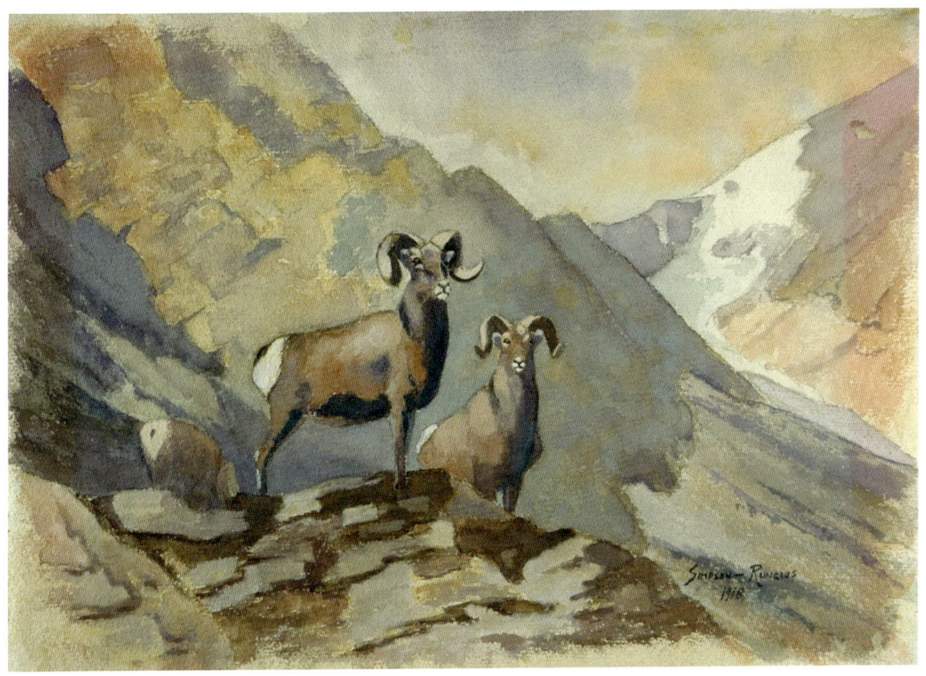

CARL RUNGIUS AND JIMMY SIMPSON. *Untitled* (Mountain Sheep), 1918. Watercolour on paper, 22.0 x 29.5 cm. Collection of the Whyte Museum of the Canadian Rockies

paintings of the natural world undoubtedly had a positive influence on his own artistic endeavours. He was fascinated by his good friend Carl Rungius at work, whether in the field on their early pack trips or in Rungius' studios, in both New York and Banff. In a magnanimous gesture, Rungius collaborated with Jimmy on a sheep painting in which Jimmy provided the background and Carl completed the two animals in the foreground. The painting, now in the Whyte Museum, is attributed to both artists, certainly an anomaly but also a strong indication of their close friendship. Jimmy welcomed other artists from Banff to his Bow Lake camp, particularly Belmore Browne and Peter and Catharine Whyte. The Whytes, Jimmy's neighbours in Banff, often visited the Simpson family at the Ram Pasture and, later, at Num-Ti-Jah Lodge.

Jimmy had always relied on his powers of observation to survive in the wilderness, and his ability to see the landscape from its immense grandeur to subtle variations in colour is apparent in his watercolours. He was certainly inspired by watching his friends work with oil, but he mainly developed his own style. In fact, he used up to three boxes of watercolours at once in order to reproduce the different hues he could see in the landscape.[129] His primary subject was his beloved Bow Lake, but Jimmy did branch out and paint other scenes, including Mount Assiniboine[130] and the pass west of Watchman Lake, an area he visited with Ian McTaggart Cowan.[131] His landscapes show all seasons, through spring breakup to fall, and different times of day, including some magical moonlit scenes.

Jimmy's unerring eye allowed him to capture the shape and scale of the mountainous landscape, despite the fact that his sketches were often small, intended as Christmas cards or accompaniments to letters. The recipients of his paintings were delighted with these unique greetings, and one acquaintance, J. Smart, comments particularly on Jimmy's ability to suggest the delightful feeling of Bow Lake.[132] In the early days, Jimmy gave most of his watercolours away. However, in his later years when the lodge was completed, his wife, Billie, started to sell his paintings in the gift shop. Watercolours by the legendary mountain man became very popular and soon Jimmy was happily engaged year-round doing commissions.[133] A photograph in the *Bulletin of the Trail Riders and Skyline Hikers* shows Jimmy in his nineties, wearing the characteristic pony Stetson and posing for the camera, according to the caption, by taking time off from his painting.[134] Jimmy's enduring love of painting, a pastime stemming from his appreciation of the Canadian wilderness, became a stimulating vocation in his retirement.

The Paintbox, Banff (1922)

Rungius and Simpson

Jimmy was a patron of the arts, not only through his valuable collection and friendships with artists, but also through the practical help he offered to Carl Rungius to establish his Banff studio, known as the Paintbox. Rungius and his wife, Louise, first came to Banff at Jimmy's suggestion in 1910, an annual pilgrimage he would repeat almost every summer and fall until 1957. During the early visits, Jimmy could offer Carl and Louise accommodation in a tack shed beside the house, but by 1920

Jimmy had a growing family and space was at a premium. In 1921, Jimmy offered to sell Rungius two lots on Cave Avenue in Banff so that the artist could build a studio and home, allowing him to spend more time each year in the mountains.[135] Rungius overcame his concerns about the cost and sent Jimmy $700 for the two lots in January 1922. Jimmy generously took on the role of contractor, hiring tradesmen and overseeing construction. A flurry of letters from Rungius in New York over the spring of 1922 reveals his anxiety about expenses, suggesting that Jimmy buy a second-hand stove and reluctantly agreeing to a necessary evil, the bathtub. Rungius gave Jimmy the authority to make small changes in the plans supplied by Fred Godwin, an architect and friend in New York, but he insisted the interior of his studio have a natural look with rafters showing, preferably without beaverboard on the walls. Rungius acknowledged the peremptory tone in some of his letters and amusingly suggested putting up a bronze tablet to honour Jimmy's efforts. In the end, Rungius was pleased with his new studio and he happily moved into his Banff home in June 1922.[136]

Art Transformed: Influence of the Canadian Rockies

Carl Rungius

Jimmy Simpson had a significant influence on the development of Rungius' career by persuading the reluctant artist to come to the Rockies in the first place and then by facilitating the creation of his Banff studio, where Rungius could work from April through October close to the animals and landscape that inspired him. As a young artist training in Germany, Rungius had a clear focus on his subject matter: creatures of the natural world, especially the majestic wild game animals.[137] He developed great skill in drawing through careful study of animal anatomy. In 1884, when an invitation arrived from his uncle Dr. Clemens Fulda in New York to go on a fall moose hunt in Maine, the young artist eagerly set out for North America. Although the two did not find a moose in the wild, the visit was extended to a year and Rungius was able to continue working in a studio in his uncle's house.[138] By using a trophy head of a moose he found in a taxidermist's shop, he completed a painting that was eventually displayed in a gallery window in New York. Fortuitously, William Hornaday of the New York Zoological Society saw Rungius' moose one evening in February 1895 and, recognizing an extraordinary talent in creating a lifelike representation of this wild animal, Hornaday contacted the young artist.[139] Their friendship eventually led to significant commissions from 1912 to 1934 for the zoo's "Gallery of Wild Animals."[140] These commissions, as well as illustrations for periodicals and outdoor magazines, sustained Rungius in his early North American career as a wildlife artist.

Another providential meeting during Rungius' stay in New York occurred when he visited a sportsmen's trade show in the winter of 1895. There, he met Ira Dodge, a buckskin-clad guide from Wyoming, who offered the wonderful opportunity to visit his ranch the following summer.[141] Rungius could now fulfill his boyhood fantasies of living like a cowboy and travelling by horseback into the wilderness with the freedom to hunt and sketch as he wished. Now he could see animals such as elk and antelope in their natural habitat. This first trip to the Wild West undoubtedly influenced Rungius' decision, in 1897, to move permanently to the United States.[142] On subsequent visits to Wyoming, he proved his ability to be self-sufficient in the wilderness. He also began the habit of doing sketches of animals and landscape for later reference in the studio.[143] When in 1910 another invitation was offered by a guide, this time from a subscriber to Hornaday's *Zoological Society Bulletin* named Jimmy Simpson, Rungius already had the wilderness experience that would allow him to make the most of Jimmy's offer to hunt and sketch mountain sheep in the Mistaya River valley. Rungius' first trip to the Rockies changed his perception of landscape. In his biography published in 1945, he describes his impression of this alpine landscape to William Schaldach:

> For the first time I felt strongly the urge to paint straight landscape – that is, landscape for its own sake. Until then, I had considered landscape only as a setting for big game animals. But the grandeur of the mountains with the marvelous atmospheric conditions in Alberta and consequent color effects changed all of that … in Alberta, with its scenic grandeur and its remarkable wealth of big game species, I felt that I had found at last the land which I had been seeking.[144]

From 1910 until 1925, when Rungius won the Carnegie Prize at the National Academy of Design in New York for his painting of Lake McArthur, the alpine landscape on its own was a primary concern of the artist.[145] He gained considerable artistic recognition through his landscapes, whereas, in contrast, his wildlife paintings were considered in the realm of zoological illustration rather than fine art.[146] When painting the alpine tundra in the Rockies, Rungius developed new techniques to reflect his different perception of light. He became bolder in his use of colour, now applying it in broader strokes so that brushwork, rather than detail, revealed the structure and volume of the subject.[147] Rungius would eventually return to his earlier concentration on big animals, but landscape would always remain an integral part of his compositions.

Artist in the Backcountry

Belmore Browne

Belmore Browne established his reputation as a great mountain climber by reaching the horseshoe-shaped ridge on the summit of Alaska's Mount McKinley with Herschel Parker in 1912. Although a blizzard prevented the men from locating a low rise on the ridge, technically the precise peak, Parker and Browne demonstrated tremendous courage and endurance to reach the summit of North America's highest mountain.[148] In view of this stellar accomplishment, Browne draws an interesting comparison between the spiritual rewards of the climber in reaching a mountain's peak and of the artist attempting to capture the image of the mountain on canvas.[149] The artist can never achieve the perfect picture of his mountain – he will never reach the absolute summit – but his attempt to create a painting is immensely rewarding because his careful observations will increase his knowledge and, thus, his awareness of the natural beauty. Browne imagines a discussion between the artist and mountain climbers:

> Across the evening campfire you will listen, with the old thrill to your companions' talk of ice-slopes and hand-holds, but on your side of the day's score sheet will be hours you stood in Nature's laboratory watching the cloud forms in their making, the bull moose with head submerged groping the floor of a sapphire lake and other forms and colors bewildering in their numbers and beauty.[150]

The artist who ventures into the wilderness will not only find unknown beauty, but he will also experience adventures of the pioneers. Browne, with his wife, Agnes, and their two children, Evelyn and George, spent 20 summers between 1921 and 1941 exploring the mountains from their summer home, Illahee Lodge on Spray Avenue in Banff. These expeditions by pack train provided wonderful family vacations and an opportunity for Browne to paint the alpine landscape. Walter Wilcox, looking back on his experiences exploring the Rockies, particularly remembers Belmore Browne's competence in taking pack trains into the wilderness and his gift for painting the landscape:

> Belmore Browne, the artist, got a tremendous amount of pleasure out of the mountains. He loved to camp out with friends or family. He could pack and ride his horses with skill, cook an excellent meal and set up a comfortable camp by himself. We became good friends as was natural between two men who were both interested in depicting the beauty of nature, I with my camera and he with his marvellous paintings.[151]

Agnes Browne kept a diary of the family trips, including several to Bow and Hector lakes. She comments sensitively on the natural beauty of the alpine landscape, the great enjoyment of the children in the outdoors and the fine sketches Belmore worked on in the backcountry. On a trip in July 1928,[152] they lost the trail north of Lake Louise and very nearly lost Belmore's painting equipment when a horse attempting to ford the Bow River was swept away. Nevertheless, they spent a happy week camped beside Hector Lake, allowing Belmore to complete three canvases. Later that summer, from August 21 to September 12, they returned to the area to stay at Jimmy Simpson's camp at the north end of Bow Lake. He had been able to lease the land around his old camping spot near the stream from Bow Pass and complete a boathouse and an octagonal log cabin, the Ram Pasture, by August 1924, followed by a second log cabin in 1925.[153] Agnes Browne marvelled at the beauty of the location and the comforts of the Ram Pasture with its fireplace and animal skins decorating the interior. Jimmy was the outfitter and guide for the Browne family and a number of their friends. He also led a sightseeing tour over Bow Pass, down to Peyto Lake and onto the glacier. Agnes later remarks on the spectacular sight of this large group departing for Lake Louise with 20 people and 50 horses making their way around Bow Lake.

In August 1929, Agnes describes an exhilarating ride through a landscape of peaks and meadows to Bow Lake.[154] While George was successful in catching trout on the fly, his father painted images of the Crowfoot Glacier, his horses and the Bow Valley. In July 1930, they also spent a week at Hector Lake,[155] where Jimmy kept a rowboat for his guests. Jimmy suggested they row to the head of the lake to see the great icefield with its two waterfalls, a scene that no one had painted. Belmore established his easel here and spent four days working on a large canvas, an exhibition piece, according to Agnes, that involved about 40 miles of rowing back and forth from their camp at the opposite end of the lake. When they returned to Bow Lake, they were the only people in camp, so they moved into the Ram Pasture.

While the Browne family was at Bow Lake in late August and early September of 1929, Frank Panabaker, an artist whom Browne knew through the Salmagundi Club in New York,[156] stayed with his wife at Illahee Lodge in Banff.[157] The young couple was delighted to move from their rented room to enjoy the Brownes' house, furnished with oriental carpets, old brass and antique furniture. Browne also helped the younger artist by offering criticism of his work and allowing Panabaker to view his own paintings in frames borrowed from Browne's collection. When the Browne family returned to Banff on September 6, the Panabakers started their expedition up the Bow Valley with a pack train provided by Pat Brewster in exchange for a sketch. Their original destination had been the Ptarmigan Valley, but a report of a grizzly in the area caused them to go to the nine-mile camp on the trail to Bow Lake instead, where they put up their tent near the warden's cabin. On September 8, Panabaker painted Mount Temple, and the next day, Hector Lake. On September 23, after eating all their remaining food, they waited in vain for the horses and guide and finally decided to embark on the five-hour trek to Lake Louise with the paintings on Panabaker's back.

Five-Day Rides

Trail Riders of the Canadian Rockies at Bow Lake

Now that Jimmy Simpson had established a permanent camp at the north end of Bow Lake, travel on horseback over the trail from Lake Louise was popular. With spectacular scenery and manageable distances between camping spots, the ride to Bow Lake was ideal for the Trail Riders of the Canadian Rockies, an organization under the guidance of John Murray Gibbon of the CPR that included prominent Banff residents such as Belmore Browne, Byron Harmon, Carl Rungius, James Simpson and Mary Schäffer Warren.

When 60 participants left Lake Louise on July 29, 1926, for the five-day ride to Bow Pass, Carl and Louise Rungius and Byron Harmon were part of the group. The plan on the first day was to follow the Bow River valley to a lunch stop that had a wonderful view of Lake Hector, nine miles along the trail. From there, they would take the upper trail along the base of Mount Hector to the first camp at the junction of the Bow River and Mosquito Creek.[158] The next day, the riders could choose to fish in Hector Lake or ride up the Bow River past the Crowfoot Glacier and Bow Lake to Bow Pass. The third day would take the trail riders over Molar Pass and down Molar Creek to camp at its junction with the Little Pipestone Creek. In order to join a powwow at the foot of Redoubt Mountain in the afternoon on the fourth day, they would travel over the summit between the Little Pipestone Creek and Red Deer River. At the powwow, some of the activities planned for guides and guests, before the evening of singing and moccasin dances, included packing competitions, horse races and wilderness tennis. On the final morning of the ride, the participants had an opportunity for photography and socializing before riding to the Chateau Lake Louise for dinner, followed by a general meeting.

Carl Rungius greatly enjoyed the songs and conversation around the campfire and consequently went on a five-day ride every summer.[159] The *Bulletin* for June 1933 advertised another ride to Bow Lake, illustrated with a Rungius painting of the lake.[160] Horses would no longer be used for the entire trip, however, because the construction of a new highway allowed the trail riders to be driven as far as Mosquito Creek before travelling on horseback to their camp at Bow Lake. After a side trip to Bow Pass, the horses would take them over the Dolomite Pass to Isabella Lake for the second camp. On the third day, the planned ride would follow Dolomite Creek to the Siffleur River and over the Pipestone Pass to their next camp on the Pipestone River. A ride down the Pipestone to Lake Louise the next day would conclude their journey. This ride covers, in reverse, the same territory that Ralph Edwards and members of the Appalachian Club journeyed through with such difficulty in 1898.

Artist of the Mountain Solitudes

A.C. Leighton

Like Carl Rungius and Belmore Browne, A.C. Leighton thoroughly enjoyed the adventures of trail life in the Rockies. His first experience as an artist in Canada had been on a visit in 1924 when he painted scenes along the railway line for the CPR. The train would drop him off in places that inspired him to paint and then pick him up on the return journey. One can imagine the feeling of wilderness solitude as the train disappeared, leaving him entirely alone to paint the mountain landscape. This desire to sketch the natural scene far from civilization became typical of Leighton. On his next visit to Canada, in 1927, he concentrated on mountains, a subject that appealed to him right until the end of his career.

Leighton was offered the position of art director at the Provincial Institute of Technology and Art in 1929, when Lars Haukaness died suddenly. Leighton's new post allowed him to stop working for the CPR and settle in Calgary. John Murray Gibbon, the publicity agent for the CPR, encouraged him to become a member of the Trail Riders in order to have access to the remote scenery that he preferred to paint on location.[161] In 1931, after Leighton married his former student Barbara Harvey, they spent their honeymoon in the Kananaskis Valley.[162] Now Leighton had a companion for his painting expeditions, and, as a result, he no longer accompanied the Trail Riders. Instead, the couple preferred to hire an outfitter, who would leave them in the mountains to work in solitude for two weeks or more.[163] Travelling by pack train in the Rockies fulfilled Leighton's boyhood fantasy of living the life of a Canadian cowboy.[164] As an artist in the wilderness, he did have adventures, such as becoming snowbound in a tent with Barbara, or very nearly falling over a cliff after his horse threw him.[165] In his Bow Lake and Bow Pass paintings, the mountains dominate each scene, suggesting the grandeur and solemnity of the wilderness. Later in his career, Leighton would have access to this area by automobile, if he deigned to take advantage of this modern invention.[166]

Since Leighton had very high standards for his work, not all of his mountain paintings have survived. Walter Phillips recognized Leighton's artistic gifts in the first Canadian exhibitions of Leighton's work in 1927. Phillips was particularly impressed by the speed with which Leighton completed a watercolour sketch – twice as fast as most artists.[167] Leighton's style is distinctive in the restrained use of colour, softened even more by his preference, in his watercolours and oils, for tinted backgrounds.[168] The subdued tones and delicate colours, however, do not detract from the great power of his paintings: Leighton captures the quiet immensity of the mountains in their remote settings.

Leighton's Kindred Spirit

Walter J. Phillips

A.C. Leighton and Walter Phillips developed their skills in watercolour painting in England before coming to Canada and discovering the mountain landscape. Phillips admired Leighton's work because it demonstrated many qualities that Phillips considered essential: superb drawing, strong composition, rich colour and a sensitive depiction of the natural scene. Phillips had high praise for

Leighton's traditional techniques and individual style that created paintings reflecting an attitude of thoughtful calm and honesty. In fact, the older Phillips suggests that Leighton has reached the summit of artistic expression in his watercolours.[169]

The praise for Leighton's painting can also be applied to Phillips' own work, as he was an artist steadfast in his belief that traditional techniques, in watercolour or woodcut, were the means to depict a realistic, natural beauty. In an article called the "Cult of Clumsiness," Phillips rejects pseudo-modern schools of art that have no use for proper technique and realism.[170] Further, he suggests that paintings by the Group of Seven, with their austere, forbidding landscapes of Georgian Bay – consisting of rocks, jack pines and lakes – are repellent in their lack of any human presence.[171] Phillips had a much gentler view of landscapes, and as such, his paintings reflect a sense of tranquility in the midst of natural beauty. The loneliness of the wilderness did not appeal to him and, in fact, he enjoyed having a companion on his sketching trips, suggesting that such company was just as important as his painting equipment.[172]

In his perceptive comments on Phillips' art, Duncan Campbell Scott points to a strong sense of design and rhythm in the naturalness and the dynamic portrayal of flowing water.[173] Phillips was fascinated by water, especially waterfalls, which encompass all the qualities of water: above the precipice, the smooth water reflects the landscape and sky, but as the water falls, these reflections are fragmented in the white water and foam, covered with a fine mist.[174] Phillips recognized the greater power of water in its transience, flowing over solid rock, wearing it away with small fragments carried by the rushing torrent.[175] Like Leighton, Phillips liked to sketch on location, revealing a wonderful spontaneity in these small images. Phillips, too, ventured into the mountains on horseback, put up with the vagaries of mountain weather and had his share of adventures with wild animals, including being followed by a mountain lion on the trail from Lake Oesa to Lake O'Hara.[176]

Artists at Bow Lake

Peter and Catharine Whyte

Peter Whyte grew up in Banff and began to study art with Belmore Browne and Nora Drummond-Davis, a British illustrator, before going, at the suggestion of a New England landscape painter,

Aldro T. Hibbard, to the School of the Museum of Fine Arts in Boston, where he met Catharine.[177] In a letter to Catharine before their marriage,[178] Peter described a painting expedition with Belmore Browne near Banff. Once the two artists found a suitable area for sketching, they would separate and work about a mile apart. Later, when the time came to return home, they would locate each other by howling like coyotes. On this occasion, Peter, still learning the artist's craft, was encouraged by Browne's praise for one of his sketches. In the same letter, Peter tells Catharine that he has been invited by his neighbour in Banff, Jim Simpson, to pack his sleeping bag and painting supplies and spend two or three weeks in June at Bow Lake, where he could paint, fish and generally enjoy himself. In addition, Peter explains to Catharine that Jim is also an artist and his art collection in his Banff house is worth a fortune. Jimmy's generous offer to Peter, an aspiring painter, is perhaps the first example of the artist-in-residence program at Bow Lake.

In his formative years as a landscape artist, Peter had the opportunity to learn from Carl Rungius and J.E.H. MacDonald, a member of the Group of Seven, with whom Peter went on painting expeditions at Lake O'Hara.[179] After Peter and Catharine's marriage in June 1930, the couple moved to Banff, where Peter's design for their new summer studio beside the Bow River was influenced by the Brownes' home. In 1939, they winterized and expanded their log house by adding a second-storey studio.[180] Catharine benefited from Peter's knowledge about landscape painting when they went sketching together, working just a few metres apart in spectacular locations such as Lake O'Hara, Mount Assiniboine and, especially, Bow Lake.

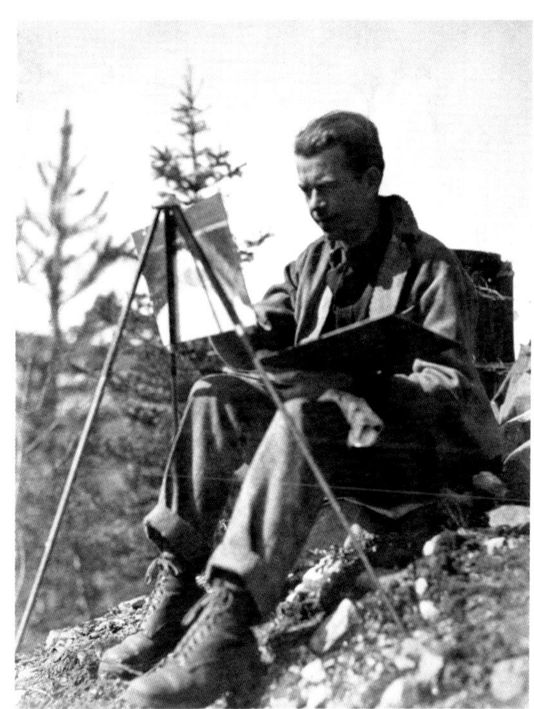

Photograph of Peter Whyte painting near Bow Lake, no date. Whyte Museum of the Canadian Rockies (v683/I.A.6.e).

Catharine's numerous letters to her mother suggest that Bow Lake was a popular destination, not only for sketching, but also because of the Simpsons' warm hospitality. In a letter of June 1937,[181] Catharine mentions that they delivered a stove to the Simpsons at Bow Lake camp because Jimmy never asked them to pay for anything. After making their delivery, which was possible by means of the new road, Peter and Catharine went up to Bow Pass to have tea, looking back to Bow Lake. One of Peter's finest paintings from this area, *Bow Lake from the Summit*, may have been sketched from a similar location on Bow Pass.

A series of letters in August 1954 describe a perfect trip to Bow Lake, providing an insight into Catharine's sense of humour and her great enjoyment of painting outdoors.[182] Most nights they slept in their Jeep and in the morning moved it from the road to a secluded spot at the lakeshore. There, Peter and Catharine cooked breakfast and lunch on the tailgate and relaxed in deck chairs, admiring the reflections in the water. Most of the mornings were taken up with sketching together, drawing the compositions carefully, and, after lunch, working on their paintings. When the light became too bright, they would retreat to shade behind the lodge. The Simpsons always invited them for dinner and, afterward, Peter and Catharine would go outside to watch the changing evening light. When the sky darkened, they would return to the lodge to talk with guests they had known for years. Catharine's charming wit is apparent in her anecdote about a humorous sketch done for the Simpsons by an artist called Boles, from Eureka, California, who, with a pretense of grandeur, signed the work as "Duke of Eureka." Catharine watched in delightful anticipation as a Calgary woman showed a friend through the lodge rooms decorated with paintings by well-known artists. When the two came to the sketch by the Duke of Eureka, the joke was complete because they were completely fooled by the fraudulent signature and accepted without question that the Duke's sketch deserved a place of importance in Jimmy's collection.

Catharine mentions only one difficulty in painting outdoors apart from the storms causing rapid changes in light: the rain. Even an umbrella over Peter's sketch box was not sufficient because the rain dripped down his neck, eventually making a slimy mess of the paint. But apart from the weather, Catharine's letters describe an ideal arrangement for the two artists: freedom and solitude during the day and a hot dinner and company at night. Although many of their canvases of the Bow Lake area are undated, the number of them indicates that they returned to this special place many times, usually painting near the lodge or in Bow Pass. They liked to begin the outdoor sketching season at Bow Lake, even arriving in June to find their camping spot with patches of snow and the lake still partly frozen.

The Tradition of the Artist in Residence

Num-Ti-Jah Lodge

By welcoming artists to his Bow Lake camp, Jimmy helped to develop the artistic legacy of this special place, particularly in the paintings of Carl Rungius, Belmore Browne and Peter and Catharine Whyte. Jimmy's dream of a permanent camp had evolved over many years of negotiating leases with the government and securing funding for construction. When work started on the Banff–Jasper highway in 1931, Jimmy realized the opportunity to provide accommodation to tourists travelling by automobile, and, as a result, he ambitiously began to build a lodge in 1937, without the requisite plans or permits.[183] He took advantage of the new road to transport logs from a burned area north of Bow Pass, near Mistaya Lake, and to salvage rock along the road allowance for his foundation. The financing for his new building came from income generated by the figure-skating careers of his two daughters. By 1940, when the new highway opened, the first version of Jimmy's lodge, which he named Num-Ti-Jah after the Stoney word for pine marten, was complete. But Jimmy had grander plans to enlarge the building substantially with a new wing, including the present dining room. This time, Jimmy's friend and neighbour in Banff, Catherine Whyte, provided the financing through a $50,000 loan. Jimmy would repay the favour many years later by giving his Banff property to Catharine for the Whyte Museum. Num-Ti-Jah Lodge was officially opened July 1, 1950, and construction was finally finished with installation of steam heat in 1954. Jimmy had fulfilled, on a grand scale, his dream of someday putting a building on his favourite camping spot. Beyond that, he also now had the perfect location to hang his art collection and his own watercolours: on the walls of the lodge with windows looking out on the scenery that inspired much of the artwork.

The current artist-in-residence program at Num-Ti-Jah started in the mid-1990s with an idea from Tim Whyte, an owner of the lodge.[184] Lee O'Donnell was the innkeeper at the time, and he enthusiastically endorsed the concept by inviting artists, giving them accommodation, and, in time, helping to organize art shows. When Lee fortuitously saw a cover on an *Avenue West* magazine with a painting by Banff artist Max Elliott, he was able to make contact with Max, who, in turn, made connections with other local artists. Max enthusiastically took part in the artist-in-residence program for the first time in 2002. In *The Banff Crag & Canyon*, Max described her great enjoyment in going to Num-Ti-Jah to become part of a long artistic tradition and to paint the amazing scenery outdoors, "happily distracted by the rumble of avalanches."[185] In return for a residency of two to four days, artists give Num-Ti-Jah a *plein air* sketch, which is then displayed at the lodge to extend the appreciation of art to the guests and staff. About the time that Lee was organizing the residencies, Brewster's Icefield Chalet discontinued its artist-in-residence program, resulting in artists going to Num-Ti-Jah. More and more artists went to the lodge, inspired by the alpine landscape and attracted to Simpson's historic building with all its warmth and comfort. The program became so successful that Lee arranged a curatorial residence to catalogue the artwork.

After her residence, Max felt a special fondness for this hospitable place, and in gratitude for so much kindness, she organized, with Lee's support, two significant art shows. The first, called *The Source*, opened on May 23, 2003, and was a multidisciplinary show including work by almost 40 artists. The exhibition's name focused on Bow Glacier, a major source of water for the Bow Valley, while the exhibition itself served to bring attention to the United Nations' campaign to preserve fresh water. Two years later, in May 2005, Max and Lee organized *The Art of History*, to commemorate Alberta's centennial with images related to the history of Bow Lake, in terms of its recreation, geology and culture. The shows brought a wide range of artists to the lodge, with the artwork remaining on display throughout the summers. Roy Andersen, a Banff photographer, organized exhibitions of black and white photographs for the summers of 2004 and 2005, extending the idea of the *Source* exhibition to include images of the disappearing glaciers in the backcountry of all of the parks in the Rockies.[186] Many other contemporary artists have become part of this vibrant tradition that spans almost a century of art at Num-Ti-Jah, a tradition that all started when Carl Rungius took a second look at Jimmy Simpson's invitation to visit Bow Lake.

Contemporary Artists Associated with Bow Lake

Carolyn Oldale Adams

Originally from Nova Scotia, Carolyn Oldale Adams attended the Nova Scotia College of Art and Design, allowing her to develop a lifelong interest in the creative arts, including clothing design, folk art, drawing, watercolour, acrylic and oil painting. She moved to Calgary in 1976 and, after raising her family, returned to her art full time in the 1990s. Subsequently, she took classes from Jean Geddes and Mike Svob and painted for years with Norm Brown, an encouraging mentor. In 2003, she met Dominik Modlinski who, as well as a friend, is an important influence on her style and use of colour. Carolyn Oldale Adams was also inspired by her 2004 experience as one the artists in residence at Num-Ti-Jah Lodge, a special place combining history and the beauty of the landscape where the innkeeper, Lee O'Donnell, offered a warm welcome. As a member of the Calgary Sketch Club since 2001, she has developed an interest in painting *en plein air*. She is also a member of the group of artists known as The New Seven.

Roger D. Arndt

Roger Arndt has a home and studio in the Okanagan, where he carefully oversees every stage in the creation of his paintings: from the preparation of the boards, by coating them with layers of oil primer and sanding them by hand to a glassy finish; to preliminary oil studies; and to the finished image, produced by applying many layers of transparent colour onto the white board. This meticulous, time-consuming process, derived from Flemish artists who used it centuries ago, creates the striking effect of luminescence in Roger Arndt's works. His concern for detail is carried over to his custom framing of each painting. The subjects are varied, including his own garden, West Coast totem poles and the landscape of the Rockies, which he discovered in his late teens and has returned to every year to hike, camp and sketch.

G.H.W. (Herb) Ashley

Born in Banff, Herb Ashley, a contemporary of Peter Whyte, developed a natural talent by taking drawing lessons from Belmore Browne and Mrs. Drummond-Davies in 1921 and 1922. To supplement his income working as a labourer for the Parks Service in the early 1930s, he taught himself sign painting and show-card writing and did freelance work in commercial art. At this time, he also learned on his own how to use oils and pastels. Carl Rungius, who had a summer studio in Banff, gave him valuable advice about painting wildlife. By 1938, he had become a warden in Banff National Park, and an important part of his job was to photograph and sketch the animals and landscape. From 1957 until 1967, his position as Park Superintendent, which did not allow him to earn extra money through commercial art, gave him the opportunity to concentrate in his leisure time on painting native peoples and wildlife. After his retirement in 1967, he focused on animal subjects, working in watercolour, oil and pastel, from his studio near Shuswap Lake, British Columbia.

Glen W. Boles

As an accomplished skier and mountaineer, Glen Boles has been able to explore the Rockies landscape over many years since his friend Heinz Kohl persuaded him to go climbing for the first time in 1957. His climbing career in the Rockies includes over 450 summits, some by new routes and some first ascents. Glen's recently published book *My Mountain Album* records his expeditions in the mountains through his photographs and drawings. While he found time for climbing, he was also employed for over 35 years by the City of Calgary's waterworks engineering department. On his retirement, he turned his energies to art, working in pen and pencil, watercolour, acrylic and oil. He now lives and paints in Cochrane, Alberta.

W.J. Bradley

W.J. Bradley was born and raised in Banff, where she now lives. As the third generation of her family in Banff, she has a strong sense of history stretching back to her grandfather, who packed supplies in to Mount Assiniboine Lodge. Her great interest lies in painting *en plein air*, trying to capture the special bond she feels with the landscape. Some of her favourite places in the mountains include Lake O'Hara, Mount Assiniboine and Bow Lake. She is mainly self-taught, but she has studied at the Atlin Art Centre and over the last 15 years has taken workshops from artists such as Dominik Modlinski and Mike Svob. W.J. Bradley has also been an artist in residence at Num-Ti-Jah Lodge, recording her thoughts and feelings in her journal for April 29, 2006: "Tonight I am full of anticipation sitting in Num-Ti-Jah Lodge at Bow Lake. My time here reconnects me with Spirit. I find clarity, comfort and growth wrapped in the folds of this place." As well as creating her own paintings, she mentors clients in their photography and sketching through her organization Artistic Journeys.

Bill Burns

Bill Burns is a Canadian artist who now lives in Ontario. Some years after studying at the Ontario College of Art and Design, he found his way to the Rockies and Bow Lake, where he was among the early artists to benefit from the artist-in-residence program established by Tim Whyte and Lee O'Donnell. While sketching near Bow Falls one day, Bill met his friend David McEown and graciously introduced his fellow artist to Lee O'Donnell. David, in turn, suggested to Dominik Modlinski that he, too, should come to Bow Lake. Now two more artists who had studied at the Ontario College of Art were able to become artists in residence. Bill's artistic explorations in the mountains were not limited to the Bow Lake area, as he also travelled to Lake O'Hara and north along the Icefields Parkway. His impressionist style captures the vitality of the alpine landscape.

Horace Champagne

Horace Champagne, who was born in Montréal and presently makes his home in Île d'Orléans, Québec, is the grandson of the artist Charles-Ernest de Belle (1873–1939). Horace decided in 1980 to leave a successful career in advertising and devote his time to painting in dry pastels. He studied art at l'École des Beaux Arts in Montréal and the School of Art in Ottawa, as well as taking workshops from Charles Movalli in New England and Daniel Greene in North Salem, New York. Recently, one of his paintings, a marvellous still life, was featured on the cover of the February 2009 issue of *The Pastel Journal*, and the accompanying article, "Joie de Vivre," by Deborah Secor, offers an insight to his artistic approach. Horace has always enjoyed the outdoors, especially when fly fishing in northern Ontario and Québec. He now paints *en plein air* whenever possible, completing the larger works in his studio. His subjects are varied, ranging from street scenes in Old Québec, to the Rockies landscape, the Pacific shore and, more recently, Newfoundland, where he owns a house at Rose Blanche, just 30 feet from the Atlantic with its drifting icebergs. Wherever he paints, he is inspired by the vitality of the landscape in its changing light and colour, and he strives to capture those moments of fleeting beauty.

C.J.M. (Max) Elliott

Born in Saskatchewan, Max Elliott was inspired by the alpine landscape at an early age. After studying art, at the Alberta College of Art and Design in Calgary and the Nova Scotia College of Art and Design in Halifax, she now lives and works in Banff. Her art focuses on the mountains but in a variety of media, including mosaics, ceramic pieces, mixed media collage and painting in oil and acrylic. Her commissions from Parks Canada include the Fenland Trail signposts in Banff, the Lake Louise entry sign and banners for Field and Lake Louise. Max paints on location, creating both abstract and representational landscapes. To prepare for her solo show *Glacier-Fed* at the Whyte Museum in 2003, she absorbed as much as possible about glaciers through the artist-in-residence programs at the Icefield Centre, the Haig Glacier Camp in Kananaskis and Num-Ti-Jah Lodge. She describes her stay at the Lodge from May 27 to June 1 as one that combines the wonders of nature and great comfort: "The last painting day was the best – I listened to a symphony of avalanches/ running water/ the chink of ice chunks falling into the water. The season's first water birds were landing on thawed patches of lake. My room is so decadent – big comfy beds, a great view, a writing desk, and no phone, no fax machine, no computer and no television." Max also organized two art shows at Num-Ti-Jah Lodge, *Source* (2003) and *Art of History* (2005), producing fascinating exhibitions of work relating to Bow Lake.

Sarah Kidner

After spending most of her childhood in Ontario and studying fine art, history and philosophy at the University of Toronto, Sarah Kidner moved to Banff in 1987, attracted by her love of skiing and hiking. She has participated in workshops led by Mike Svob, among others, and studied figure drawing with Holly Middleton. Some significant influences on her style of oil painting are the French Impressionists, Tom Thomson and the Group of Seven. Sarah is intrigued by the effects of changing light on the colours of the mountain landscape. She does paint on location, but most often she works in her studio in Canmore where she now lives. Her subjects extend beyond the alpine landscape to include urban scenes in Venice, Banff or Canmore, and often she includes people, capturing a moment from their everyday lives in an enduring image.

Donna Jo Massie

Donna Jo Massie left a position in Fort Myers, Florida, to come to the Bow Valley in 1976 and teach for the program in Environmental Education for Kananaskis Country. A decade later, she started to paint, and turned to watercolours full time in 1988. She continued in her role as an educator and naturalist by teaching watercolours to adults in Canmore and Banff, as well as by leading workshops for corporations and in the backcountry. Her teaching is complemented by her Canadian bestseller *A Rocky Mountain Sketchbook*, a guide to painting the alpine landscape in watercolours. She has been an artist in residence at the International Peace Park in Glacier National Park, Montana, and at Bow Lake. An enjoyment of hiking in the mountains gives her the opportunity for painting on location. She is inspired not only by the high alpine landscape but also by flowers. A member of the Alberta Society of Artists and the Society of Canadian Artists, Donna Jo has been recognized by her hometown of Canmore with an Artistic Achievement Award and the Honorary Chair of ArtsPeak.

David McEown

David McEown's artistic journeys have taken him literally to the ends of the earth through his recent residencies on cruise ships travelling to the high Arctic and Antarctica. He seeks remote and endangered landscapes, hoping to increase awareness of their fragile natural beauty. Born in Toronto, David developed his love of art and nature by spending time in Muskoka, in northern Ontario, on his great-grandparents' homestead. After studying at the Ontario College of Art and Design, he spent his graduation year at the Algoma School of Landscape Arts, and the area appealed to him so much that he stayed for five years, living in a cabin and creating watercolours of the natural world. His accomplishments earned him two Elizabeth Greenshield Foundation grants, in 1994 and 1999, allowing him to extend his search for beautiful places that are under threat of change. When he is at home in Toronto, David also teaches watercolour classes at the Royal Ontario Museum. He has recently established another studio in Vancouver.

Janet (Holly) B. Middleton

Holly Middleton has worked in a variety of media over her long artistic career, including stained glass, woodcuts, murals, oils and watercolours. Her training began at the Winnipeg School of Art (1941–1943), followed by the Provincial Institute of Technology and Art in Calgary (1943–1946) where she studied with H.G. Glyde and Walter J. Phillips, moving with them to the Banff School of Fine Arts. During the years 1961 and 1962, she travelled to London to study graphics at the Slade School of Art. At this time in her life, she also had the opportunity to study in France, Italy, Japan and the United States. Holly Middleton's teaching career is also extensive, including many years in the Extension Department, University of Alberta (1948–1964) and 23 summer terms (1948–1971) as a painting instructor at the Banff School.

Dominik J. Modlinski

Dominik Modlinski, born in Warsaw, Poland, began his artistic training at the age of 7 by studying with a master printmaker. He came to Canada when he was 16 and studied painting and drawing at the Ontario College of Art. After graduation in 1993, he moved to Algoma to live and paint at the Algoma School of Landscape Arts. In 1994, he set out on a painting trip to western Canada, sketching the landscape in watercolours. On a four-month bicycle trip in the spring of 1995, from Whitehorse to Vancouver, Dominik discovered Atlin and the Kluane mountain landscape, a great inspiration for him. His latest adventures include residencies on cruise ships bound for the Arctic, Antarctica and Patagonia. The artist-in-residence program organized by Tim Whyte and Lee O'Donnell at Num-Ti-Jah Lodge offered him the wonderful opportunity to paint the landscape around Bow Lake, especially in the late fall and winter when he could hike and snowshoe, sketching *en plein air*. Dominik strives through his art to bring joy and a better understanding of the environment.

Zelda Nelson

Born in Saskatoon, Zelda has moved west over the years, to Calgary in 1971 and to her present home in Canmore in 1987. She has studied art at the University of Calgary and the Banff Centre. Her contribution to the artistic world is not only through her painting but also in her dedication to the Canmore Artists and Artisans Guild, serving as president in 1996 and 2001. Zelda paints on location whenever possible, working in watercolour, acrylic or oil, and her main goal is to express her strong feeling for the landscape – her sense of the underlying power of nature in creating such magnificent beauty. The alpine landscapes of Lake O'Hara and Mount Assiniboine have a particular fascination for her. In 2005 as an artist in residence at Num-Ti-Jah Lodge, she had an opportunity to paint at Bow Lake, a place that inspires her with its abundant history as well as natural beauty.

Erica Neumann

A graduate of the Ontario College of Art in drawing, painting and sculpture, Erica Neumann now lives in Okotoks, Alberta, where she has a studio and the Neumann Gallery. She promotes the study of art by teaching in her gallery and by creating DVDs about artists. In her own art, she emphasizes a respect for wildlife, with paintings of wolves, deer and bears. She is well known for her remarkable images of bears and made a significant contribution to the show at the Whyte Museum when the *Year of the Great Bear* was announced in 2001. Erica also likes to paint the mountain landscape on location using lively colours and energetic brushstrokes. She has been an artist in residence at Num-Ti-Jah Lodge several times and was commissioned to create a portrait of Blondie, a grizzly who lived in the Bow Lake area for many years. At Bow Lake, she has had an opportunity to see more bears than anywhere else, although fortunately not when she has been painting *en plein air*.

Ralph Edward Oberg

Ralph is an artist who enjoys mountaineering, backpacking and taking trips with horses into remote areas. He often travels with his wife, Shirley, also an artist, to create sketches on location, which are later enlarged in his studio. Born in Biloxi, Mississippi, he grew up in Colorado, studying art at Colorado State University (1968–1970). After a short time working in commercial illustration, he began his career in art in 1974 by painting wildlife. By 1987, he wanted a different focus, moving away from an emphasis on photographic realism to study with the *plein air* artists, especially landscape painters. He feels that working on site allows him to capture the varied light and colours in nature, and he is now a member of the Plein-Air Painters of America. Carl Rungius is an important influence on his work, and like Rungius, he has an interest in both wildlife and landscape. More recently, animals have returned to his art, portrayed with an impressionistic technique. Bow Lake is a favourite destination in the fall, with Num-Ti-Jah Lodge providing a comfortable base for his painting expeditions into a landscape that stimulates his artistic energy: "I'll never tire of painting on site at Bow Lake and its vicinity as it always seems to bring out my best. The Rockies have been superbly suited to the sensibilities of artists for generations. The grandeur of the mountain shapes, colors, contrasts and textures provide aesthetic elements that often seem to compose themselves effortlessly and joyfully."

Alice Saltiel-Marshall

Originally from Toronto, Alice Saltiel-Marshall studied with Doris McCarthy at The Art Centre in the Central Technical School (1966–1969). After her marriage and honeymoon in Europe, she lived in England for a year, working as a commercial artist. Shortly after returning to Canada, the young couple moved to Alberta and created a company, Saltiel Originals Inc., which continues to reproduce and distribute reproductions of Alice's paintings. For over two decades, since 1986, Alice and her husband, Bill, have lived in Canmore, where the alpine landscape has inspired her. She also enjoys backpacking in the mountain parks and sketching in areas such as Lake O'Hara, Mount Assiniboine and the Tonquin Valley. She especially enjoys Bow Lake because all the elements of the alpine landscape – a beautiful lake surrounded by trees with glaciers and peaks above – are so easily accessible without hiking for hours. Her love of adventure and travel has also taken her on painting expeditions to France and the west coast of Vancouver Island. In 2008, Alice created a show called *Wild!* – paintings of big cats, a subject she returned to after many years. While living in Canmore, Alice played an important role in the arts community by acting as the president of the Canmore Artists and Artisans Guild (1986–1987) and as a trustee on the board of the Whyte Museum (1994–1997). Recently Alice and Bill moved to Claresholm, Alberta.

Mike Svob

Mike Svob was born in Ontario and educated at Niagara College and the University of Western Ontario. He now lives on Canada's west coast in White Rock, British Columbia. As well as being a past president of the Federation of Canadian Artists, he has made a significant contribution to the teaching of art through his writing on artistic techniques, for example in *Paint Red Hot Landscapes That Sell*, and through workshops for fellow artists. In a painting career of more than a quarter century, he has explored nature's relationship to people, recording his impressions of light on the landscape using strong colours. His subjects vary, from the canals of Venice to the Rockies of Canada, and the size of his works ranges from an average canvas to commissioned murals. Mike is a strong believer in sharing his artistic knowledge. His vibrant, impressionist style has influenced many contemporary artists.

Elizabeth M. Wiltzen

Elizabeth Wiltzen was born in Portage la Prairie, Manitoba. About 20 years ago, her love of hiking, climbing and skiing in remote mountain places inspired her to paint the landscape. While she is mostly self-taught, she has taken workshops with prominent artists. Her subjects now vary and include flowers, portraits, animals and landscapes – urban and coastal in addition to alpine. After 15 years painting in watercolours, she decided that the texture and colours of oils were better suited to her perception of the landscape, allowing her to create a greater impact on large canvases. She enjoys the immediate connection with the landscape when sketching on location, and with oils she has the ability to change the painting as it develops. In March 2005, Elizabeth was given senior signature status in the Senior Federation of Canadian Artists. As well as larger canvases, she has recently been creating 6 × 8 in. sketches in a project called "100 *plein air* paintings in 100 days."

Rob Zeer

Rob Zeer, born in Weyburn, Saskatchewan, is mainly self-taught, but he has received some instruction in art at the University of Calgary and the Alberta College of Art and Design. He likes to work in charcoal and acrylic on canvas or paper, and he attempts to capture the rugged quality of the Canadian landscape by painting solely *en plein air*, a purist's approach similar to that of the Group of Seven and the French Impressionists.

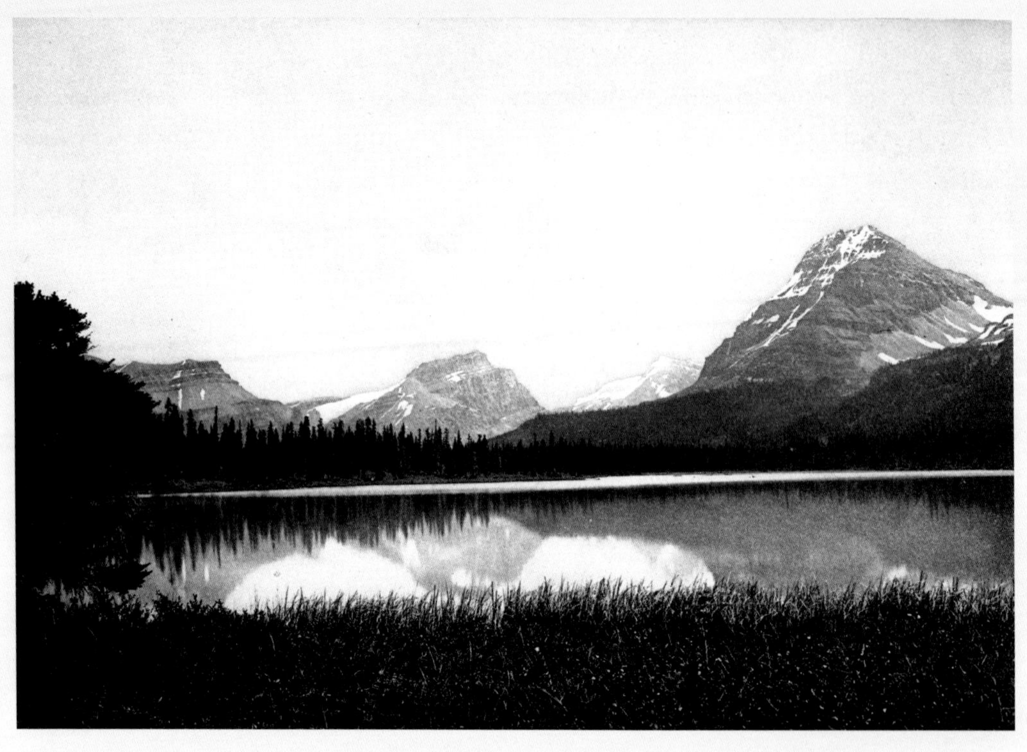

Walter Wilcox

Photograph of Upper Bow Lake (looking east), 1895.
Whyte Museum of the Canadian Rockies (v85/na66-559).
Bow Peak on far right; Mount Hector in distant centre;
Molar Mountain left of centre.

BOW PASS

All through that halcyon day we travelled northwards – across streams and meadows, through the chequered shades of pine groves and past where the wonderfully sculptured Crowfoot Glacier thrusts down its icy talons towards the flashing waters of the Lower Lakes. By late afternoon we found ourselves on the sandy beach, where the trail comes out upon Bow Lake itself – a great basin of green, glacial water, two miles across. On the left, shattered limestone precipices and talus fans fall steeply to the water, but the eastern shore is low and swings northward in a gradual curve to the north-east corner of the lake. Here a wide treeless moorland bounded by dark woods and converging mountains rises to the summit of Bow Pass three miles beyond.

— B.S. Darling, "Up the Bow and Down the Yoho,"
Canadian Alpine Journal, III (1911), 161–62.

Peter Whyte

Bow Lake from the Summit, n.d.

Oil on Canvas, 63.5 × 76.5 cm
Collection of the Whyte Museum of the Canadian Rockies

The title of this stunning view from Bow Pass does not reflect the emphasis on Crowfoot Mountain with its magnificent glacier. The viewer's eye follows the winding stream, one of the sources of the Bow River, down through the meadows and then moves across the lake to Crowfoot, which fills almost half of the painting. Bow Lake seems insignificant in contrast to the majestic presence of the mountain looming above, but Peter Whyte draws the two together by repeating the shape of the glacier in the expanse of water below. He offsets the sombre gray sky, with just a hint of good weather in the narrow band of blue, by introducing vibrant splashes of colour beside the stream closest to the viewer and in the trees. This powerful image encompasses the extremes of alpine beauty, from the meadows and lake to the rugged terrain high above.

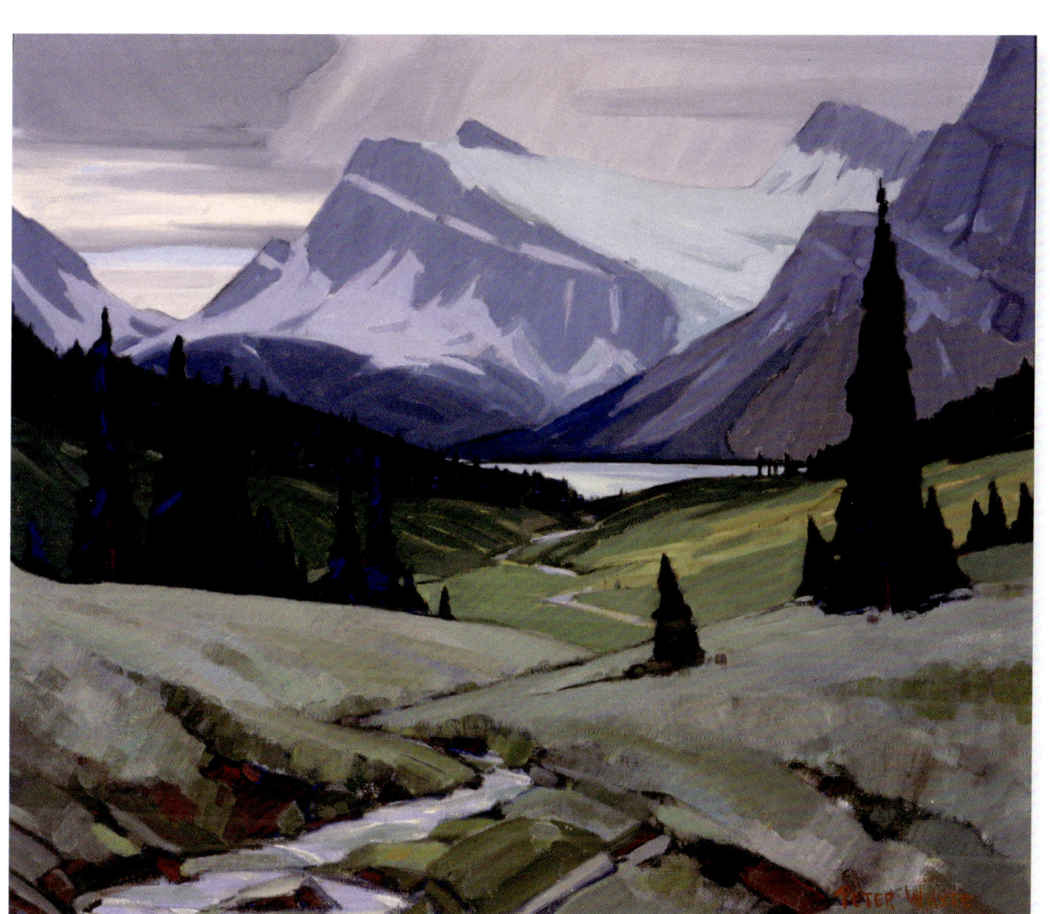

A.C. Leighton

Bow Pass – Early Morning, n.d.

Watercolour, 28.5 × 37.5 cm
Collection of the Whyte Museum of the Canadian Rockies

Early explorers mention the wonderful perspective from Bow Pass, made even more spectacular by climbing the spur of Mount Jimmy Simpson, shown on the right in the background of Leighton's painting. From such a vantage point, one can see the broad, green valley containing Bow Lake and the surrounding mountains. Leighton, however, chooses to give an impression of alpine solitude, a landscape of rock and snow. The morning sun illuminates the eastern flank of the mountain, and its imposing height is in striking contrast to the undulating terrain of the foreground, much of it still in shadow. Another spire is just visible in outline beyond the sunlit mountain. The high elevation of the pass results in heavy snowfalls, and Leighton's image suggests late spring or early summer with snow patches lingering on the ground. Leighton's subtle values, with the different effects of light on the terrain, show various shades of the reddish-brown rock. His image is realistic in the limited use of colour, and it also captures a feeling of austerity in the high alpine landscape.

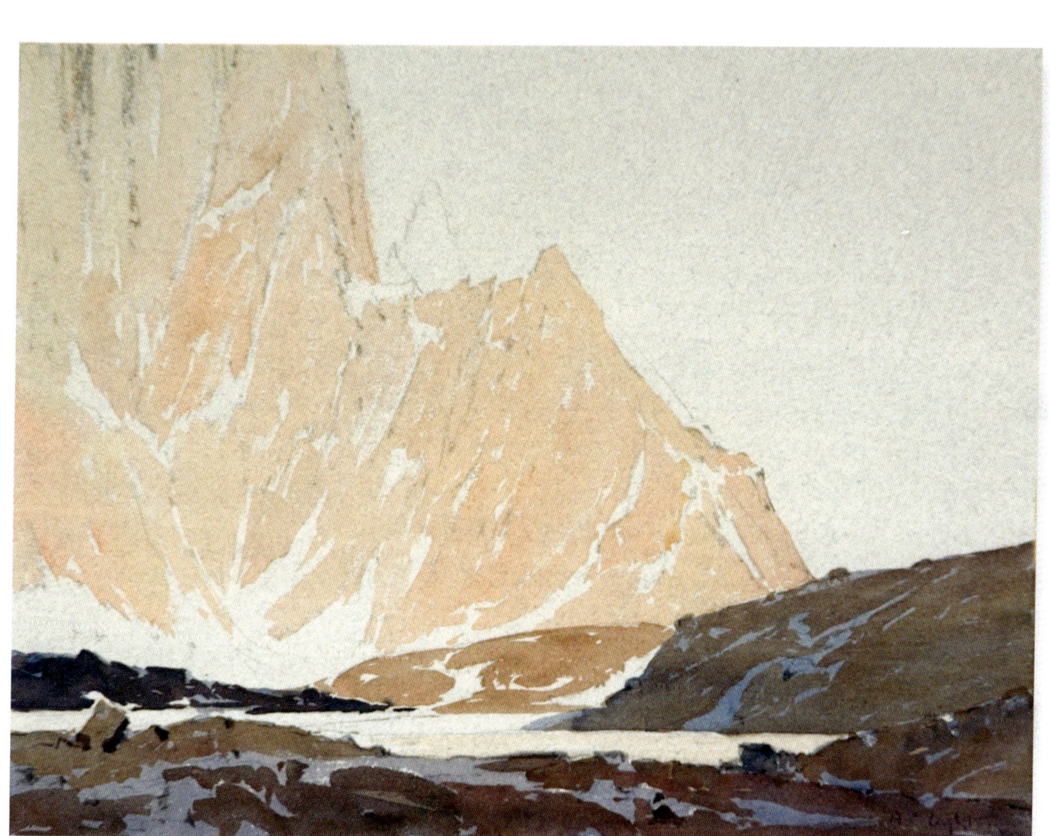

Catharine Whyte

Bow Panorama, n.d.

Oil on Canvas, 14.2 × 35 cm
Collection of the Whyte Museum of the Canadian Rockies

Catharine Whyte's breathtaking panorama from the north end of Bow Lake epitomizes summertime in the Rockies. The focus in her sketch is Bow Peak, right of centre, with Mount Hector just behind and to the left. Flanking these great summits are Molar Mountain, left, and the slope of Crowfoot Mountain just showing on the right. The glacial blue water of the lake and the softer blue in the sky frame the four mountains. Catherine's horizontal format is balanced by the vertical lines of trees below and the peaks above. Catharine is fascinated by transitory clouds, and here she playfully arranges them on an angle to counter the horizontal emphasis in the foreground.

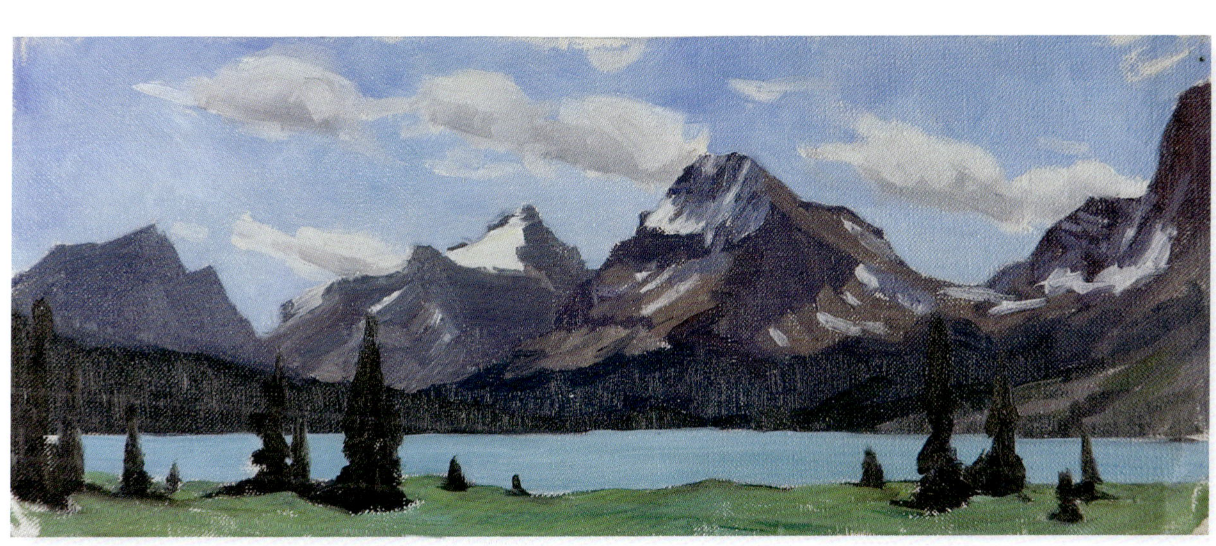

Jimmy Simpson

Bow Lake, 1962

Watercolour, 29.0 × 37.8 cm
Collection of the Whyte Museum of the Canadian Rockies

Jimmy Simpson portrays the clouds floating in a summer sky over the peaks that can be seen from the meadows leading to Bow Pass. Mount Hector is on the distant left, with its distinctive glacier leading to the summit, the route of the first ascent by Abbot and members of the Appalachian Club. Dominating the valley in the centre background is Bow Peak, with Crowfoot Mountain to the right. The firm lines of the peaks reaching into the sky are in contrast to the ridges sweeping down to the lake with its curving shoreline. Jimmy's sensitivity to colour is particularly evident in the gentle slopes of the foreground meadows. Here the single tree leads the eye to the imposing mass of Bow Peak. Jimmy captures a summer idyll – the soft beauty of the valley and Bow Lake with the inspiring mountains in the distance.

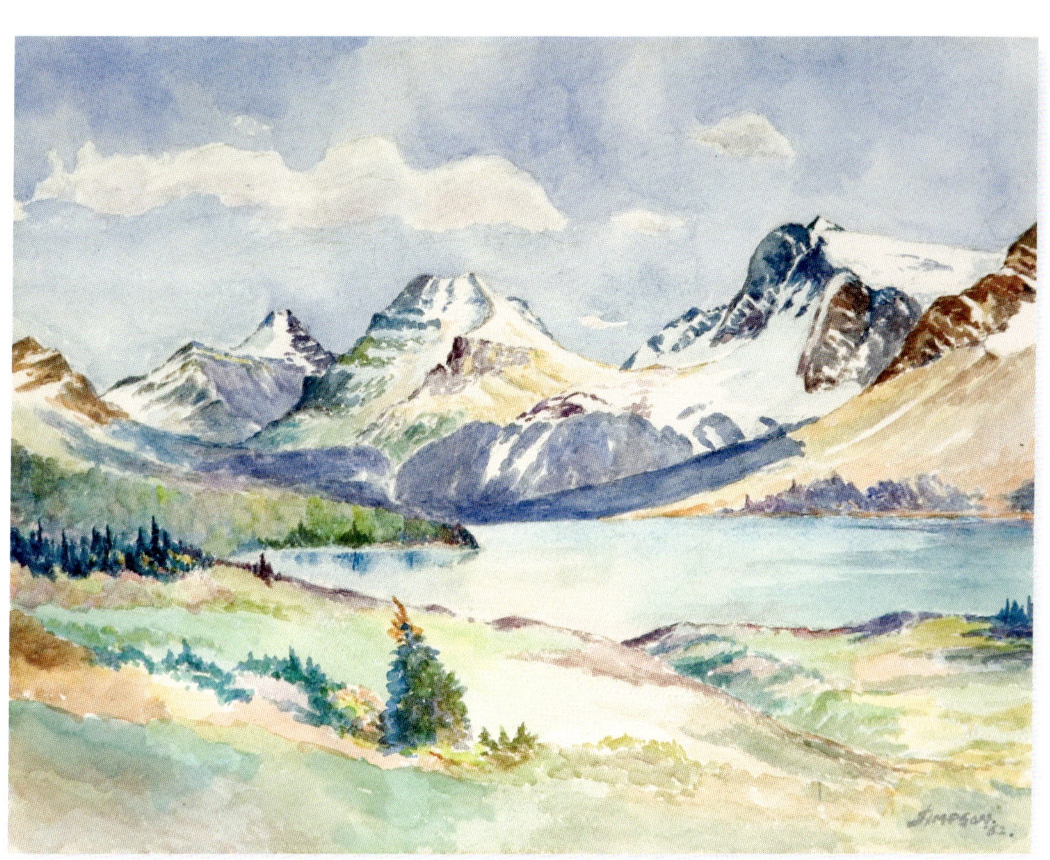

Peter Whyte

Mount Hector, Bow Lake, n.d.

Oil on Canvas, 27.6 × 34.8 cm
Collection of the Whyte Museum of the Canadian Rockies

Peter Whyte's sketch captures the fleeting moments of sunlight illuminating Mount Hector, to the right of centre, and Molar Mountain, to the left. The steep ridge of Bow Peak rises out of the picture on the right. Trees in the foreground frame the view over Bow Lake to the distant peaks, and a dramatic contrast in colour between the various shades of green in the meadow and the warm tones of the mountains set against a stormy sky gives the painting great energy. A small patch of blue above the cloud bank may soon disappear, obliterating the sunlight and with it the warm colours. Broad brushstrokes suggest that Peter was sketching quickly to portray this ephemeral beauty before the light changed.

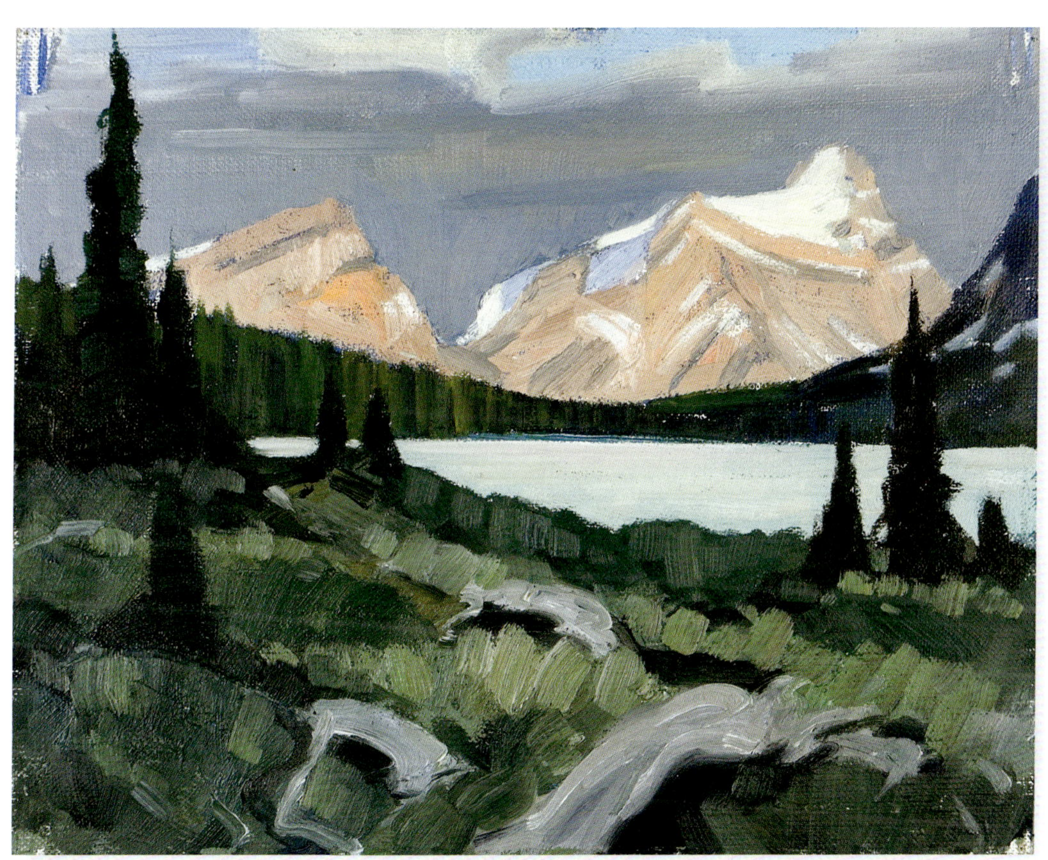

Horace Champagne

Bow Lake, Always Fresh with Nature's Surprises, c.2003

Pastel on Paper, 61.0 × 45.7
Private Collection

Horace Champagne's painting depicts the wild beauty of the alpine lake with snow-clad mountains towering behind. His vantage point is near the shore of Bow Lake, looking past the precipitous shoulder of Bow Peak to magnificent Mount Hector with its distinctive glaciated summit. An early snowfall is melting in the sunshine, but larger patches linger, especially in the shade of the trees closest to the viewer. The red paint-brush beside the snow suggests late summer. Meadow grasses and bushes are portrayed in warm colours and with great delicacy of line, while the ancient clump of trees in the foreground reaches with withered trunks toward the summits. The viewer's eye follows the snow patches, in the direction of the deep-green water, sparkling in the sunshine, and across to the narrow channel between the upper and lower Bow Lakes. A red canoe floats to the left of the channel, while the mountains rise steeply above the treeline, a sharp contrast to the world below. The wonder of this scene, which epitomizes the remote wilderness, is its close proximity to the Icefields Parkway.

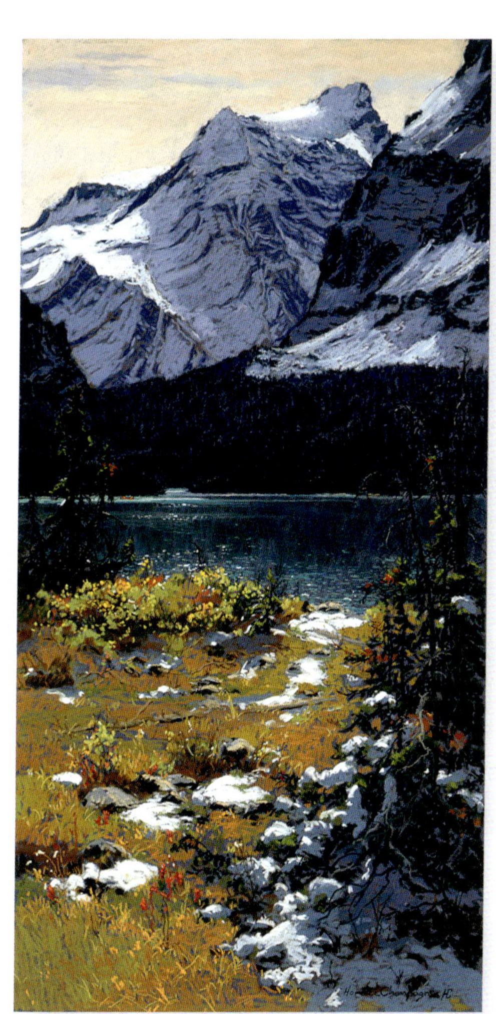

Belmore Browne

Hector Lake, Canadian Rockies, n.d.

Watercolour on Paper, 10.8 × 16.6 cm
Collection of the Whyte Museum of the Canadian Rockies

Belmore Browne liked to explore on horseback with his family in the summers, and Agnes Browne's diaries record several trips to Bow Lake, which also included camping at nearby Hector Lake. Belmore probably completed this sketch from their campsite beside the lake, looking across to Pulpit Peak. Jimmy Simpson kept a rowboat at Hector Lake that the Browne family frequently used to row across to the outlet stream flowing from Lake Margaret, which is tucked in below Pulpit Peak and enclosed by the green ridge on the right in the watercolour sketch. While the Browne children, George and Evelyn, fished in Lake Margaret, Belmore and Agnes rowed to the end of Hector Lake, with a view of the Balfour Glacier, to find suitable painting spots. Belmore has created a powerful image of the escarpment on the eastern edge of the Waputik Range rising from left to right, culminating in Pulpit Peak. This diagonal thrust is balanced by the trees in the foreground, which lean slightly in the other direction; the contrary motion gives the watercolour a great deal of energy, supported by the vigorous application of colour. The rugged beauty of the mountains across the lake is softened by the small bay with its lush vegetation in the foreground.

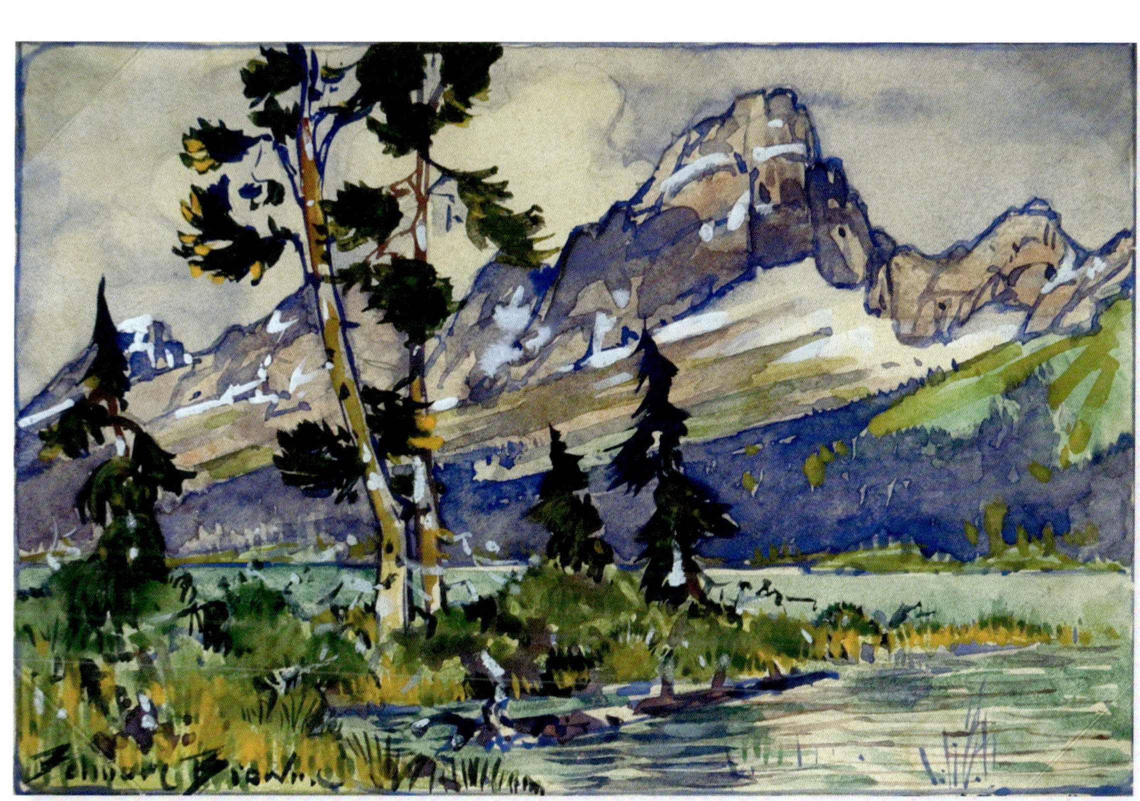

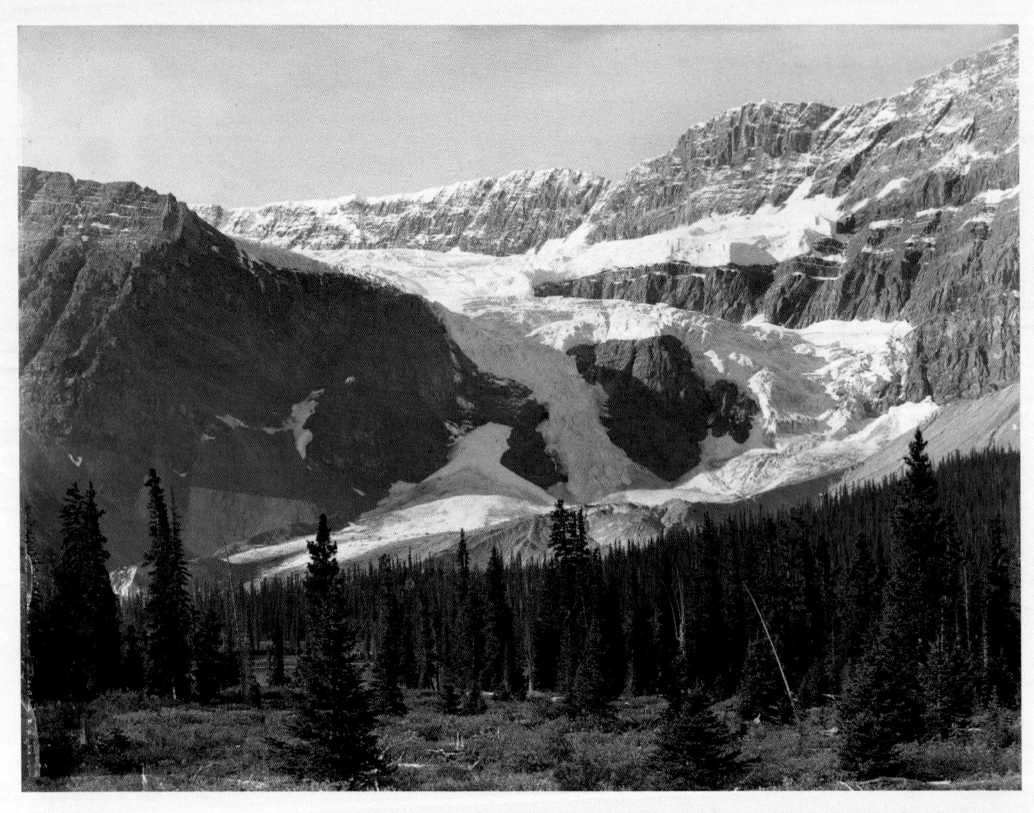

Vaux Family

Photograph of Crowfoot Glacier (No. 158), 1902
Whyte Museum of the Canadian Rockies (v653/na80-1136).

CROWFOOT GLACIER

We crossed a wide meadow which led by a gentle slope to the shore. The beauty of water, trees, and rugged mountains is here combined to make one of the most charming situations. Our camp was pitched on the border of a small lake, less than half a mile in length, which proved later to be a land locked cove of the main body of water, and separated from it by a narrow channel. In the distance, through this connecting waterway, a glimpse of the larger lake appeared. Toward the east, the small lake, upon which our camp was placed, contracts into a shallow stream, which falls a few feet by a succession of gentle rapids and enters another lake about three-quarters of a mile long. This rests against the very base of the glacier-bearing mountain west of our camp.

— Walter Wilcox, *The Rockies of Canada* (1909), 144.

Carl Rungius

Spreading Glacier Tongues, n.d.

Oil on Canvas, 22.7 × 27.9 cm
Collection of Glenbow Museum

Carl Rungius sketched the three icy tongues of the Crowfoot Glacier from a high vantage point across the valley; he was looking past the treetops and over the lower end of Bow Lake. Rungius shows the lowest tongue, or talon in the crow's foot, reaching well down the talus slope, perhaps even to the water's edge. Although the painting is not dated, today one can see from the viewpoint on the Icefields Parkway that only the two upper talons remain. Rungius applied the paint in broad strokes with an impressionist style, suggesting various colours in the sloping shoulder to the left and in the glacier, with its illuminated surface in contrast to the bluish walls of ice immediately above the supporting ledges. The ice flows from the top left diagonally down and around the resistant rock that contains the dynamic glacier as its immense power moulds the landscape.

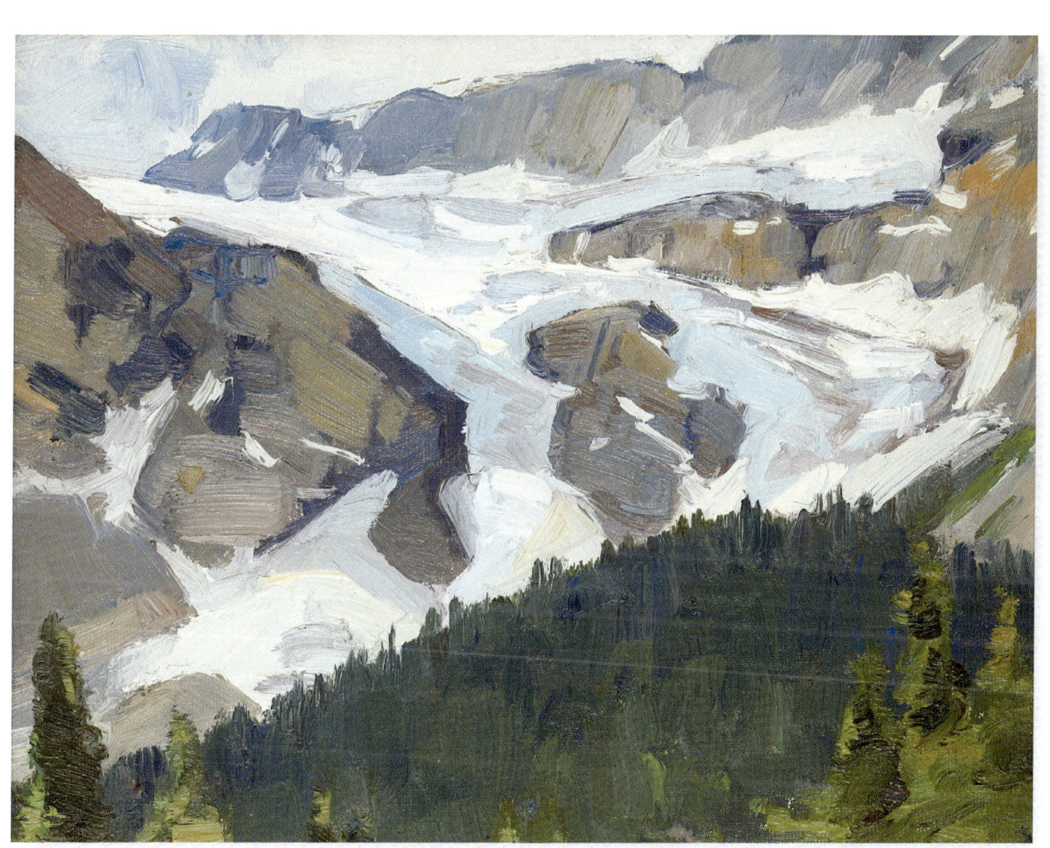

Catharine Whyte

Crowfoot Glacier, 1940–1960

Oil on Canvas, 27.7 × 35.2 cm
Collection of the Whyte Museum of the Canadian Rockies

Catharine Whyte has almost abandoned the sky in this painting and filled most of her canvas with the amazing glacier shaped like a crow's foot. The three claws are enclosed and supported by vertical rock faces, although the lowest claw, which in the days of Wilcox and Outram reached down to the water, is much diminished. Catharine's vantage point, just above the lower end of Bow Lake, allows the viewer to look up to the magnificent glacier. This dramatic view is emphasized by the strong contrast in colour between the rich brown rock and the shimmering white of the ice, which seems to flow and yet is like a river frozen in space and time. Sunlight illuminates the horizontal shapes of the rocky ridge above and the lake below, balancing the dark diagonals on either side in the middle of the painting. Catharine has created a powerful image of one of the most striking glaciers in the Rockies.

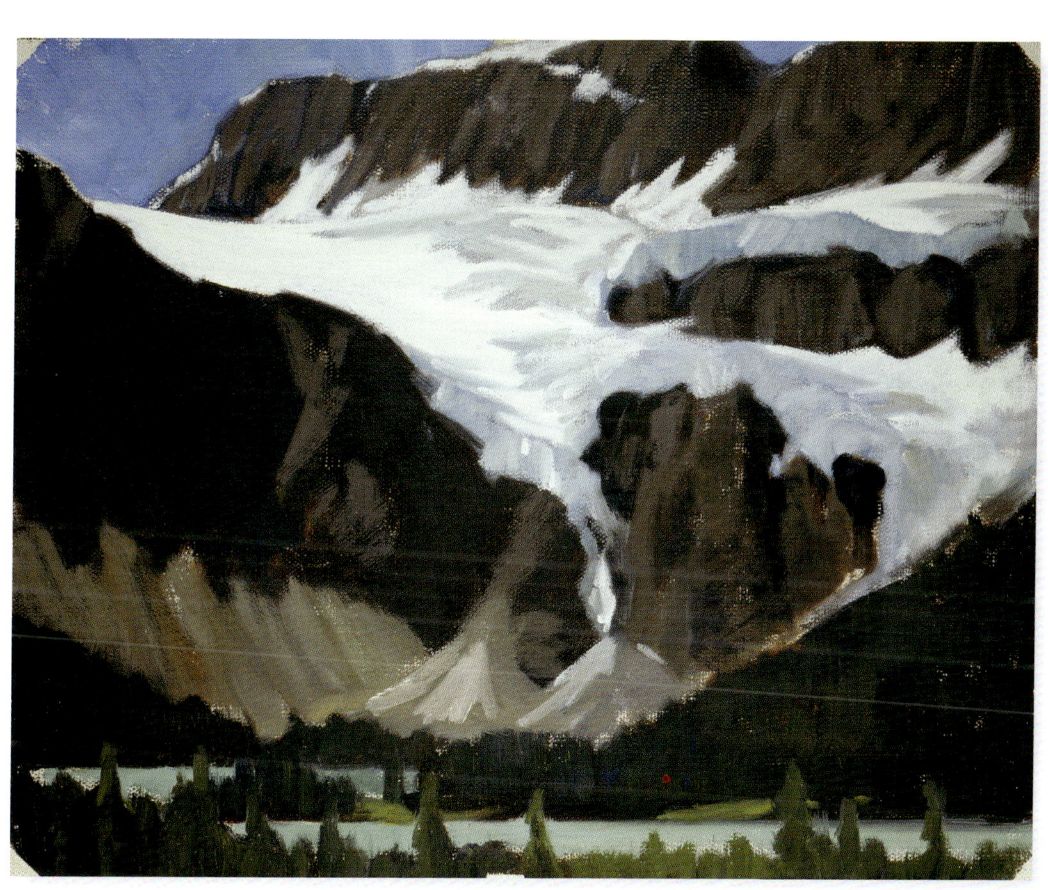

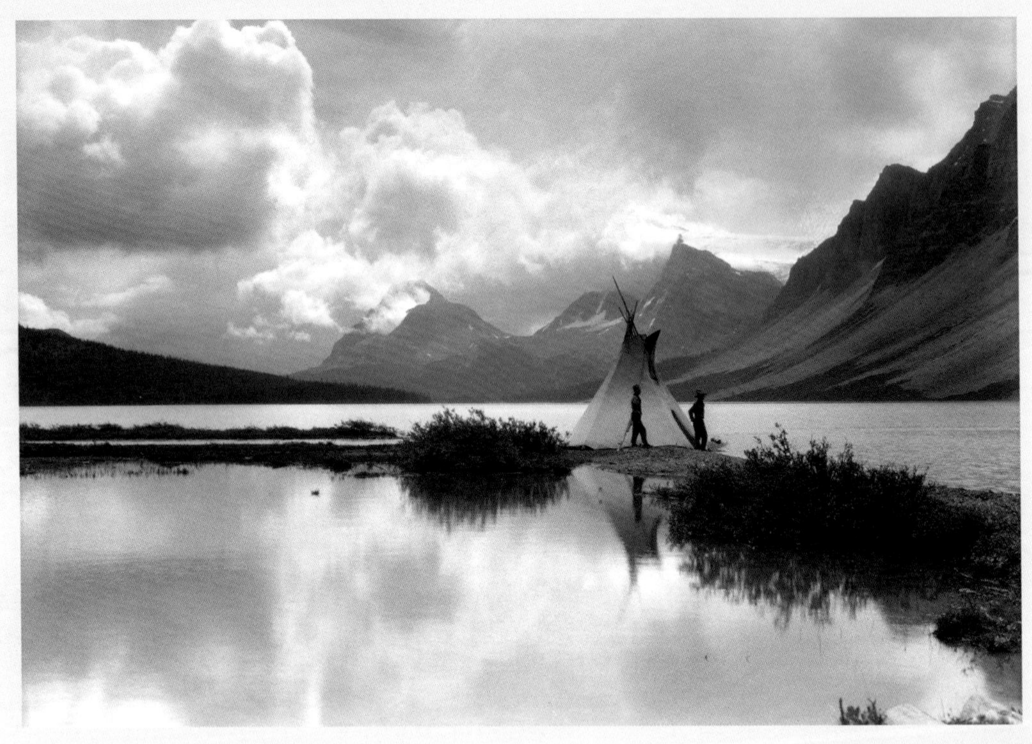

Byron Harmon

Photograph of Teepee at Bow Lake, Columbia Icefield Expedition, 1924
Whyte Museum of the Canadian Rockies (v263/na71-2274).
Looking toward Crowfoot Mountain with glacier, distant right;
Bow Peak, shrouded by cloud, distant centre.

CROWFOOT MOUNTAIN

The next day we reached the Upper Bow Lake. The first glimpse was a strip of blue water far in the distance. Dark cliffs tower above the lake, and glaciers descending from unseen snowfields appear on shelves of rock between the precipices. In warm weather the ice is crowded so rapidly over the cliff that the valley echoes almost constantly to the thunder of avalanches.

— Walter Wilcox, *The Rockies of Canada* (1909), 143.

Belmore Browne

Clouds Over Crowfoot Glacier, n.d.

Oil on Canvas, 63.5 × 76.2 cm
Collection of Glenbow Museum

Belmore Browne appears to have sketched the scene for this large oil painting on the shore of Bow Lake, near the present picnic area. He has captured an image of the landscape as it seems to be changing: the delicate puffs of mist appear to rise, revealing the ridges that enclose the massive glacier. The sunlight has broken through the clouds, shining on the ice above and the deep glacial green water of the lake below. This striking image is further unified through the composition: the sunlit shoreline in the foreground leads the viewer's eye around the lake and then up the draw to the mass of ice between the intersecting diagonals of Crowfoot Mountain. The serenity of the wilderness in the foreground is combined with the majestic, forbidding terrain of rock and ice.

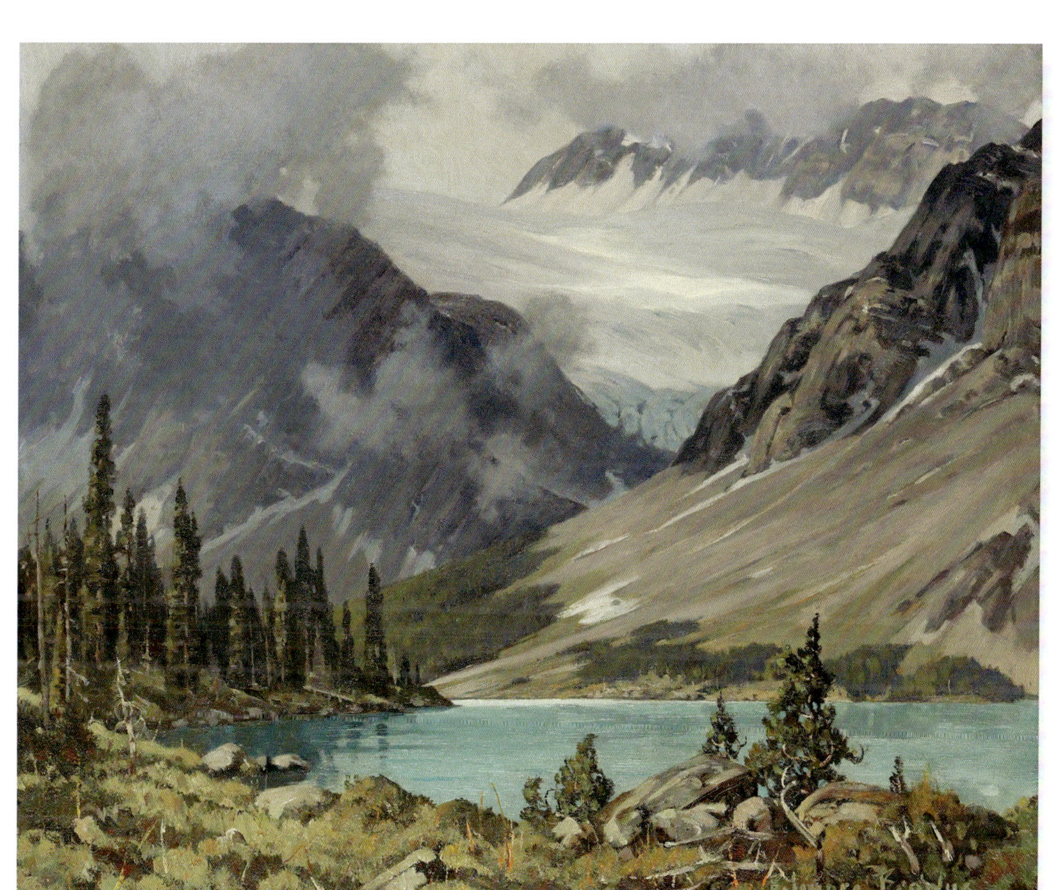

Jimmy Simpson

Crowfoot Glacier, Bow Lake, 1943

Watercolour, 24.0 × 35.0 cm
Collection of the Whyte Museum of the Canadian Rockies

Jimmy Simpson painted this view of Crowfoot Mountain, with its magnificent triangular glacier, by looking southeast from the north end of Bow Lake. Although threatening clouds are accumulating behind Crowfoot, the painting is filled with light in the lake's reflections and with the warmth of summer in the vegetation and the distant rock faces. Jimmy's sensitivity to colour in the landscape is evident, along with his keen powers of observation. The solitary tree in the foreground balances the horizontal lines, leading the viewer's eye to Crowfoot's peak in the centre background. The scene, so familiar to Jimmy over many years, nevertheless has a wonderful freshness in his depiction of the natural beauty.

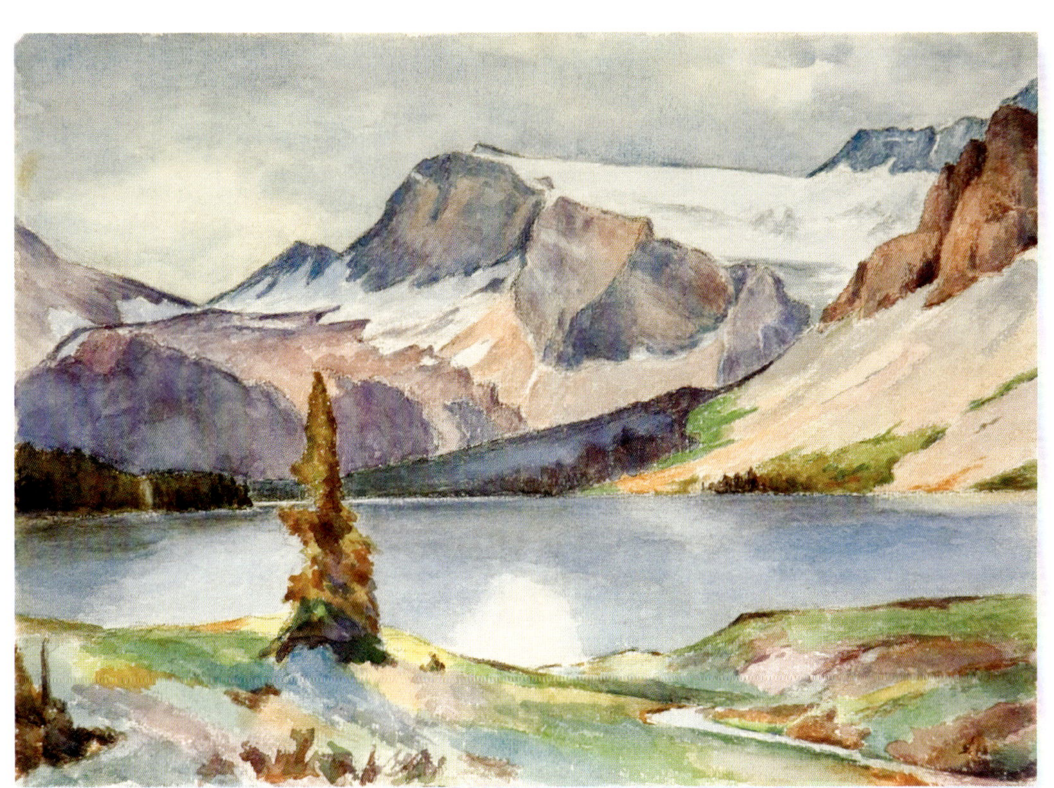

A.C. Leighton

Untitled (Bow Lake), n.d.

Oil on Canvas, 45.8 × 56.2 cm
Art Gallery of Alberta Collection
Gift of Archibald H. and Grace A.M. Dickson

A.C. Leighton captures the dramatic, pyramidal face of Crowfoot Mountain from a vantage point beside Bow Lake. His sketch emphasizes the sense of the mountain's sudden vertical rise beyond the horizontal planes of the foreground. The majestic presence of the shadowed cliffs is emphasized by the lighter values above and below – the glacier merging with accumulating clouds overhead and the warm tones of the talus slopes at the base. Gentle, natural colours combine with Crowfoot's imposing shape to give Leighton's image its great power.

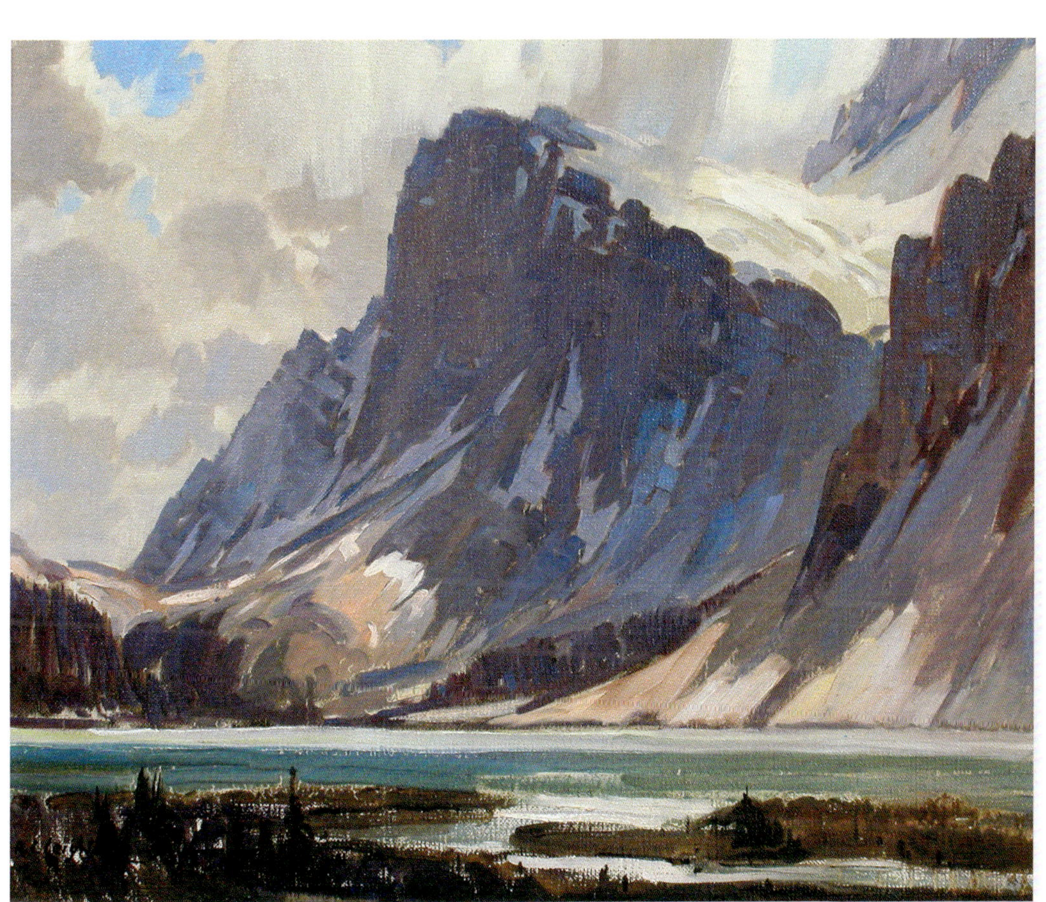

Jimmy Simpson

Winter Break-Up, 1957

Watercolour, 26.7 × 34.8 cm
Collection of Glenbow Museum

Jimmy Simpson presents the first signs of the spring thaw in the meadows near the Ram Pasture. The landscape is still mainly snow covered, but the pool in the foreground reflects the blue sky, and around the edges, beside the snowbank, brown earth is beginning to show. From the pool, the viewer's eye travels across the frozen Bow Lake to Bow Peak on the left and on the right to the glacier-covered Crowfoot Mountain. Jimmy balances his composition with the ancient tree, a survivor of many winters, competing in height with the massive ridge of Crowfoot in the middle ground. The painting is filled with light and soon the melting snow will give way to spring's vitality.

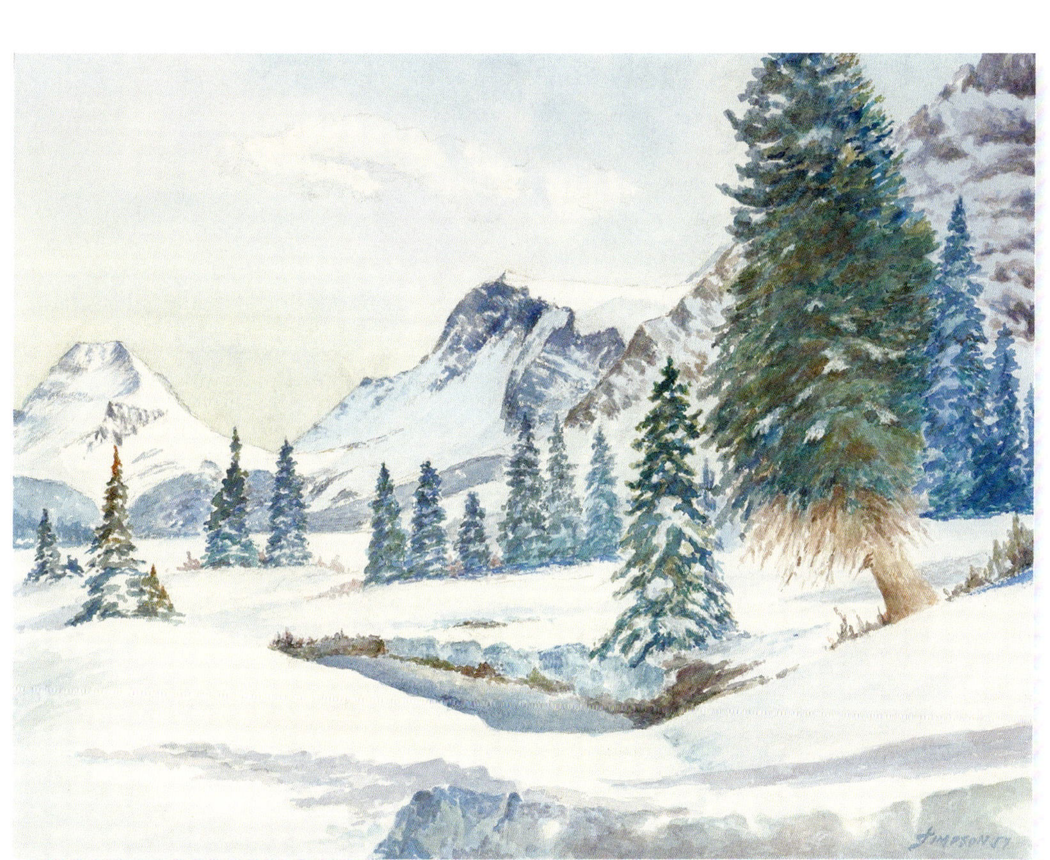

Dominik Modlinski

Creation, 2009

Oil on Board, 40.6 × 50.8 cm
Collection of the Artist

Dominik Modlinski captures the spectacular beginning of a day at Bow Lake. The sunrise brings glorious colours to the clouds and the talus slopes of Crowfoot Mountain in the middle ground, as well as to the reflections in the partly frozen lake. The summits of Crowfoot, Bow Peak and Hector Mountain stretch into the distance, the shadows of their rock, ice and snow etched against the vibrant sky. The enduring mountains separate the ephemeral colours in the sky and lake. As a whole, the painting seems to encompass the elements of creation: earth, air, water and fire. The striking portrayal of colour in its subtle gradations unites the image and, at the same time, brings out the difference between the piled clouds, the solid rock and the watery reflections. This is an inspiring painting of the wondrous beauty of early morning.

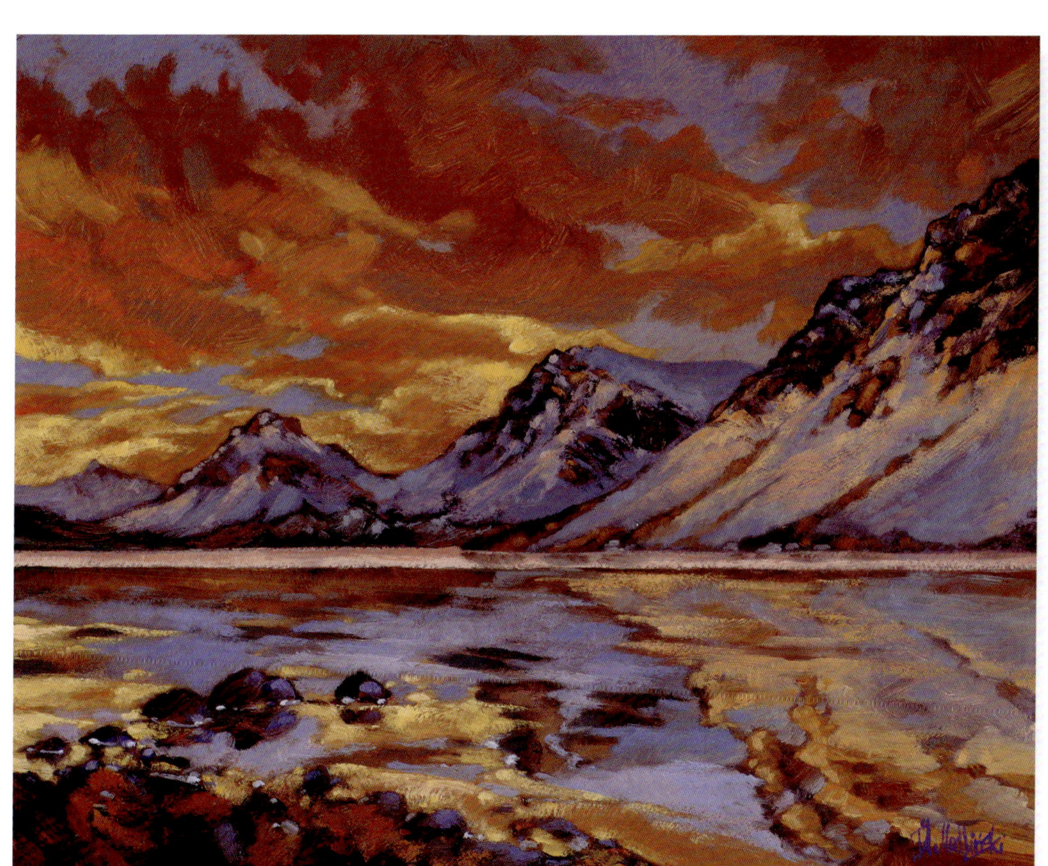

David McEown

Sunrise on Bow Lake, 2009

Watercolour on Paper, 38.1 × 55.9 cm
Collection of the Artist

David McEown portrays the precious moments of sunrise on a September morning beside Bow Lake. The fiery colours in the sky and the line of mountains extending to meet the rising sun in the southeast are reflected in the absolutely smooth water. The chill of the landscape at dawn is evident in the mist hanging along the shoreline and in the deep shadows, but the sun's rays have reached the sheer face under Crowfoot's glacier, giving the rock a warmth in the morning's early light. Beyond Crowfoot are the distinctive shapes of Bow Peak, Mount Hector and, farthest away, Molar Mountain. The sky and the lake are filled with glorious light. The undulating lines of vibrant colour above are somewhat softened in the watery element below, but both provide a dramatic contrast to the vertical shapes of the mountains in the middle of the image. Bow Lake is a mirror to nature's beauty at the beginning of a new day.

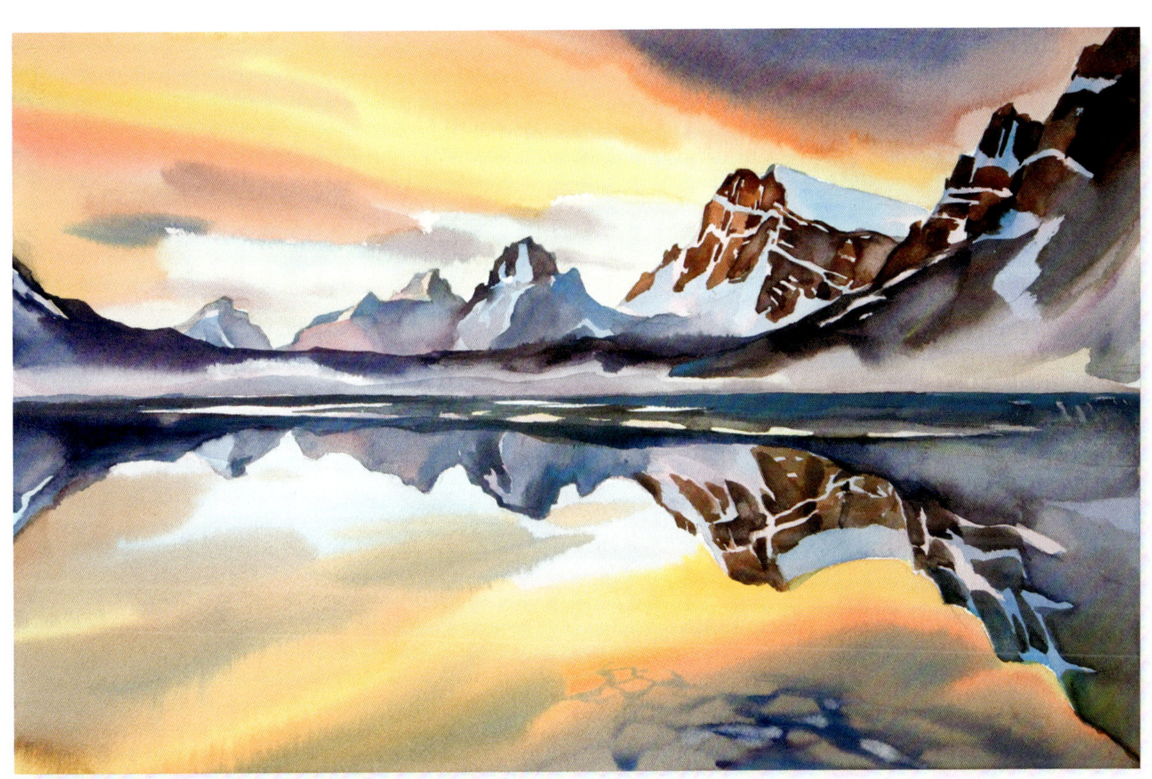

Rob Zeer

Bow Lake in March, 2005

Acrylic on Canvas, 77.4 × 100.0 cm
Collection of Num-Ti-Jah Lodge

Rob Zeer has a vivid memory of seeing a beam of light on the frozen lake early one morning when he was an artist in residence at Num-Ti-Jah Lodge. The sun was just rising behind the shoulder of Crowfoot Mountain as he hiked across the lake to start his drawing. Although he usually sketches on site, the intense cold on this occasion forced him to retreat to the lodge where he could observe the blues and grays from a window. The magical light that inspired him is the focus in his painting – a sudden radiance over the ridge, falling on the talus slopes and the lake. The rest of the snowy landscape beyond the beam of light has the bluish cast of a very cold morning. The frosty trees in the foreground seem to reach for the sunlight and the suggestion of warmth.

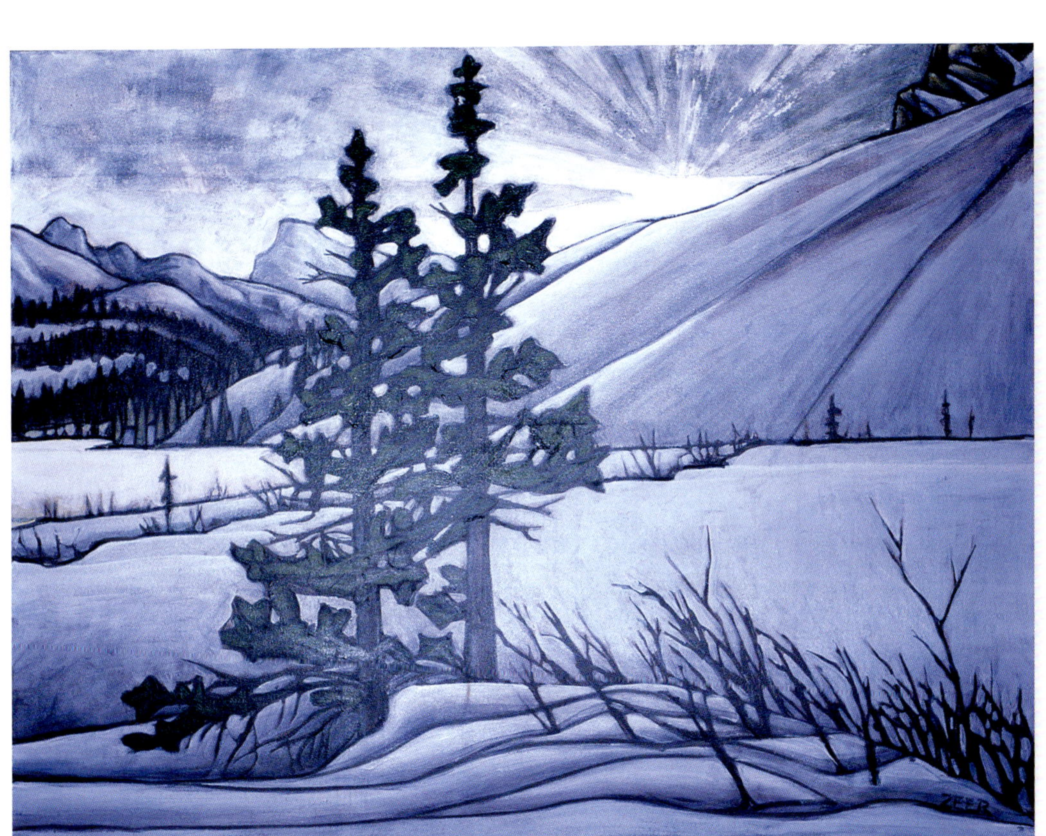

Carolyn Oldale Adams

April on Bow Lake, 2004

Oil on Canvas, 44.5 × 34.3 cm
Private Collection of Lee O'Donnell

Carolyn Oldale Adams presents an inspiring image of early spring at Bow Lake, looking past the ancient tree and across the thawing expanse of water to the majestic Crowfoot Glacier. The sunshine lends a warmth to the distant clouds, the surface of the lake and the leaning tree in the foreground with its withered foliage glowing a brilliant red. The shadowed piles of snow remind one of winter, while the light's warmth brings the promise of melting and growth to the landscape. The red tips of the branches on the old evergreen lead the eye to the great glacier, joining two images of enduring alpine beauty in the weathered tree and the mountain.

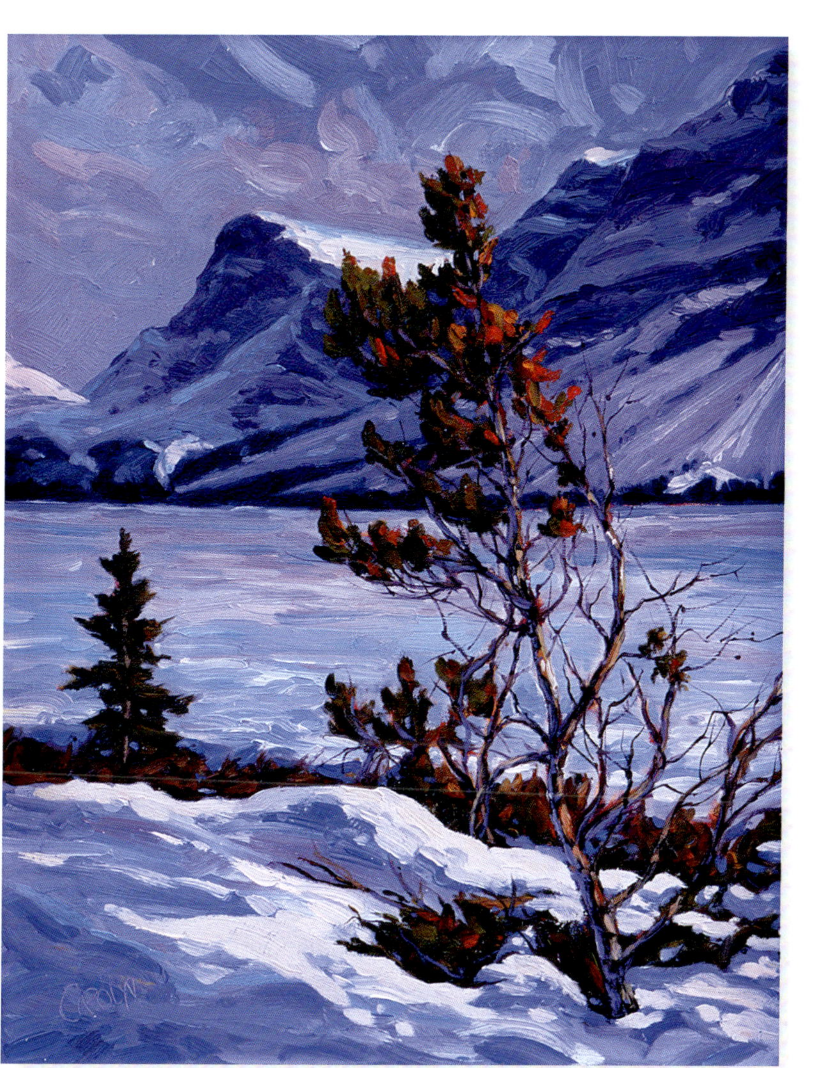

Walter J. Phillips

Mountain Landscapes (Bow Lake, Early Spring), 1959

Watercolour and Pencil on Paper, 16.5 × 27.3 cm
Collection of Glenbow Museum

The spontaneity of this image from Walter Phillips' sketchbook *Mountain Landscapes* seems suited to the portrayal of a sparkling spring day as winter releases its grip on the earth. The free brush strokes delineate the scene from the north end of Bow Lake, near Num-Ti-Jah Lodge, with Crowfoot Mountain on the right, its cliffs in shadow, and Bow Peak, in the sunshine to the left. Bow Lake is still frozen with patches of snow between pools of meltwater, but the sun warms a newly revealed stretch of brown earth along the shoreline. The vibrant blue sky is reflected in the foreground pool, and the dominant tree rising beyond the edge of the paper leads the viewer's eye to the soaring peaks beyond.

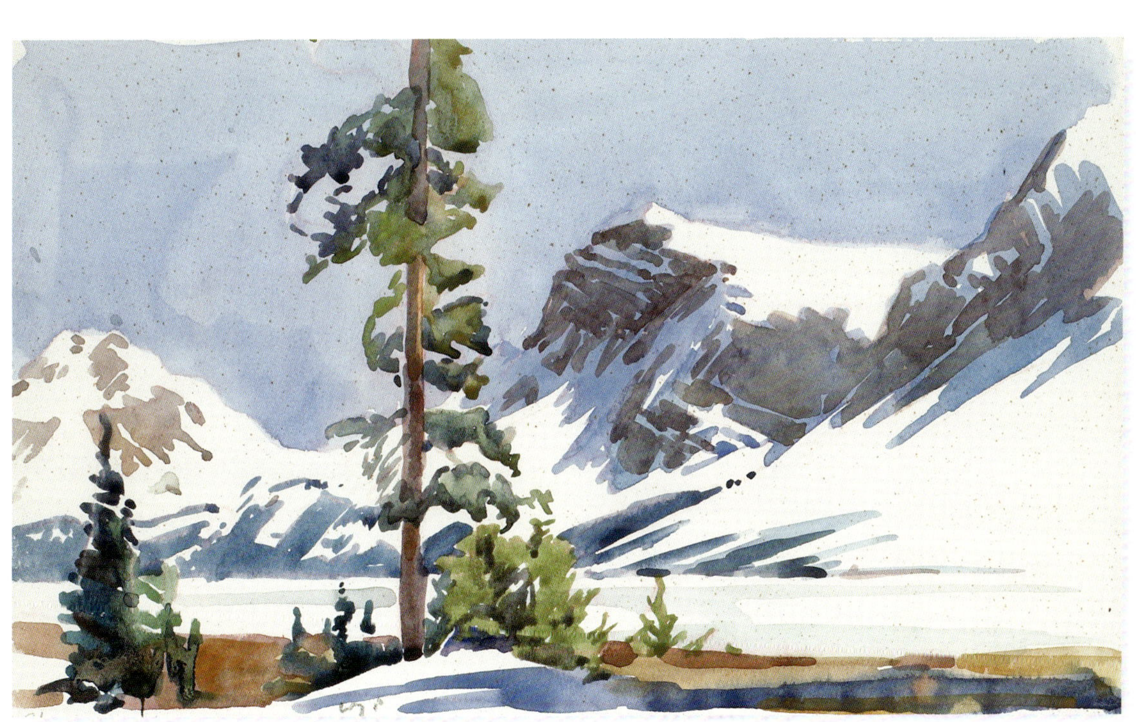

Jimmy Simpson

Autumn Evening, 1958

Watercolour, 29.5 × 34.5 cm
Collection of the Whyte Museum of the Canadian Rockies

Jimmy Simpson portrays a fleeting moment of beauty as the full moon illuminates the evening landscape before disappearing behind the shifting clouds. Hovering over the pass, the moon casts a magical glow over Bow Peak, left, and Crowfoot Mountain, right. The peaks seem higher and more majestic in this light, as the viewer's eye travels across the level expanse of Bow Lake and up past the summits to the main focus, the celestial body in the night sky. Jimmy achieves a wonderful symmetry with the pass between the mountains framing the moon, which is just peeking through one of two oblong breaks in the cloud cover. The nocturnal blue tones contrast with the moonlight, but warm touches of colour are evident in the yellow glow on the distant water and in the reddish tones of the foreground vegetation. Jimmy offers us a rare glimpse of the stillness and serenity of Bow Lake under a full moon.

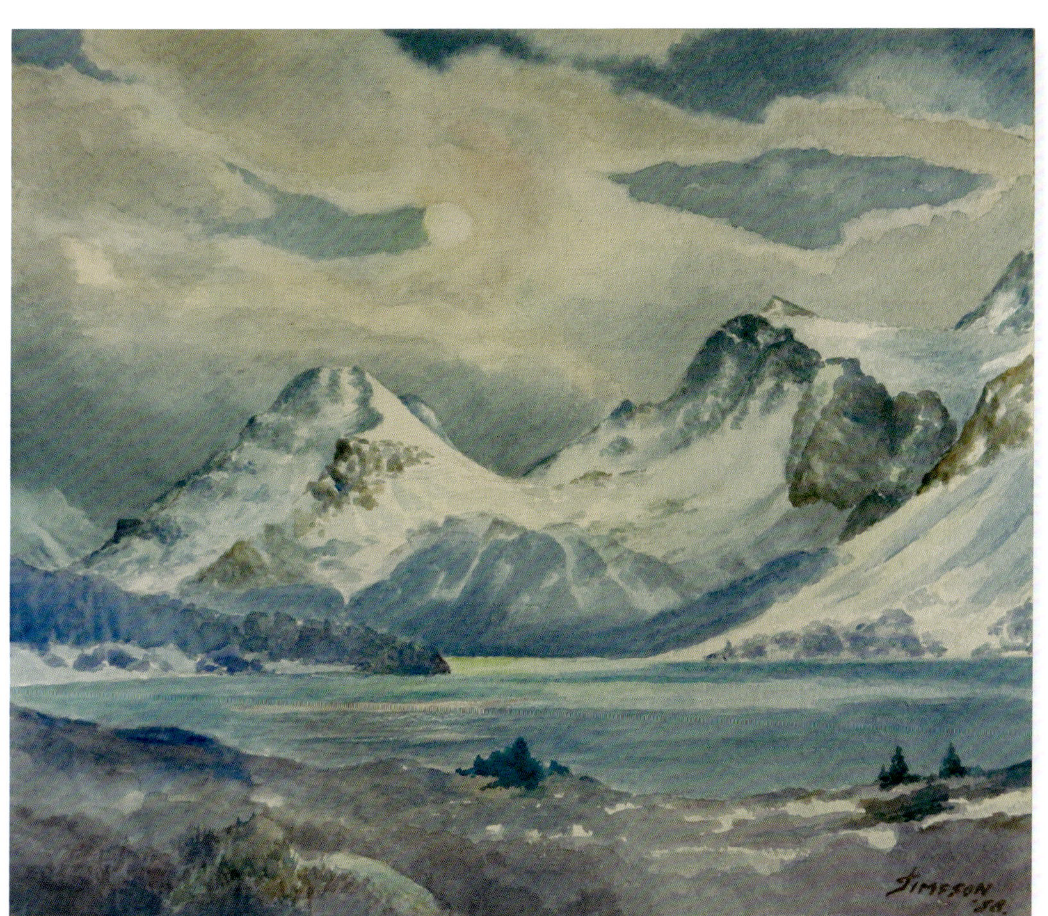

Holly Middleton

Fireweed at Bow Lake and Crowfoot Glacier, 1996

Watercolour, 54.6 × 75.6 cm
Private Collection

A profusion of red blooms nestled into a hollow in the meadow provides a vibrant contrast to the blue tones of the lake and mountains beyond. Bow Lake is completely still on this August day, reflecting the steep talus slopes of Crowfoot's shoulder on the right, while in the background the glacier, supported by shadowy, precipitous cliffs, catches the summer sunshine. Across the snowy Crowfoot Pass, Bow Peak soars into a hazy blue sky. Mount Hector, with its distinctive glacier near the summit, is in the distant left. The vertical shapes of the fireweed and trees in the foreground lead the viewer's eye to the magnificent peaks. The warmth of the meadow and the calm water create a peaceful beauty in the midst of ice and rock. From delicate wildflowers to enduring mountains, Holly Middleton has captured the essence of Bow Lake's charm.

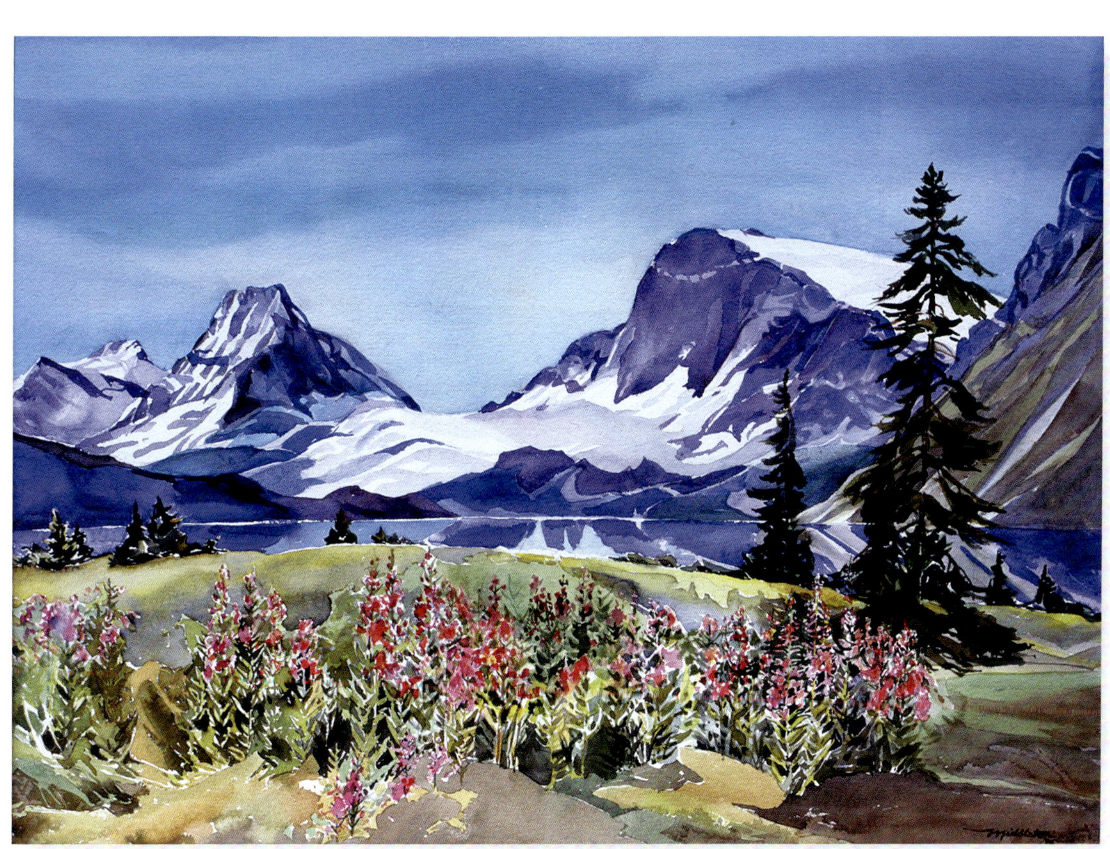

Donna Jo Massie

Bow Lake, 2006

Watercolour on Board, 35.6 × 68.6 cm
Private Collection of Bob and Colleene Peterson

Donna Jo Massie was an artist in residence in September 2006 when she painted this spectacular scene from her vantage point beside Num-Ti-Jah Lodge. The morning sunlight illuminates the eastern slopes of Crowfoot Mountain, and the fresh snow in the crevices reveals the rocky ramparts of the wall supporting the shadowed glacier above. An icy blue line of a bergschrund stretching across the glacier is visible from the end of the lake. Across Crowfoot Pass, the snowy western faces of Bow Peak are still in shade. This expansive view directly down Bow Lake emphasizes the grandeur of the mountains flanking Crowfoot Pass. The lively colours of the fall foliage in the foreground and the deep-blue glacial waters of Bow Lake complement the inspiring presence of the mountains.

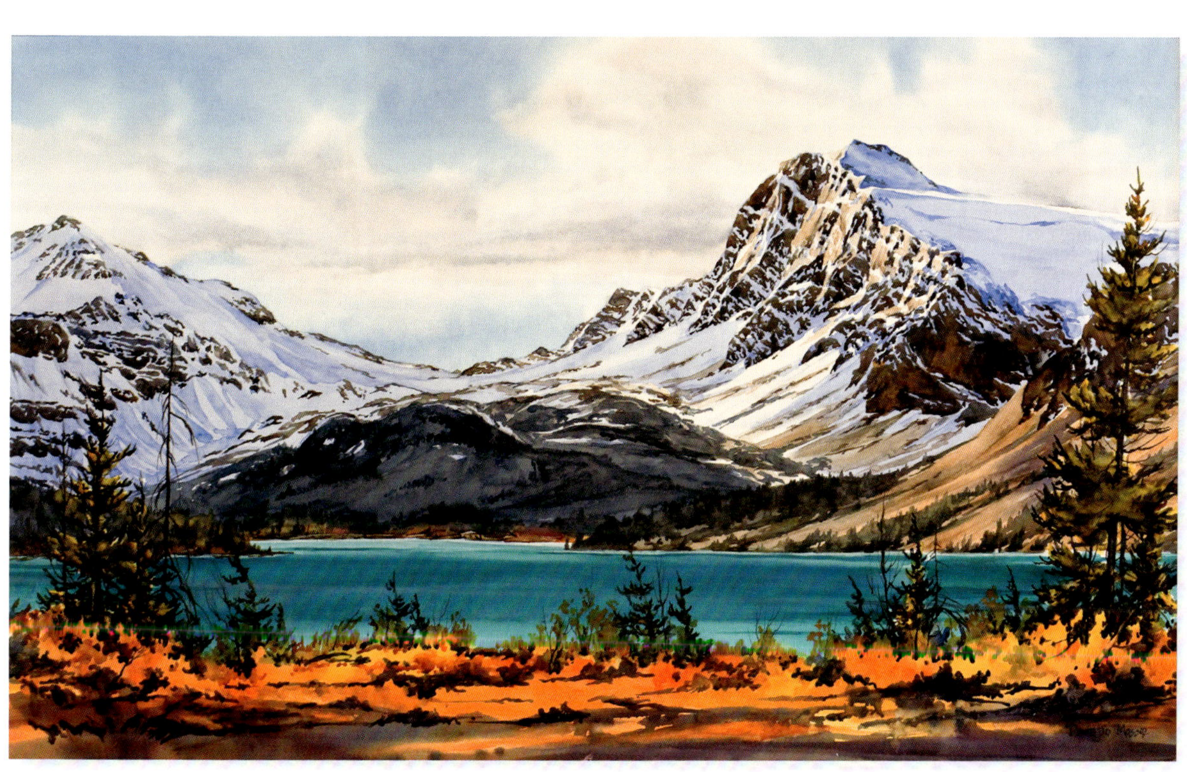

Max Elliott

May Afternoon, Crowfoot Glacier, 2006

Oil on Canvas, 40.6 × 40.6 cm
Private Collection of Tim Whyte

Max Elliott painted this powerful image of Crowfoot Mountain while sitting by the lakeshore, not far from Num-Ti-Jah Lodge. Intrigued by the patterns of snow and shadow created by the May sunshine, she decided to concentrate on a close-up view of the mountain. Brilliant snowfields on three sides enclose the dark, precipitous cliffs above and the diagonal line of forest stretching up from below. The intricate design of snow clinging to the dark face of Crowfoot and the wonderful silhouette projected onto the lower snowfield give the image great vitality. Right at the top of her painting, against the blue sky, Max portrays a white triangle created by snow and rock, but one can also imagine this shape marking the summit of the dramatic cliff face.

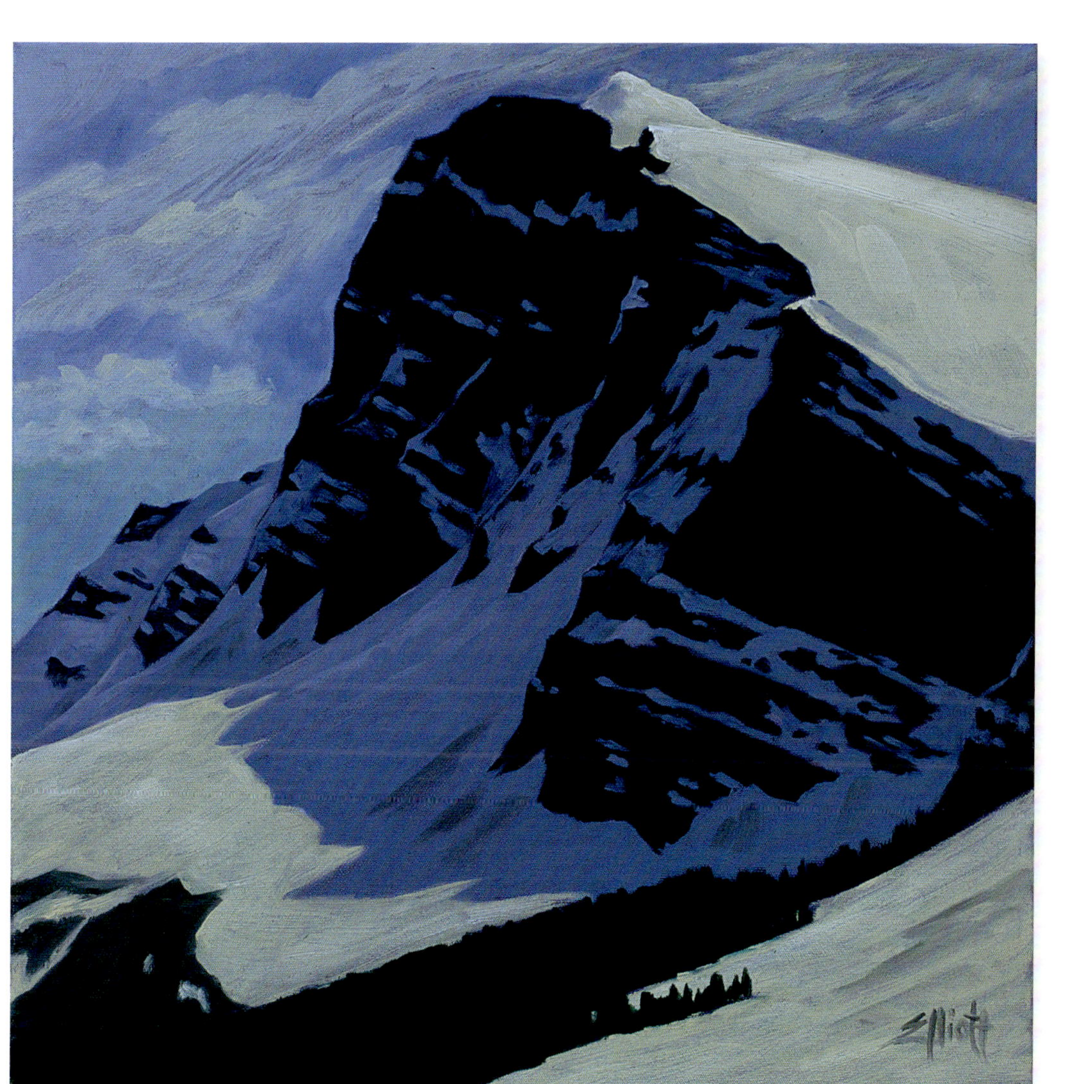
Elliott

Elizabeth Wiltzen

Bow Lake, 2003

Studio Watercolour, 35.6 × 53.3 cm
Private Collection of Tim Wiltzen

Elizabeth Wiltzen has created an exhilarating painting of Crowfoot Mountain from the shoreline of Bow Lake on a day in June. This image, the last she painted in watercolour before switching entirely to oil, surprised her with the intensity of the colour. The massive bulk of Crowfoot presents a fascinating interplay of triangular shapes with the shadowed cliff faces enclosing the sparkling expanse of the glacier. Behind these solid shapes, the delicate clouds move across the sky as the weather changes, revealing for a moment a patch of blue. The ephemeral clouds, along with the lake's reflections, contrast the fixed mass of Crowfoot's rock and ice – a landscape inspiring in its energy.

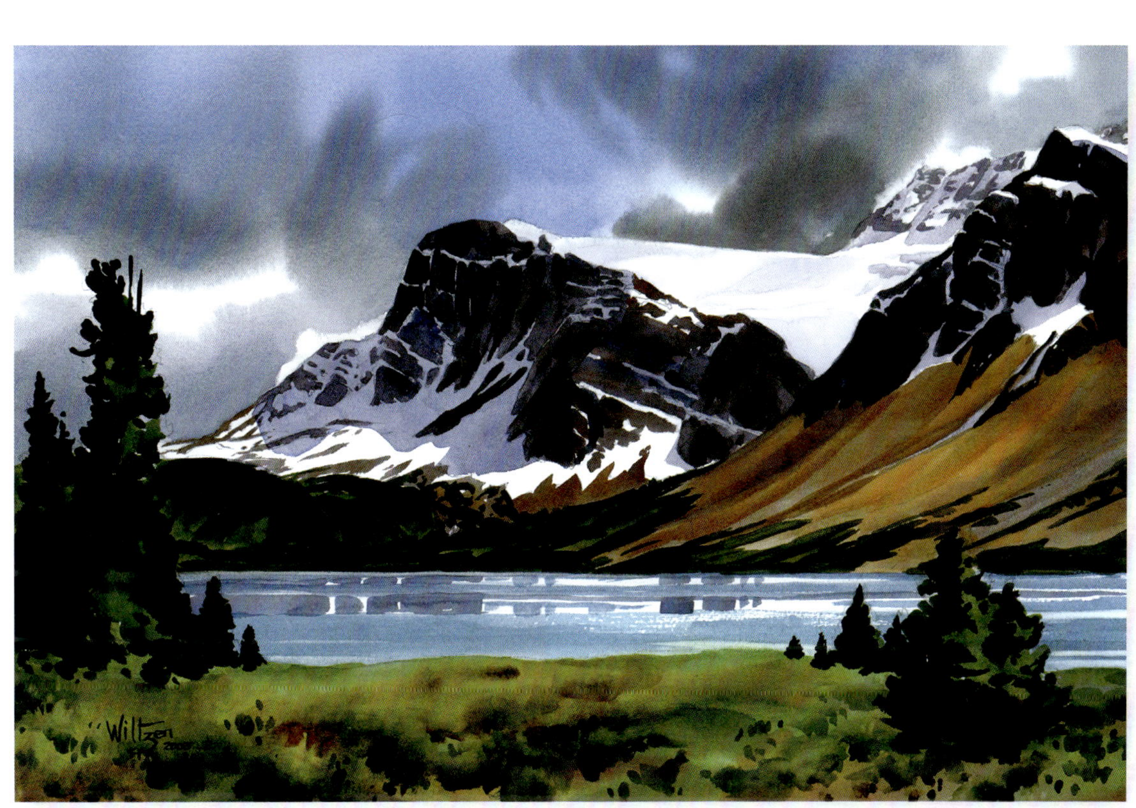
Wiltzen

Sarah Kidner

Trees at Bow Lake, 2008

Oil on Linen Board, 45.7 × 61.0 cm
Private Collection

Sarah Kidner's perspective on Crowfoot Mountain is from the shore of Bow Lake near Num-Ti-Jah Lodge on an overcast June day. Beyond the colourful line of trees and across the pale water, the looming presence of Crowfoot and its glacier rises into the mist. In comparison to the foreground, the mountain shapes have more delicate colours, but the close-up view, with the strong intersecting diagonals framing the glacier, creates a powerful image. The intricate outlines of branches in the foreground contrast dramatically with the massive mountain beyond, but both combine to create a striking alpine landscape.

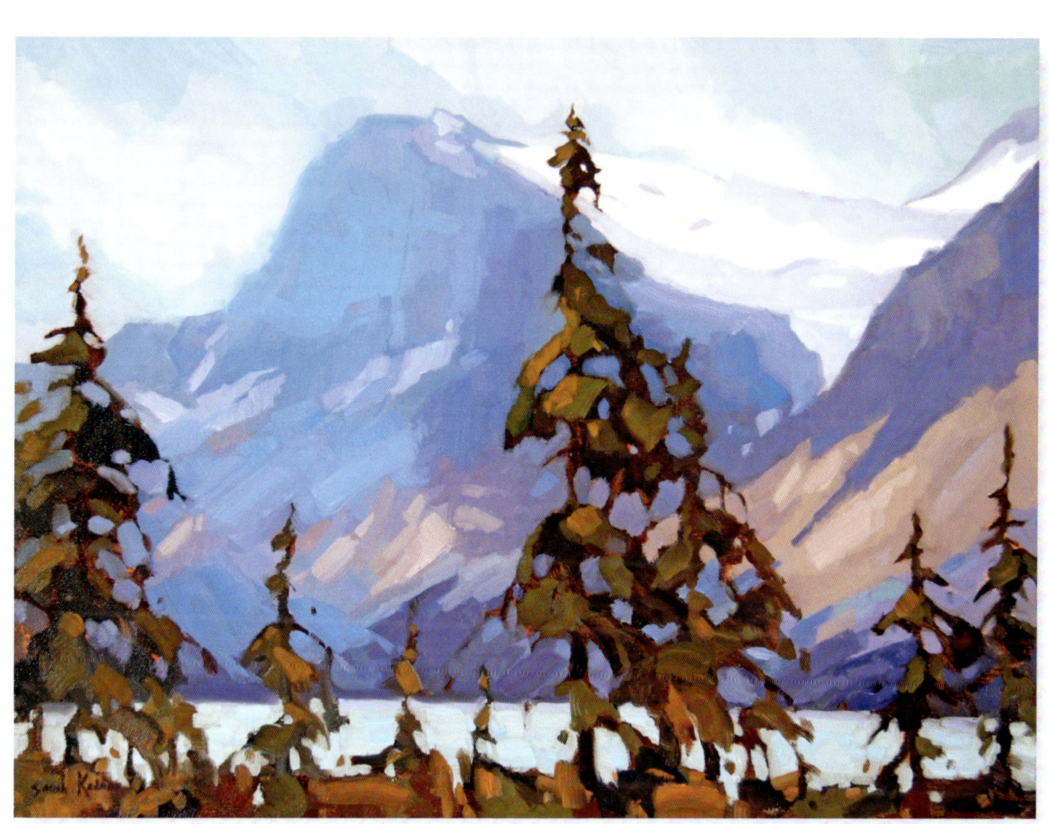

Alice Saltiel-Marshall

Crowfoot Mountain through the Looking Glass, 1999

Studio Oil, 91.4 × 137.2 cm
Private Collection

Alice Saltiel captures a special moment when the distant peak of Crowfoot Mountain is reproduced in a precise mirror image in the nearby pool. Through the title of her painting, Alice playfully suggests that Lewis Carroll's wonderland can also be found in a beautiful summer scene at Bow Lake, and she leads us into the landscape through her looking glass. This stunning reflection, in its crispness and absolute stillness, has been taken out of the flow of time by Alice the artist, allowing us imaginative enjoyment of this fleeting natural beauty. The sunlight illuminates the top of Crowfoot with its great glacier and reveals the clear, fresh colours of the meadow, lake and talus slopes in the middle ground. The intriguing cloud hanging over Crowfoot is reflected in the deep blue pool, balancing the image. All the ephemeral qualities of light, cloud and watery reflection come together to reveal the wonderful landscape of Bow Lake.

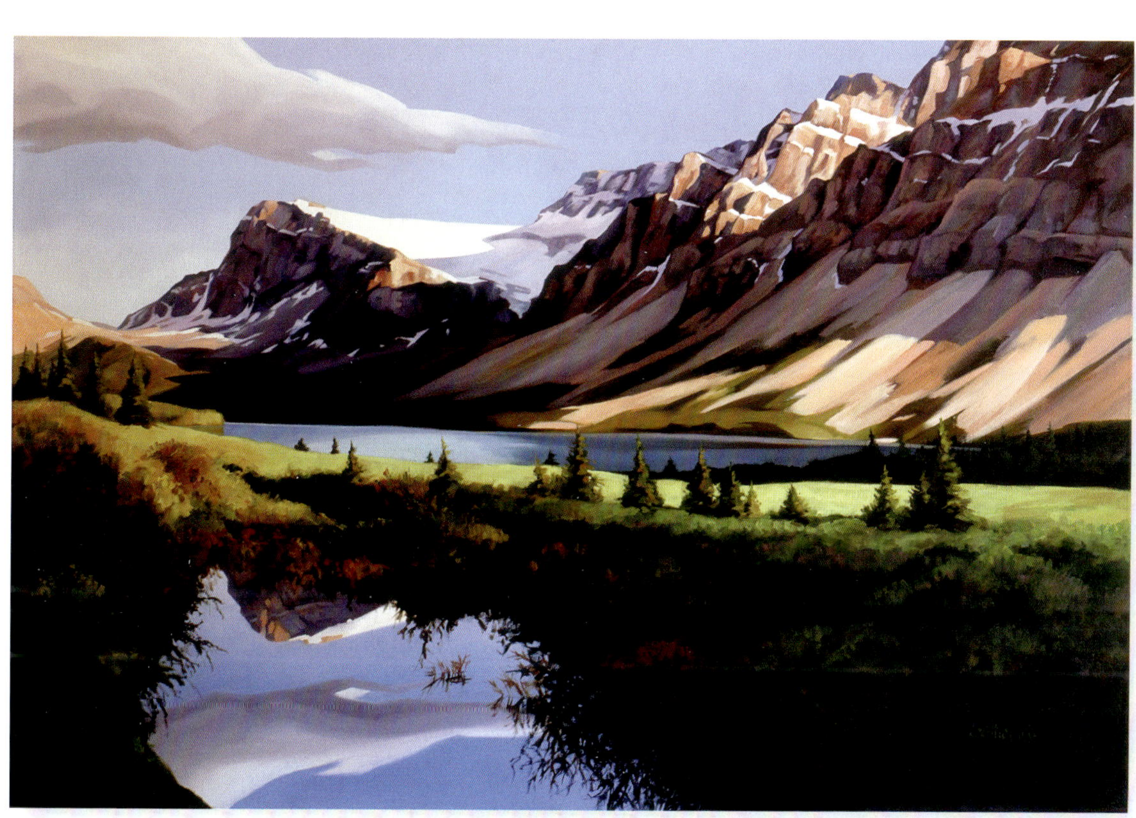

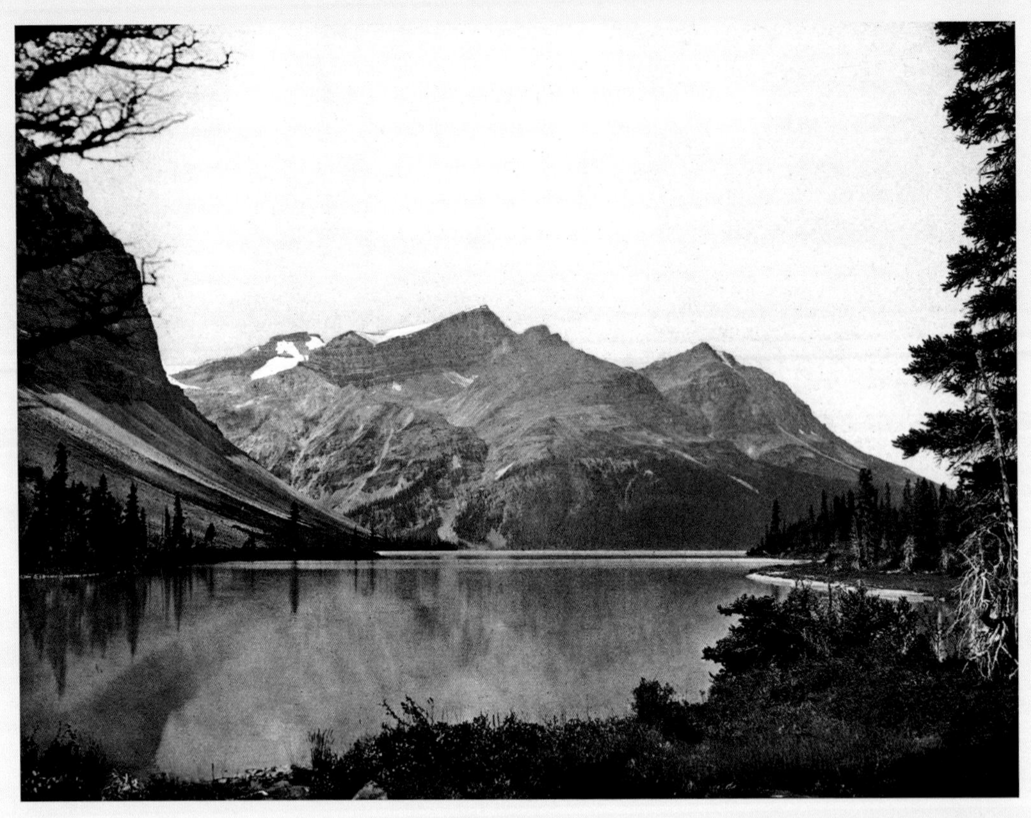

Walter Wilcox

Photograph of The Bow Lake, c.1900
(from *The Rockies of Canada*, 1909)
Whyte Museum of the Canadian Rockies (v85/na66-579).
Mount Jimmy Simpson on distant right; Mount Thompson in centre;
talus slopes on Crowfoot Mountain, centre left.

BOW LAKE

Walls without pictures do tend to imprison the mind; they crowd in upon one and crush the spirit …

Put a window in the wall, however, and you have a way out; you no longer feel cribbed, cabined and confined, you are in contact with the world of colour and movement; your outlook is enlarged and your spirit refreshed.

Pictures also are windows open to life and nature.

— Walter J. Phillips, "Art and Artists," *Winnipeg Evening Tribune*, May 13, 1939, 8.

Carl Rungius

Bow Lake, n.d.

Oil on Canvas, 27.9 × 33.0 cm
Collection of Glenbow Museum

Carl Rungius climbed high up on the east side of the Bow Valley opposite the towering bulk of Crowfoot Mountain to sketch the distinctive shape of Bow Lake as it widens toward its northern end and bends to the west in the direction of its source in the Bow Glacier. Mount Jimmy Simpson, named in 1973, looms over the head of the lake, where the Ram Pasture and, later, Num-Ti-Jah Lodge will eventually be located. The massive shoulder of Crowfoot on the left hides the peak of Mount Thompson in the background. Snow lingering near the peaks suggests the summertime, but the overcast sky creates the pale glacial blue in the water below. Rungius appears to have been working quickly, applying the warm colours of rock and talus with wide brushstrokes. The same technique is used for the foreground trees and grasses, with the exception of the more carefully delineated stump and tree trunk, fallen out of the frame to the right. Rungius' sketch gives the sense of the serene beauty of the rugged wilderness.

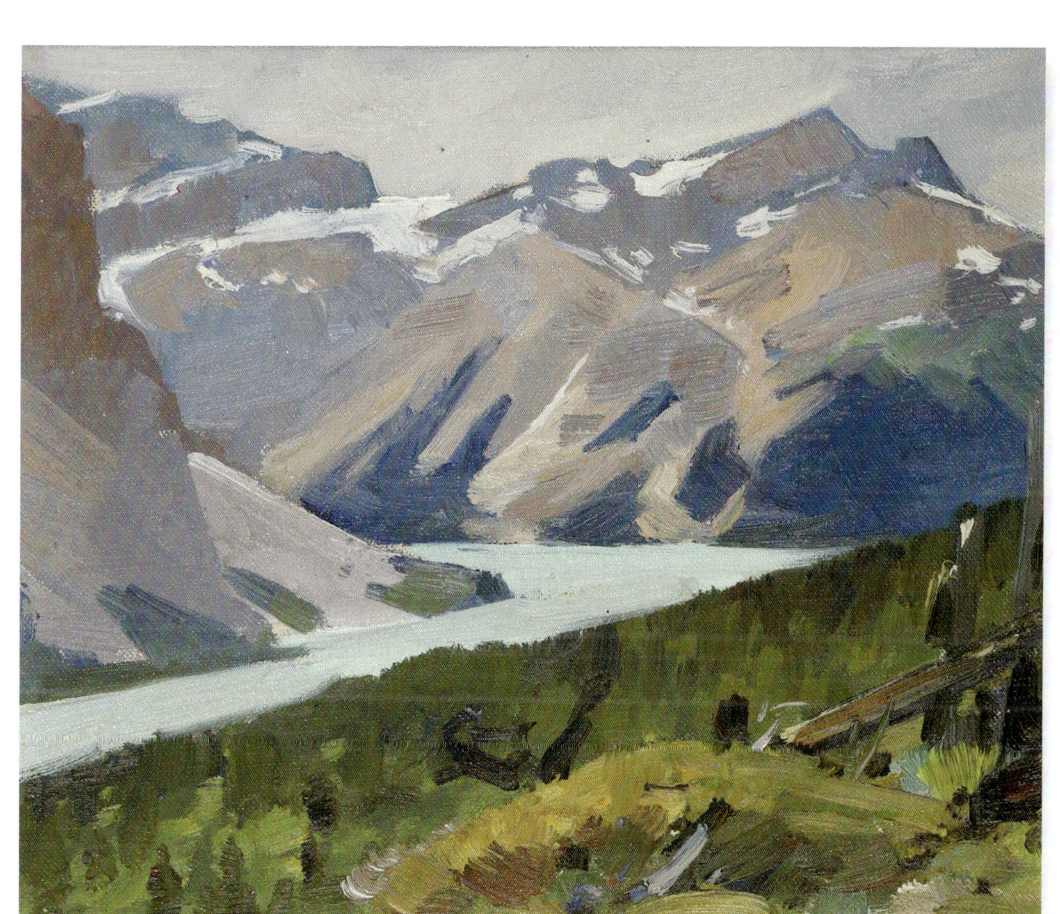

Ralph Oberg

Fall Morning at Bow Lake, 2001

Oil on Canvas, 24.1 × 29.2 cm
Collection of Num-Ti-Jah Lodge

Ralph Oberg's *plein air* sketch depicts the special warmth of early fall, a precious time before the long winter's snow. His view of the dramatic peak of St. Nicholas soaring out of the glacier into a cloudless blue sky is framed by the grove of trees beside the lake and, across the water, the shadowed cliff of Crowfoot Mountain. The morning sunlight brings energy and colour to the scene, leading the viewer's eye to the striking white glacier and, below, the yellow leaves near the deep blue lake. The painting is infused with immediacy and vitality, the promise of a perfect fall day at Bow Lake.

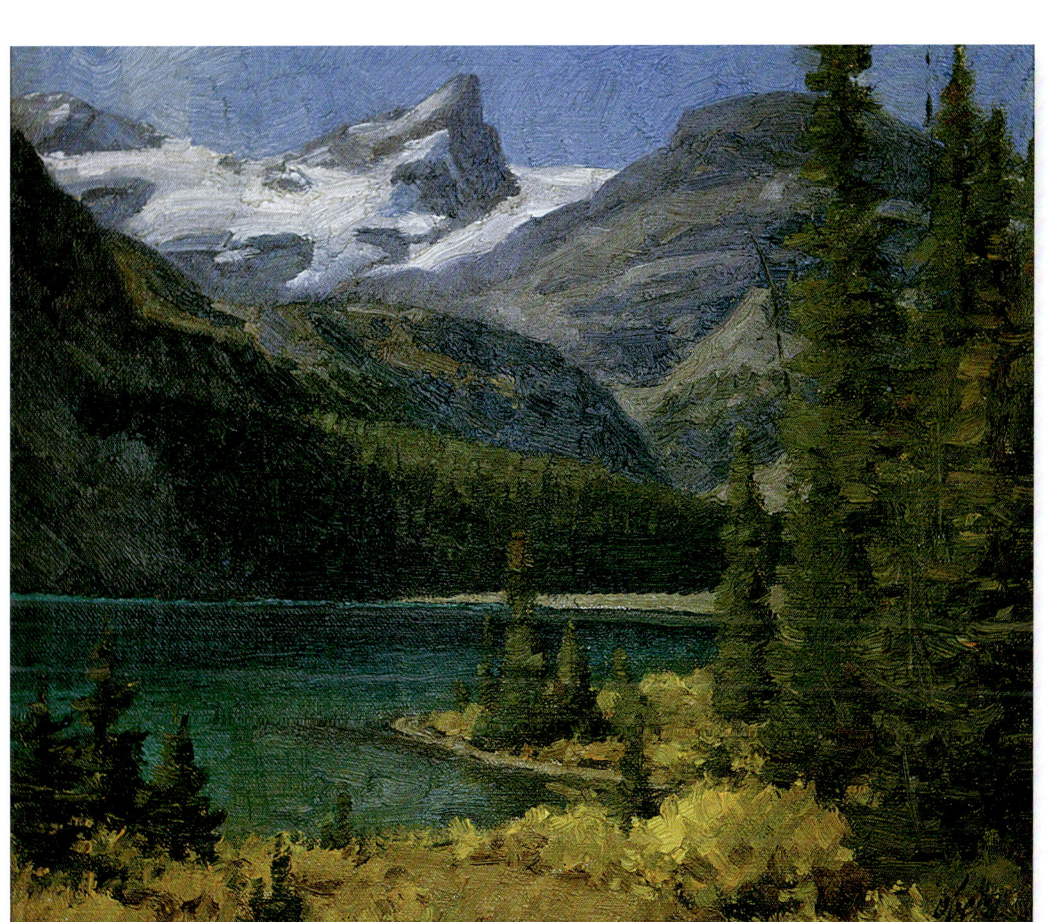

Barbara Leighton

Evening, Bow Lake, n.d.

Linocut, 31.0 × 37.2 cm
Collection of the Whyte Museum of the Canadian Rockies

An evening stillness pervades this view of the great Bow Glacier, between the rounded rock formation known as the Onion in the background on the left and the sloping shoulder of Portal Peak on the right. The glacier is seen past the framing trees on the other side of a small cove on Bow Lake. Deep, muted colours of blue and green in the foreground suggest the fading light, creating dark reflections in the water. The rocky shoreline still has a light colour, as does the distant glacier against the overcast sky. One marvels at the shadowy mass of ice towering over the headwall. Bow Falls seem to be just visible tumbling over the cliff beneath the glacier. Barbara Leighton has chosen the quiet moments of evening to portray this tranquil scene.

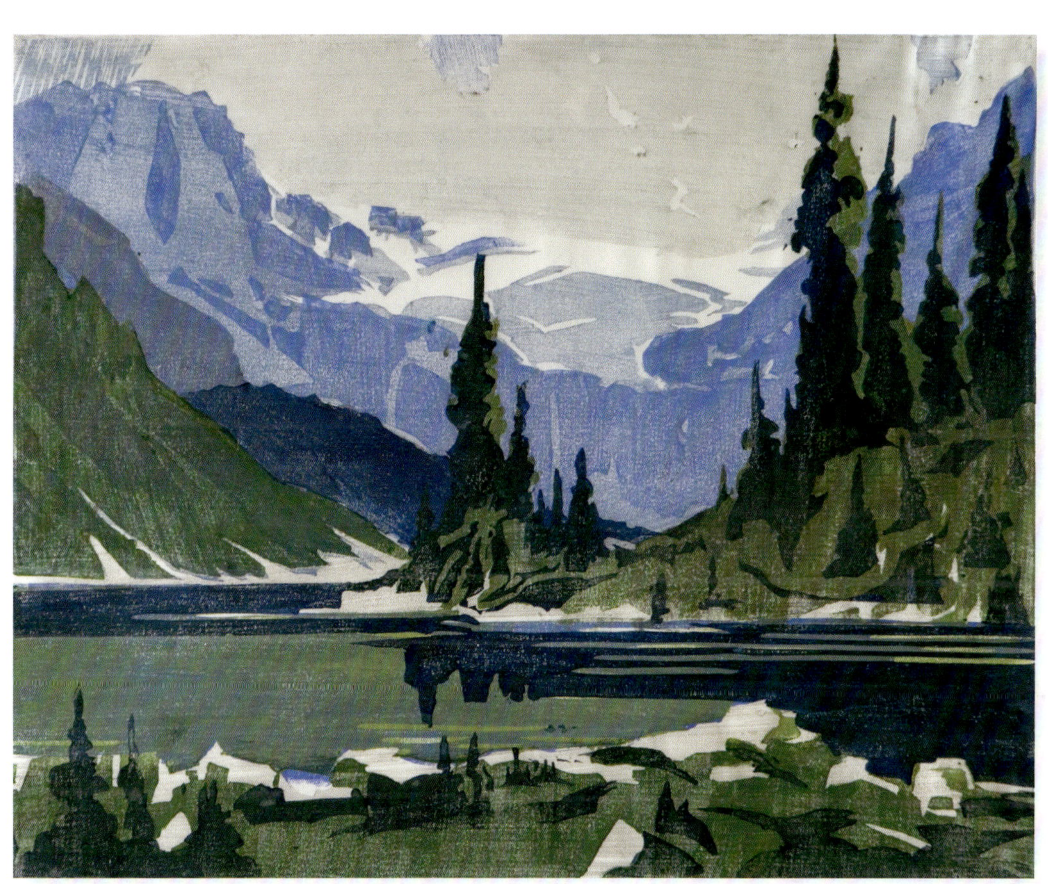

Glen Boles

Bow Lake, 2008

Acrylic on Canvas, 22.9 × 30.5 cm
Private Collection of Maxine Herbert

Glen Boles has created a stunning view of Bow Lake from the picnic ground, just off the highway, looking past the buttress at the north end of Crowfoot Mountain to the two peaks in the background: Mount Thompson under the dark cloud and Mount Jimmy Simpson to the right. The water is absolutely still, providing an amazing mirror image; the watery reflection reverses every detail of the mountains. The sweeping lines of the immense talus slopes at Crowfoot's base are particularly striking as the sunlight brings the warm tones of the rock out of the purple shadows. The reflection in the foreground just hints at the intriguing shapes of the clouds over the distant mountains, their curling whiteness in contrast to the horizontal wispiness of the curious dark cloud, a natural anomaly on this peaceful summer's day in the mountains.

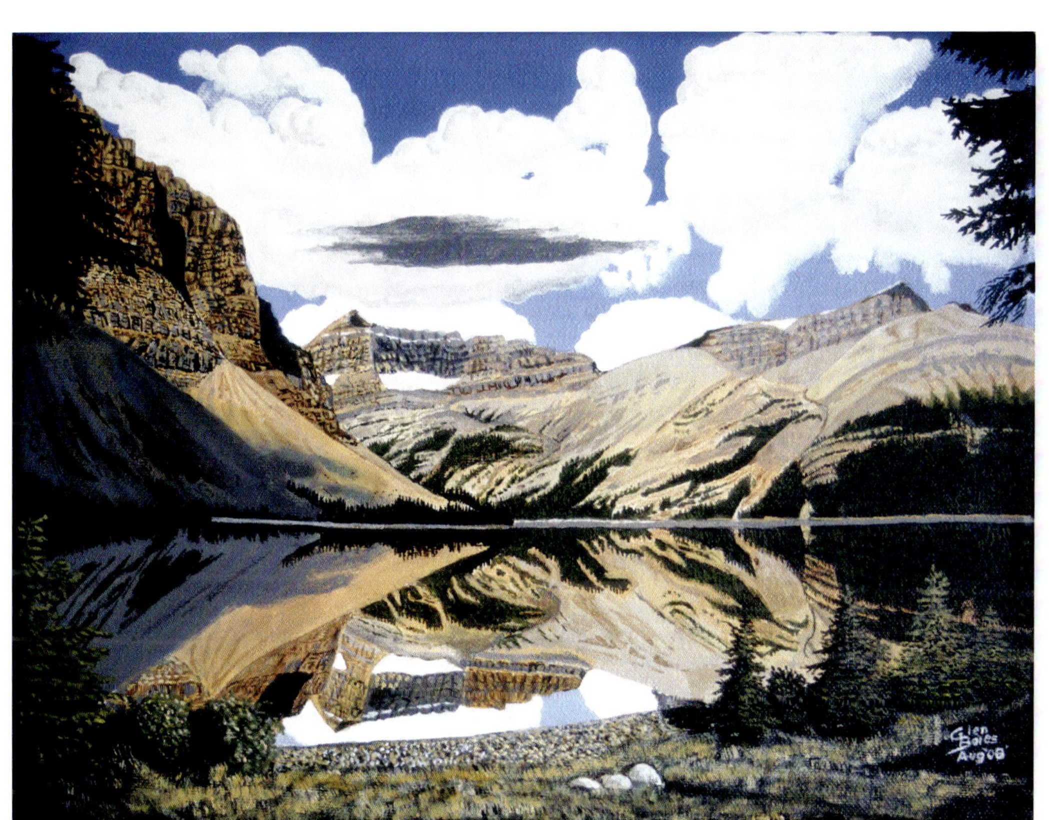
Glen
Boles
Aug'08

Zelda Nelson

Saint Nicholas Peak, 2005

Oil on Canvas, 61.0 × 91.4 cm
Private Collection of Nick J. Kuzyk

Zelda Nelson is drawn to St. Nicholas Peak because of its graceful shape and prominence on the skyline. Her portrait of the mountain, from the edge of the river flowing from Bow Glacier, is filled with light and energy. The sunlight on the water in the foreground leads the viewer's eye along the winding riverbank, past the dark shoulder of Crowfoot and the forest wall and up to the illuminated expanse of ice and rock, with St. Nicholas Peak projecting into the sky. The glacier sweeps up one side of the peak almost as if the mountain is leaning under the weight of the ice. The undulating lines of the glacier are repeated in the bare rock below, drawing the eye up to the rounded mass of the Onion with its great segments splitting apart. The sense of motion in the delineation of the mountains is repeated in the wind-blown wisps of cloud in the sky. Zelda counters our expectation that mountains are rigid and still, while foliage easily blows in the wind, by anchoring her composition in the foreground with motionless autumn leaves. With sweeping lines and vibrant colours, Zelda's wilderness landscape has great vitality.

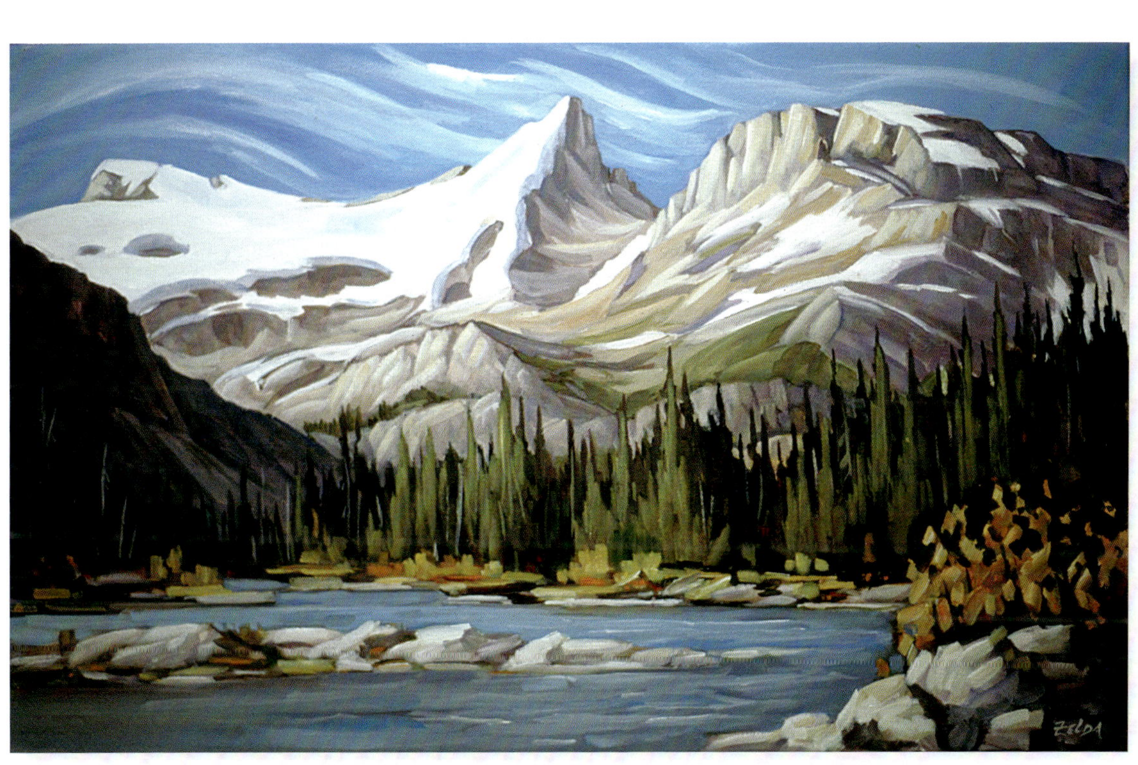
ZELDA

Walter J. Phillips

Mount Nicholas, 1963

Woodcut, 11 × 12.5 cm
Collection of the Whyte Museum of the Canadian Rockies

Walter Phillips' woodcut focuses on the dramatic shape of St. Nicholas Peak on the boundary between Alberta and British Columbia. The summit is a striking triangle soaring up from the graceful lines of the glacier. Snow and ice reach right to the top on one side, emphasizing the characteristic lean, while on the other, the bare cliff rises vertically from the talus slope. Despite the demanding medium of the woodcut, Phillips is able to create the subtle gradations of light and shade, particularly in the colours of the rock. The peak is seen against a vast expanse of sky, which takes up more than half the painting. The power and solidity of rock contrast with the ephemeral clouds that create intricate shapes out of the blue sky. Phillips' mastery of the woodcut and his optimism are evident in this image.

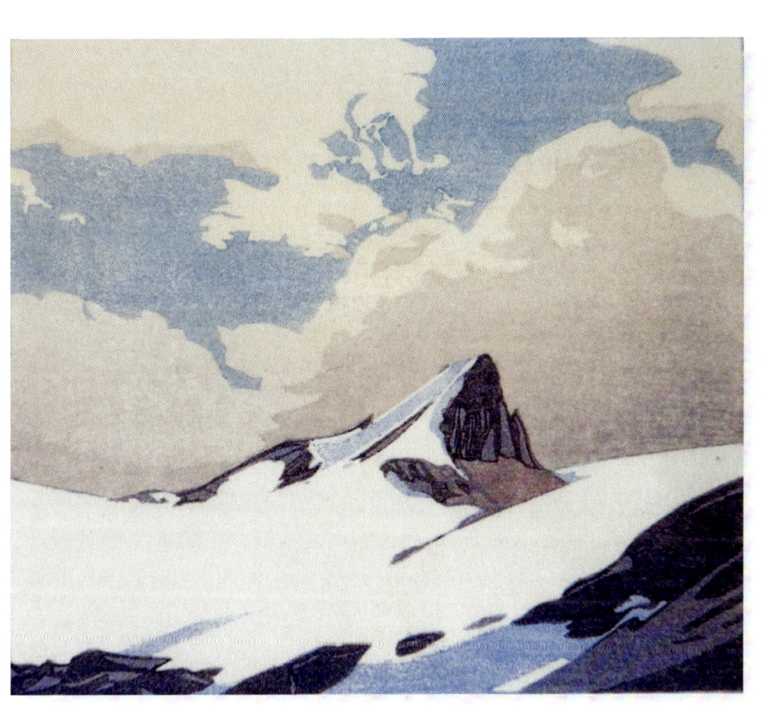

Alice Saltiel-Marshall

Saint Nicholas Peak, 1993

Watercolour on Paper, 12.7 × 17.8 cm
Private Collection of Rick and Lynn Dale

Alice Saltiel created her image from a perspective at high elevation and at close range, revealing the detail of this distinctive summit on the Continental Divide. The sunlit peak rises sharply out of the glacier like the crest of a wave thrust out of a frozen sea. A shaft of light illuminates the northwest face, showing its irregular surface, while to the west an intriguing triangular sub-peak just catches the sunshine. The crisp, vertical lines of the rock faces are in contrast to the undulating shapes of the snow-covered ice. Rich shadows on the Onion's ridge, in the lower right corner, and the even darker line of trees emphasize the radiant peak reaching into a blue sky. Alice brings a great deal of energy to the enduring presence of peak and glacier through her sensitive use of light and colour.

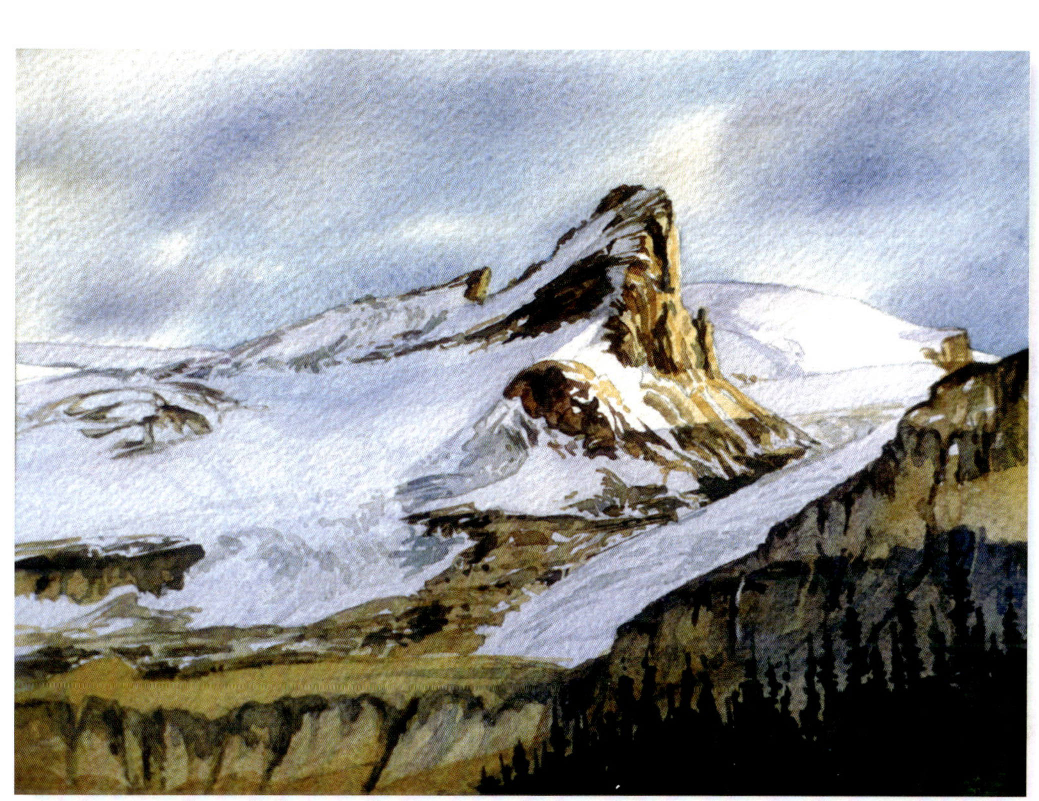

Bill Burns

Rockies #6, 2003

Oil on Board, 24.5 × 30.0 cm
Private Collection of Lee O'Donnell

Bill Burns sketched this inspiring image of St. Nicholas Peak in the meadows not far from the Ram Pasture. The trees on either side of the painting direct the viewer's eye over the end of Bow Lake and up past the sloping shoulder of Crowfoot Mountain, on the left, to the brilliant white glacier, with St. Nicholas Peak reaching into a vibrant blue sky. The painting has tremendous vitality in the use of colour, as the sunlight falls on the exposed rock and the meadow, and in the energetic style. The curving lines of the glacier surrounding and partially covering the peak are repeated in the clouds overhead. The sketch gives one an immediate sense of the rejuvenating influence of the alpine landscape.

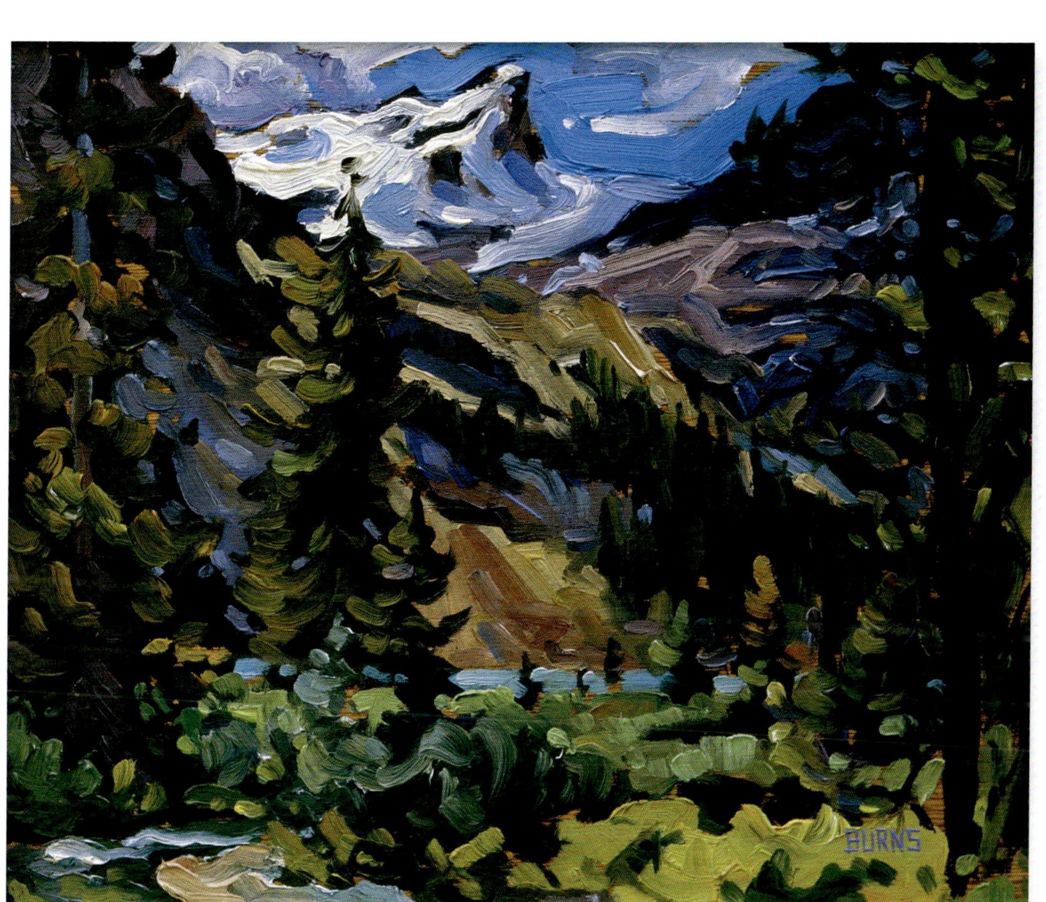
BURNS

Horace Champagne

Saint Nicholas Peak, My Favourite Point of View, c.2003

Pastel on Paper, 61.0 × 45.7 cm
Private Collection

In the foreground of his painting, Horace Champagne shows the popular trail winding beside Bow Lake leading to Bow Falls, which are just visible as the lower waterfall draining the glacier. The upper waterfall spills into Iceberg Lake. Above the glacier, the sunlight reveals St. Nicholas Peak in all its glory, with its sharp, icy ridge separating the two sheets of ice, and its prominent summit soaring into a blue sky. Below, the light sparkles on the amazing, bluish-green glacial lake. The warmth of a summer's day is evident in the wildflowers in the foreground, their vibrant colours in contrast to the blackened branches of the dying tree. Hikers have paused on the point in the middle of the painting, perhaps to watch the canoe just off the mouth of the creek. From wildflowers to glaciers, this painting epitomizes the enjoyment of Bow Lake.

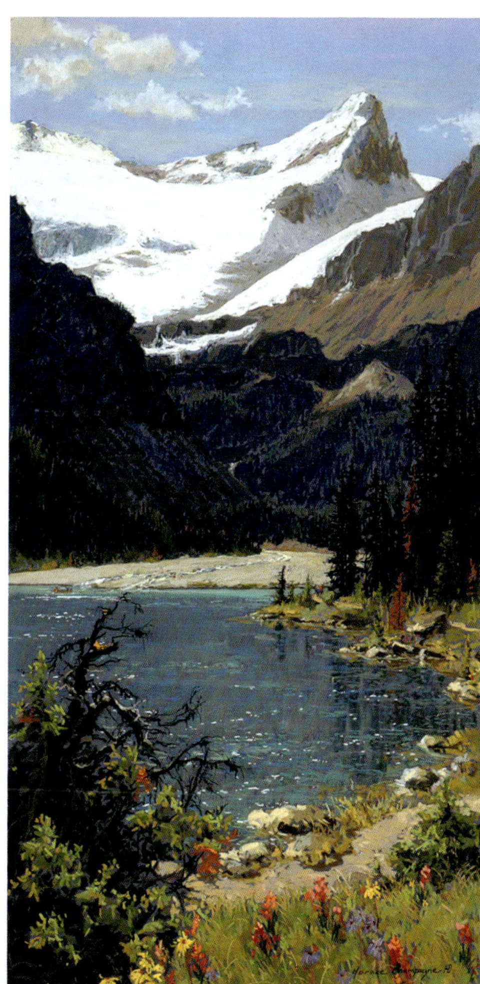

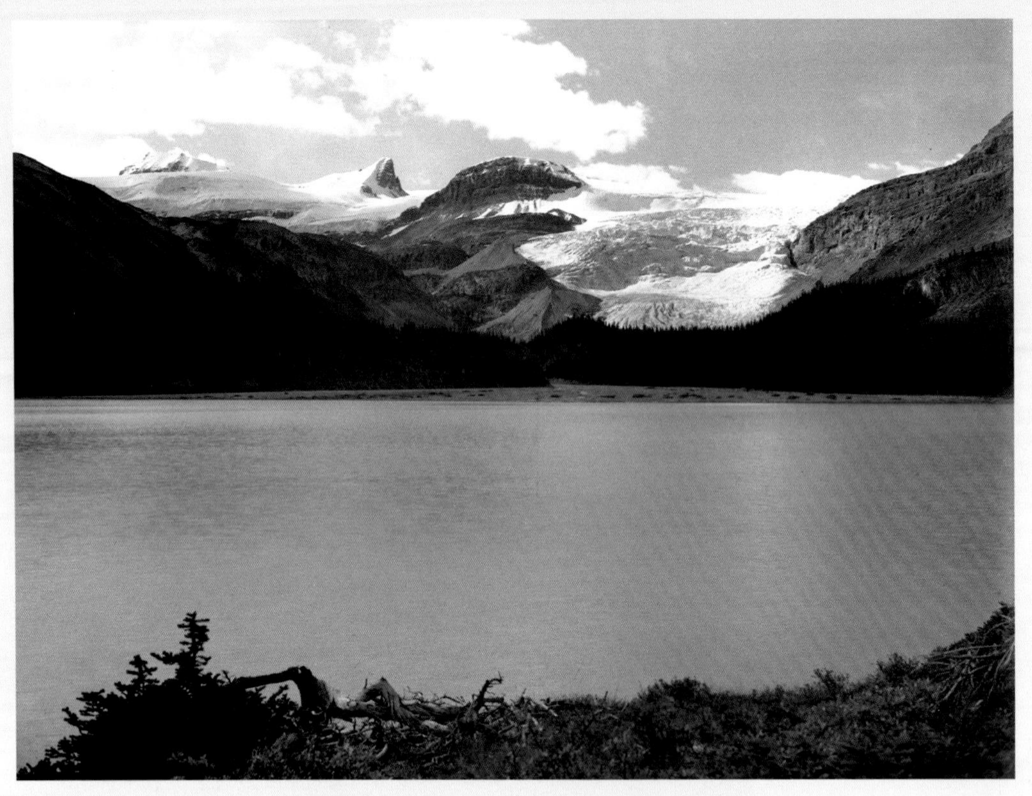

Vaux Family

Photograph of Upper Bow Lake [Bow Lake and Bow Glacier] (No. 145), 1902
Whyte Museum of the Canadian Rockies (v653/na80-1121).
Rounded shape of the Onion to left of Bow Glacier; pyramid of Saint Nicholas Peak just to left of the Onion; peak of Mount Olive far left.

BOW GLACIER

We headed westward for the woods bordering the stony flats through which the glacial outflow enters the lake, and were soon so close to the huge and sinuous stream of the glacier that we could see the séracs projecting from the icefall. In the direction of Mt. Gordon, whose crest just topped the skyline a new expanse of névé lay revealed. Billowy and sunset flushed, it broke in great waves against the cliffs of Nicholas Rock, which thrust itself like a black tusk through the ice.

— B.S. Darling, "Up the Bow and Down the Yoho,"
Canadian Alpine Journal, III (1911), 162.

Belmore Browne

Bow Glacier, c.1928

Oil on Board, 29.0 × 40.0 cm
Collection of the Whyte Museum of the Canadian Rockies

Belmore Browne's painting offers a spectacular view of the Bow Glacier from the meadows near the Ram Pasture. This scene had not only inspired Jimmy Simpson to establish his permanent camp at the north end of Bow Lake, but many early explorers had also set up their tents here for a brief rest before continuing over Bow Pass. The diaries of Agnes Browne record camping trips to Bow Lake in 1928 and 1929, and Belmore may possibly have completed his painting at that time. The extent of Bow Glacier in this image is astonishing to our eyes almost 80 years later. The ice, then, totally covered the area behind Bow Falls, now Iceberg Lake, and even flowed over the cliff where we see the falls today. The glacier is contained between the rounded shape of the Onion on the left and the sloping shoulder of Portal Peak on the right. In the upper left corner, St. Nicholas Peak is set against a cloudless summer sky. The afternoon sunlight falls on the upper slopes of the glacier and, in the middle ground, on the northern buttress of Crowfoot Mountain, which is beside the pale, glacial water of Bow Lake. Sunlight also illuminates the foreground meadow, painted in warm colours with broad impressionistic strokes. This serene summer meadow is the perfect vantage point to admire the magnificent mountains and glaciers.

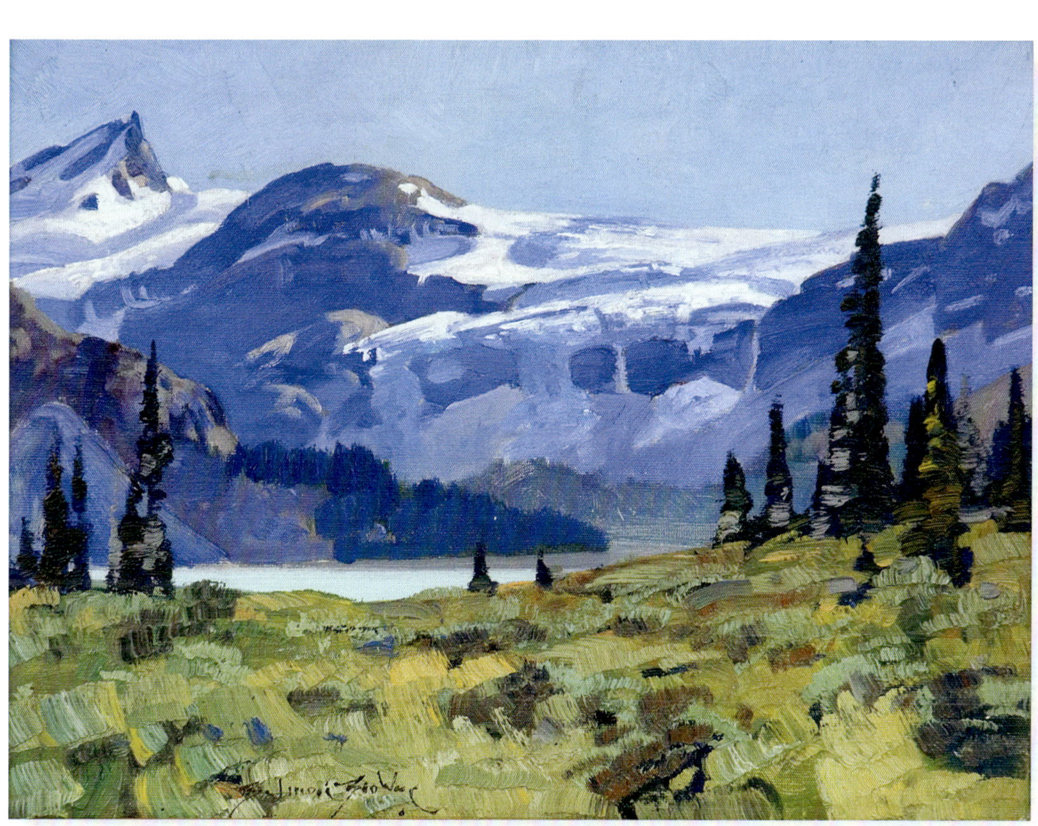

Catharine Whyte

Mount Nicholas, n.d.

Oil on Canvas, 25.1 × 30.0 cm
Collection of the Whyte Museum of the Canadian Rockies

The sturdy trunks of ancient trees frame this scene and lead the viewer's eye over the stream meandering through the willows to Bow Lake and up to the ribbon of falling water draining Bow Glacier. Despite the title of her painting, Catharine's focus is on the magnificent glacier. The ice is a dazzling white in the summer sunshine and stretches between the lower slopes of the Onion on the left – St. Nicholas Peak is out of the frame on the far left – and the shoulder of Portal Peak on the right. The sky is divided between an enormous grey cloud and a patch of blue. Catharine's image shows that the glacier is somewhat diminished; the ice that once extended to the base of the shadowed headwall has been replaced by Bow Falls, but the level area just above the cliff is still frozen and has not yet become Iceberg Lake. Branches of the foreground trees hide the distant peaks. Catharine captures this inspiring view using the soft, natural colours of a summer's day.

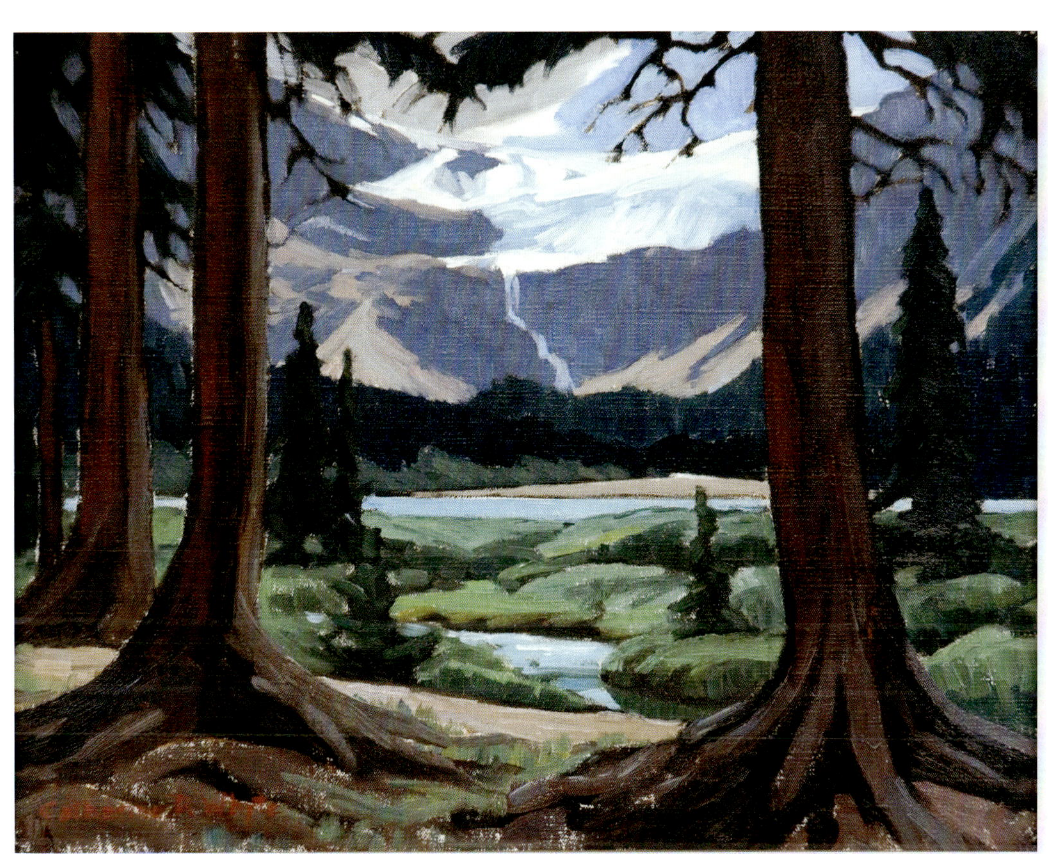

MAX ELLIOTT

Iceberg Lake (detail mixed-media collage), *2006*

ACRYLIC ON PAPER, 12.0 × 18.5 CM
PRIVATE COLLECTION OF EMMA AND JOE ANDERSON

Max Elliott's perspective is from the top of the headwall near the magnificent Bow Falls. The view across Iceberg Lake, formed by the retreating ice, reveals Bow Glacier and Portal Peak, with its summit in the shadow of a passing cloud. In the early 20th century, as shown in the Vaux family photograph, Bow Glacier filled the entire area, reaching up the sides of the mountain and extending over the present waterfall to the moraine below. Max portrays a stark landscape of rock, water and ice before any vegetation has taken hold. The vibrant colour of the glacial water is set against the reddish-brown rock of Portal Peak, an enormous illuminated slab resting on a triangular pedestal. Above the lake, an irregularly shaped oval of blue sky allows the sunshine to bring warmth and colour. The ephemeral, shape-shifting clouds provide a contrast to the slow but powerful changes to the landscape wrought by the glacier. The painting reveals a dramatic setting infused with great energy and a stunning beauty.

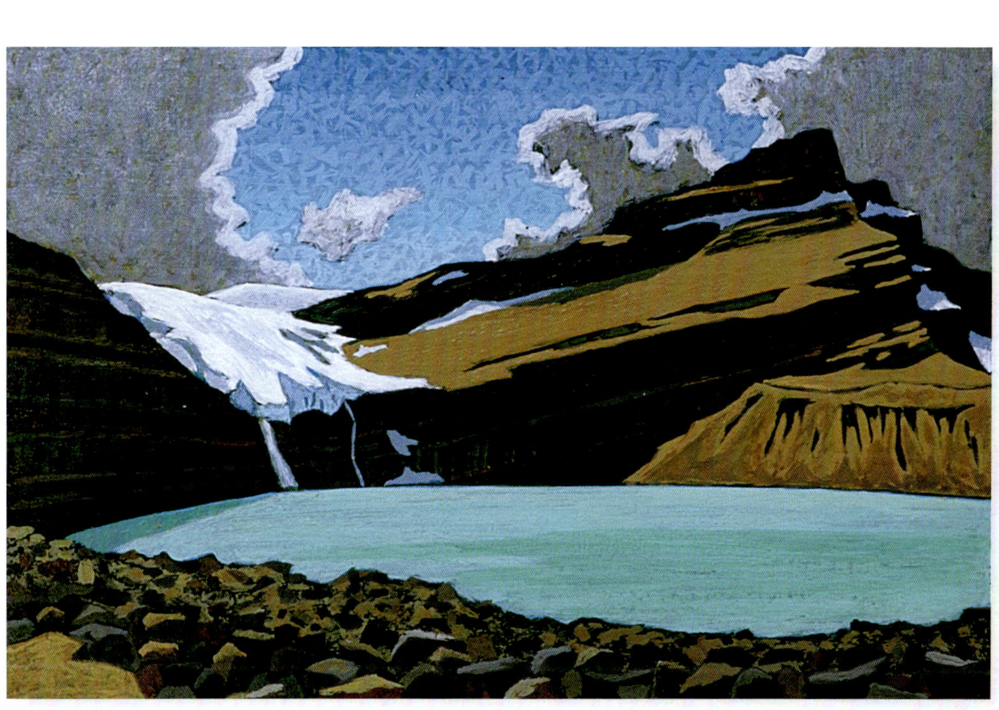

Mike Svob

Winter, Bow Glacier, 2007

Acrylic on Thick Canvas Wrap with Black Painted Sides, 61.0 × 121.9 cm
Private Collection of Kenneth and Heidy MacLeod

Mike Svob's image captures the exhilarating effect of winter sunshine on the frozen landscape. The great width of the canvas emphasizes the contrast between the brilliant line of trees, with scarlet foliage rising from peach-coloured snow, and the dazzling white of the illuminated Bow Glacier in the background, draped between the Onion on the left and the sloping ridge of Portal Peak on the right. The rock on the shadowed faces of the mountains is grey, enlivened by touches of red where the snow is tinged with light. The northern buttress of Crowfoot, however, receives the direct sunshine, bringing out the warm, rich tones in the rock and various colours in the snow, from blue to mauve and startling white. The vibrant colours in Mike's landscape allow us to see the winter landscape differently – not just a static environment waiting for the spring thaw, but an inspiring place of great vitality.

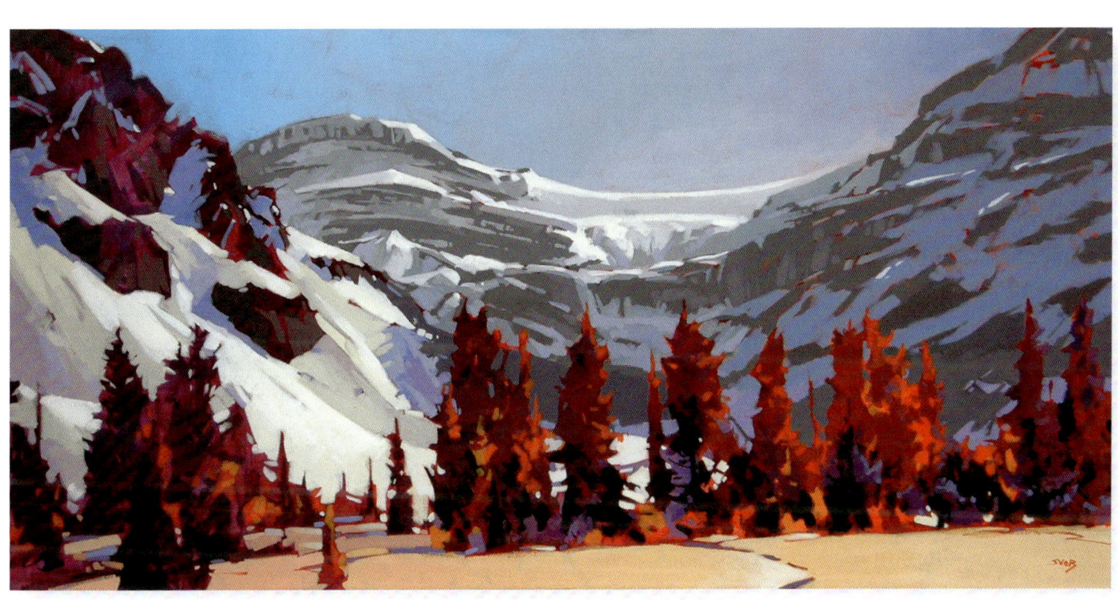

Jimmy Simpson

Untitled (Moonlight, Bow Glacier), 1968

Watercolour, 8.9 × 17.8 cm
Collection of the Whyte Museum of the Canadian Rockies

Jimmy Simpson expanded his image horizontally to provide a moonlit panorama. The painting extends from the distinctive spire of St. Nicholas Peak rising out of the glacier on the left to the rounded shape of the Onion and Bow Glacier under the moon toward the centre. On the right is Portal Peak, with a ridge extending to Mount Thompson's summit that is just out of the painting. The full moon dominates the landscape, casting a warm light over the mountains and creating golden pools in Bow Lake. Jimmy enjoyed working in watercolours because he could reproduce the various tones that he saw in the natural world. In this painting, the moonlight brings out the colour in the scene almost as if it were viewed in daylight. Jimmy captures the magical effect of the moon, illuminating the landscape so completely with a soft, yellow glow.

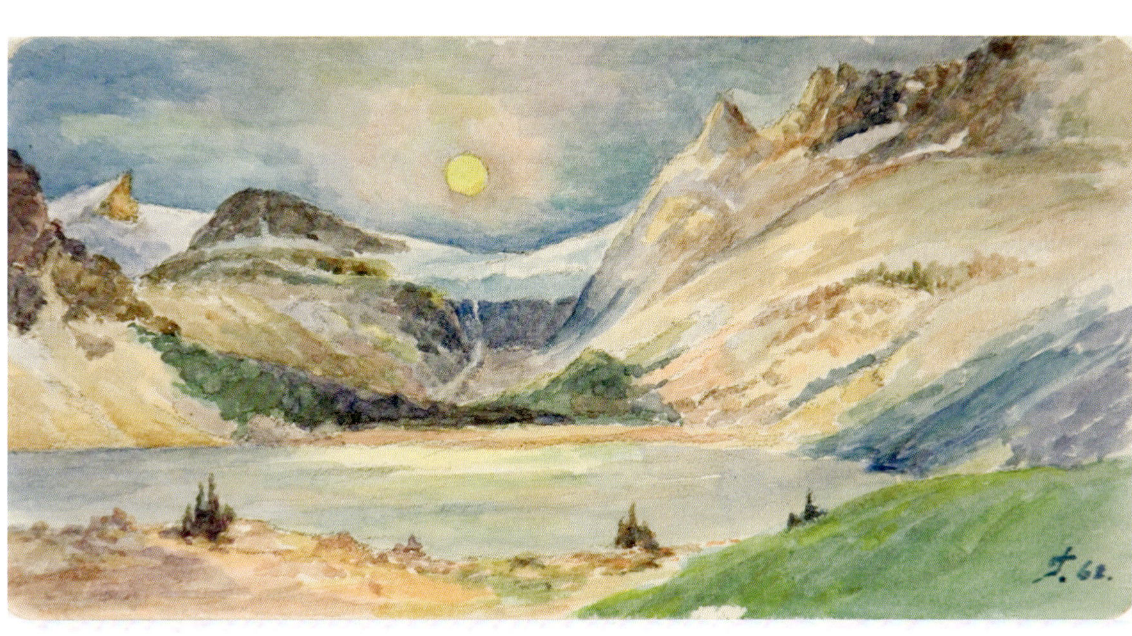

W.J. Bradley

Blue Notes, 2007

Oil on Canvas, 40.6 × 50.8 cm
Private Collection of Christie Saunders

W.J. Bradley completed her *plein air* painting on a bitterly cold January evening, using a headlamp and standing in deep snow near Num-Ti-Jah Lodge. This image is the first in a series devoted to exploring the effect of moonlight, to discover, as she explains, "in the cool moonlight, how the landscape differed in colour and shape from how it appears in the sun's light and warmth." She was surprised to find that "although the shapes are considerably simplified, the colours are complex and varied." In *Blue Notes*, the moonlight lends an enchantment to the still, cold landscape. With the sparkling stars in the deep blue sky as a backdrop, the snow-covered slopes of Saint Nicholas Peak and the rounded Onion, rising out of the glacier, are a brilliant white. The middle ground, in contrast, reveals the long buttress of Crowfoot Mountain with its intricate shadows set beside the lighter talus slopes. Across the frozen lake, the mounds of snow in the foreground reflect more shades of blue in the shadows and icy ski tracks. The moonlight illuminates the landscape in remarkable colour and detail.

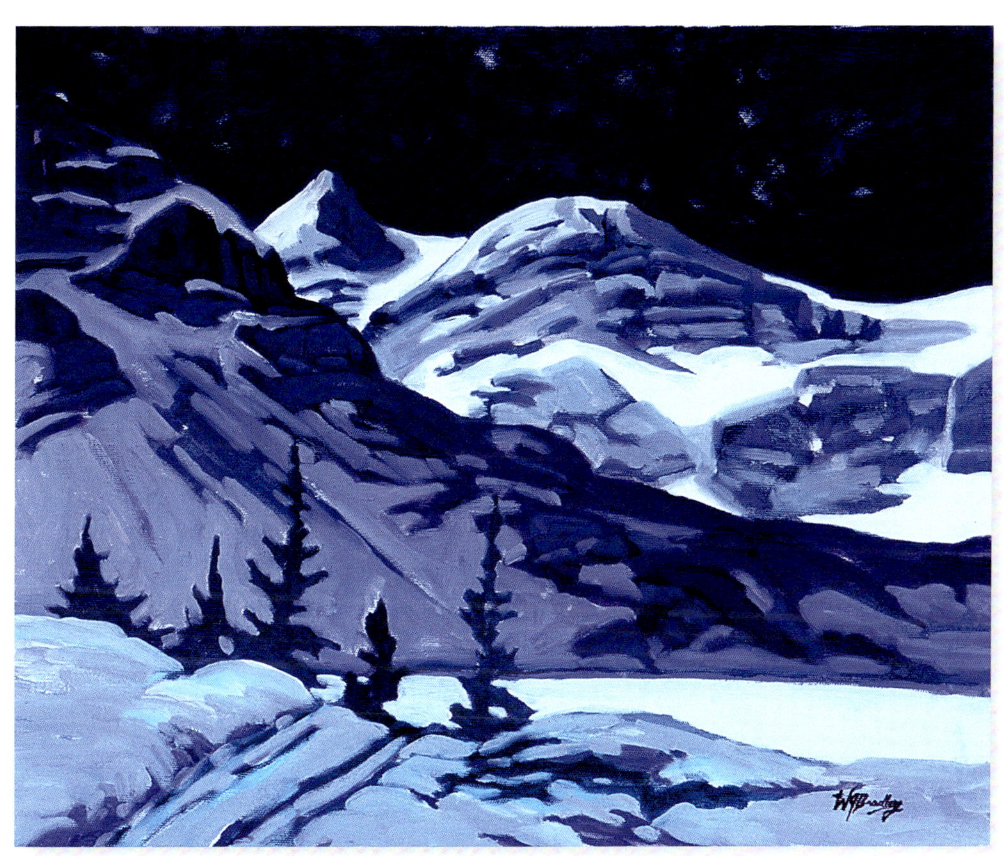

Roger D. Arndt

Winter Canyon, 2005

Oil on Prepared Panel, 40.6 × 40.6 cm
Collection of Num-Ti-Jah Lodge

The wonderful luminescence in Roger Arndt's landscape is achieved through a laborious technique derived from 15th-century Flemish painters. Many transparent layers of colour are applied onto a specially prepared white board so that the light travels through the layers and reflects off the panel beneath. This time-consuming approach allows Arndt to reproduce atmospheric effects such as the suggestion of an ephemeral mist. In this image, two figures are following the trail beside the creek that drains the vast amphitheatre below the Bow Hut. The afternoon sunlight, touching the glacier on the Continental Divide and falling on the snowbanks beside the figures, seems to evoke a light haze in the canyon. Our eye is led into the painting by the striking colour of the creek, and we follow the path of the tiny figures, dwarfed by the rocky bluffs on either side and, especially, by the majestic headwall ahead. Above the glacier, the sky has a roseate tint, a touch of warmth in this wintry landscape. The subtle interplay of light and colour, giving a sense of the atmosphere in the painting, is intriguing.

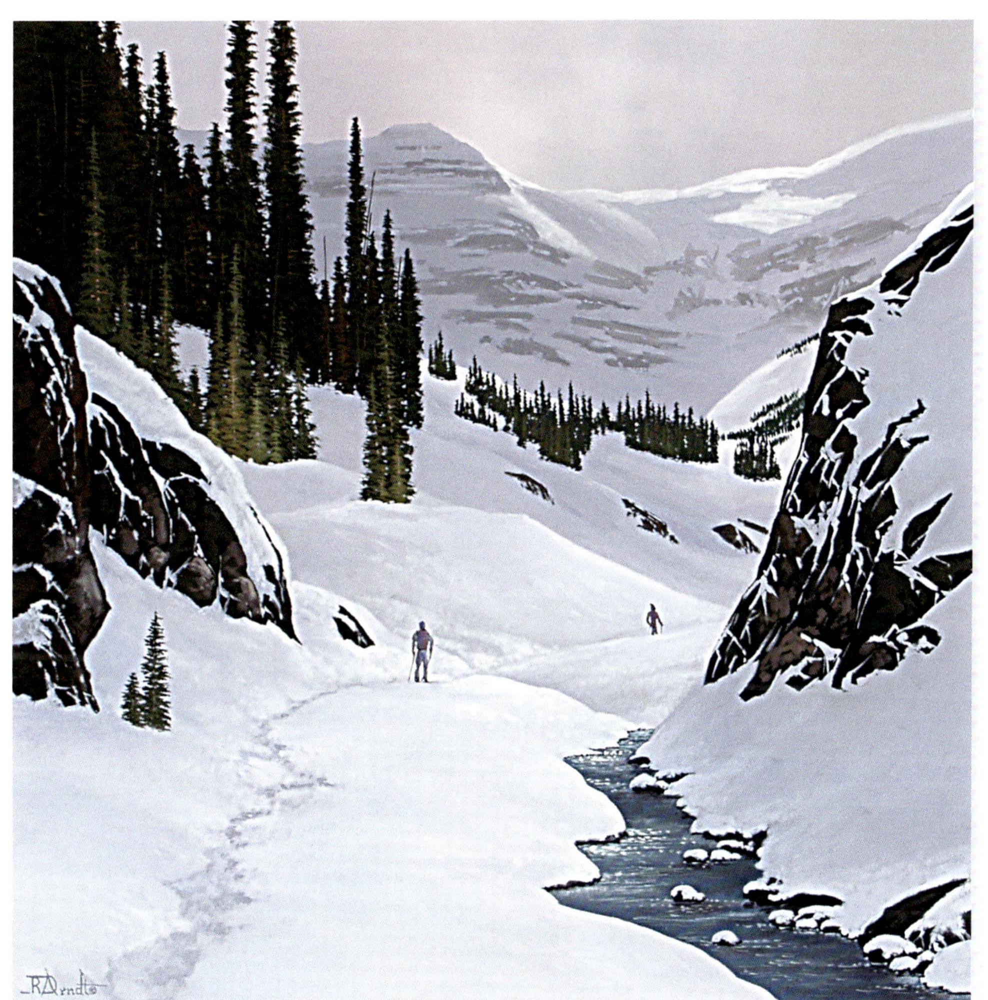

Walter J. Phillips

The Source of the Bow, n.d.

Wood Engraving, 16.0 × 10.0 cm
Collection of the Whyte Museum of the Canadian Rockies

The water that plunges over Bow Falls cuts its way through a terminal moraine by way of a narrow gorge before reaching the level, gravel plain at the entrance to Bow Lake. The sides of the ravine are at times so close together that the turbulent water below is hidden from view. Early explorers remarked on an immense boulder acting as a natural bridge and a spectacular viewpoint over the swift and tortuous course of the river below. Walter Phillips appears to have captured the torrent just as it leaves the depths of the canyon. The transience and great power of running water to wear away bedrock fascinated the artist. In this dramatic image, the swiftly flowing water catches the light as it finds its way past the dark, jagged sides of the gorge. The scene has great energy with the water escaping from the leaning walls and starting on its journey through the Bow Valley.

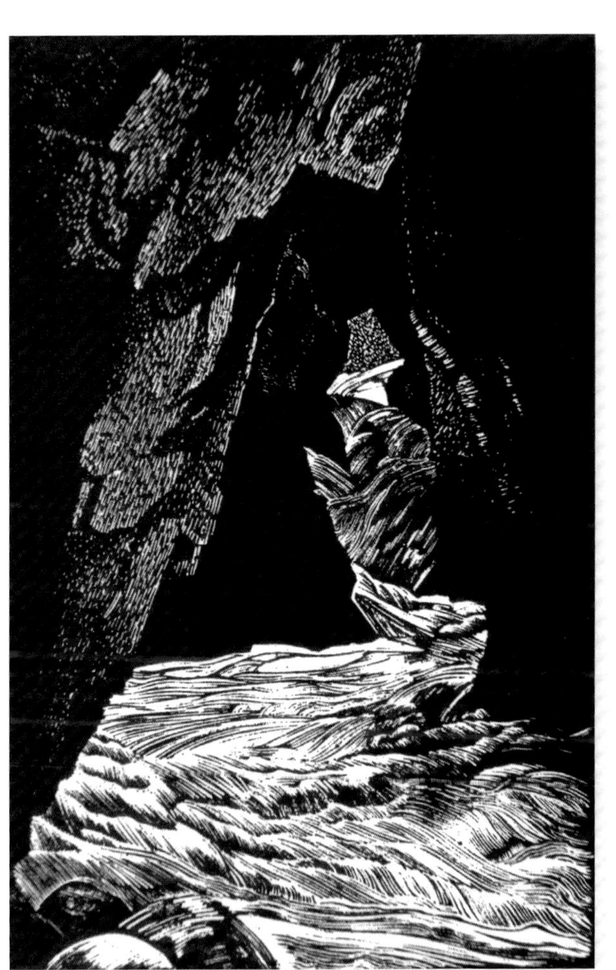

David McEown

Bow River Headwaters, 2003

Watercolour, 139.7 × 91.6 cm
Private Collection of Lee O'Donnell

David McEown remembers how at the end of a tiring day of sketching, he happened to glance back at the ridges he had just descended to see a golden light illuminating the headwaters of the Bow. Despite his fatigue, he was inspired to capture, in his words, "the transparent veils of light coming from the dark canyons." The viewer's eye follows the flowing water back past the intersecting ridges to its source in the great glacier on the Continental Divide, presided over by Saint Nicholas Peak. Autumn sunshine highlights the river's beginning, just touching the tops of the rock walls surrounding the gorge as the water winds through the rich shadows below. Where the river spills out into the open and flows toward Bow Lake, the stand of trees in the foreground is turned to a brilliant gold. The dramatic use of colour and composition is a tribute to the vitality of the Bow at its source.

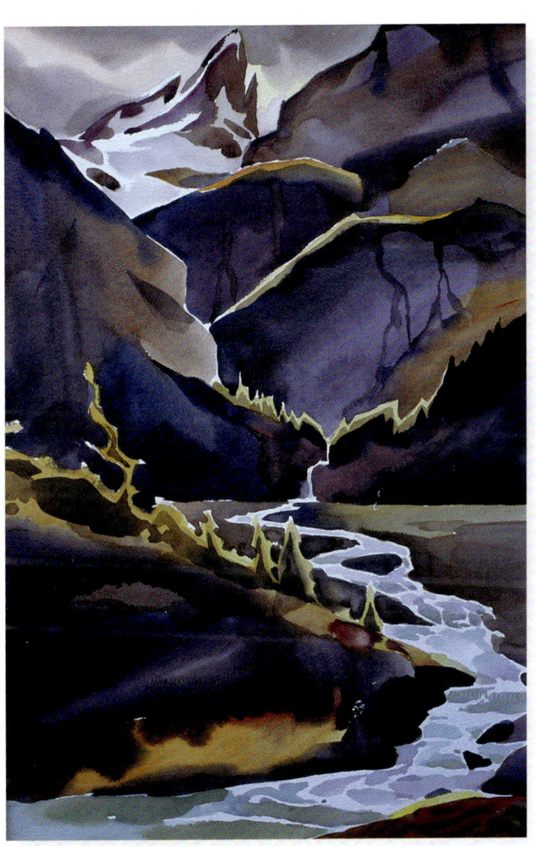

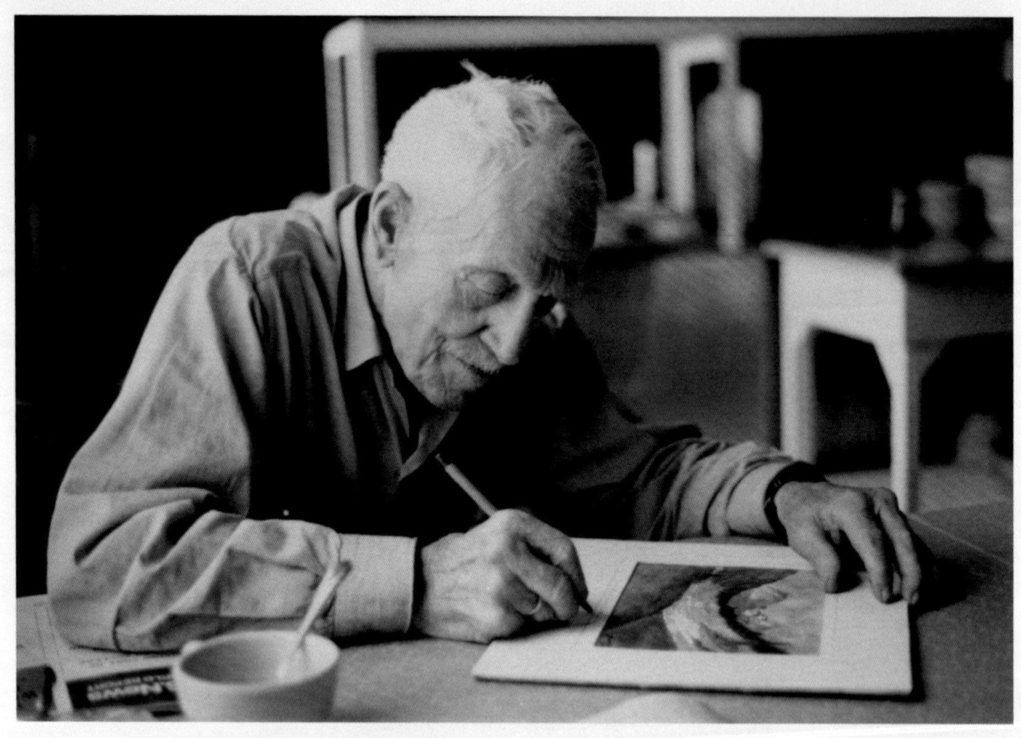

Photograph of Jimmy Simpson painting at his kitchen table, n.d.
Whyte Museum of the Canadian Rockies (v577/11d/pa27).

CAMP AT BOW LAKE

Bow Lake. I took up the site in 1920 when the first Commissioner of Parks was J.B. Harkin, but I had to expend $5,000 of work before they would grant a lease. That made me pack timber and building material through the sloughs from Laggan to Bow Lake. In 1922, Palmer and Thorington were the first tourists to use the cabins. Ladd and Thorington came in the following summer while the octagonal cabin near the lakeshore was being completed.

— Jimmy Simpson, "Days Remembered,"
The American Alpine Journal, XIX, 1 (1974), 53.

Carl Rungius

A Camp in the Rockies, c.1925

Oil on Canvas, 100.5 × 125.5 cm
Collection of Glenbow Museum

Carl Rungius probably camped many times in these meadows, whether to visit with his good friend Jimmy Simpson or for a short rest before continuing north on a hunting trip. The teepees are nestled among the trees with a spectacular view of Bow Glacier: the ice is thick at the top of the headwall and it extends down the cliff into the basin below. Nowadays, Bow Falls can be seen from this location, as the water flows out of Iceberg Lake and plunges over the cliff. To the left of Bow Glacier is the rounded shape of the Onion, and in the top left corner, just visible above the tall trees, is the distinctive shape of St. Nicholas Peak. The whole scene is filled with sunshine: parts of the glacier are a sparkling white and the meadow is painted with the warm colours of summer. This is truly an idyllic camping spot, a fitting reward after struggling through the muskeg on the trail from Lake Louise. Rungius completed a large landscape of this scene, revealing his interest in landscape for its own sake, not just as a background for wild game.

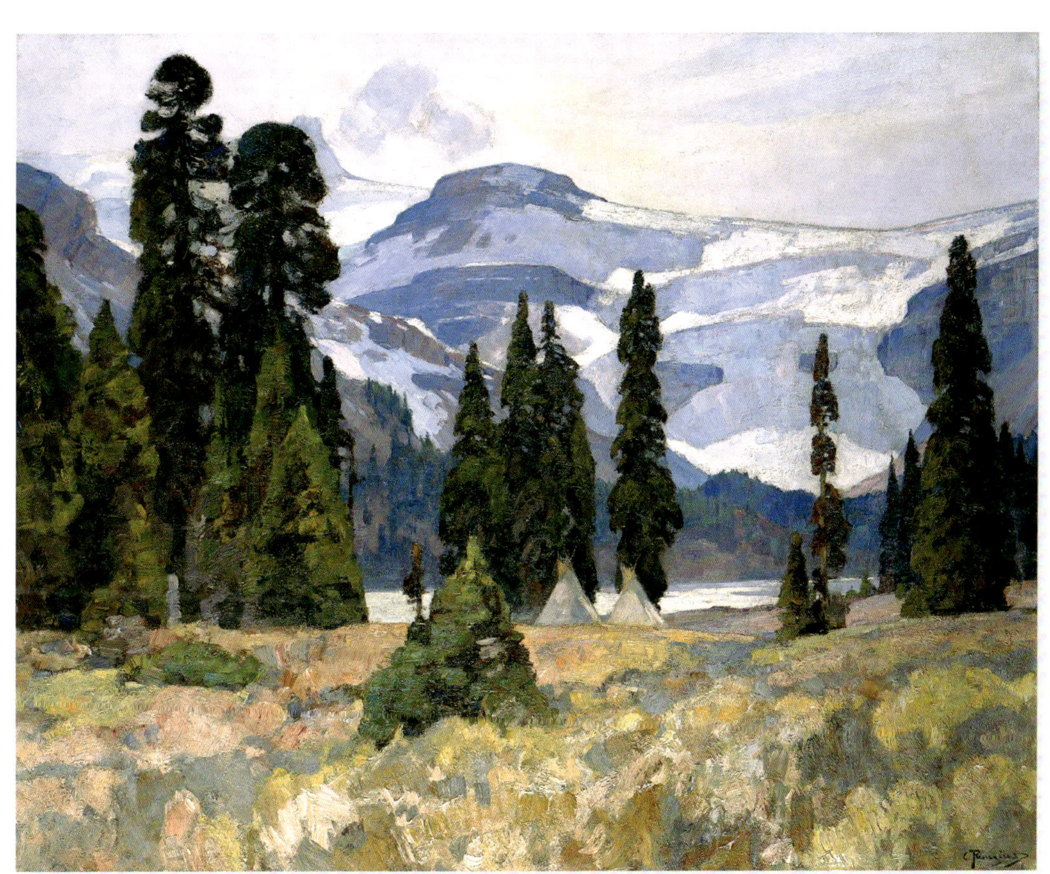

Belmore Browne

Pack Horses, Bow Lake, n.d.

Oil on Canvas, 40.6 × 50.8 cm
Collection of Glenbow Museum

Belmore Browne took his family to Bow Lake several times by horseback, and his wife mentions in her diaries that the artist liked to paint images of the horses. Browne was a wildlife artist as well as a painter of landscape. In this image, the central focus – the white horse – is turned away from the viewer, looking across the broad valley to the east, toward Cirque Peak. The sun is directly overhead, illuminating this patient group of horses waiting in the cheerful meadow. Either the other three horses will be loaded with boxes or the white horse will soon be relieved of its burden. In any case, without horses to transport gear and supplies, early exploration in the mountains would have been restricted.

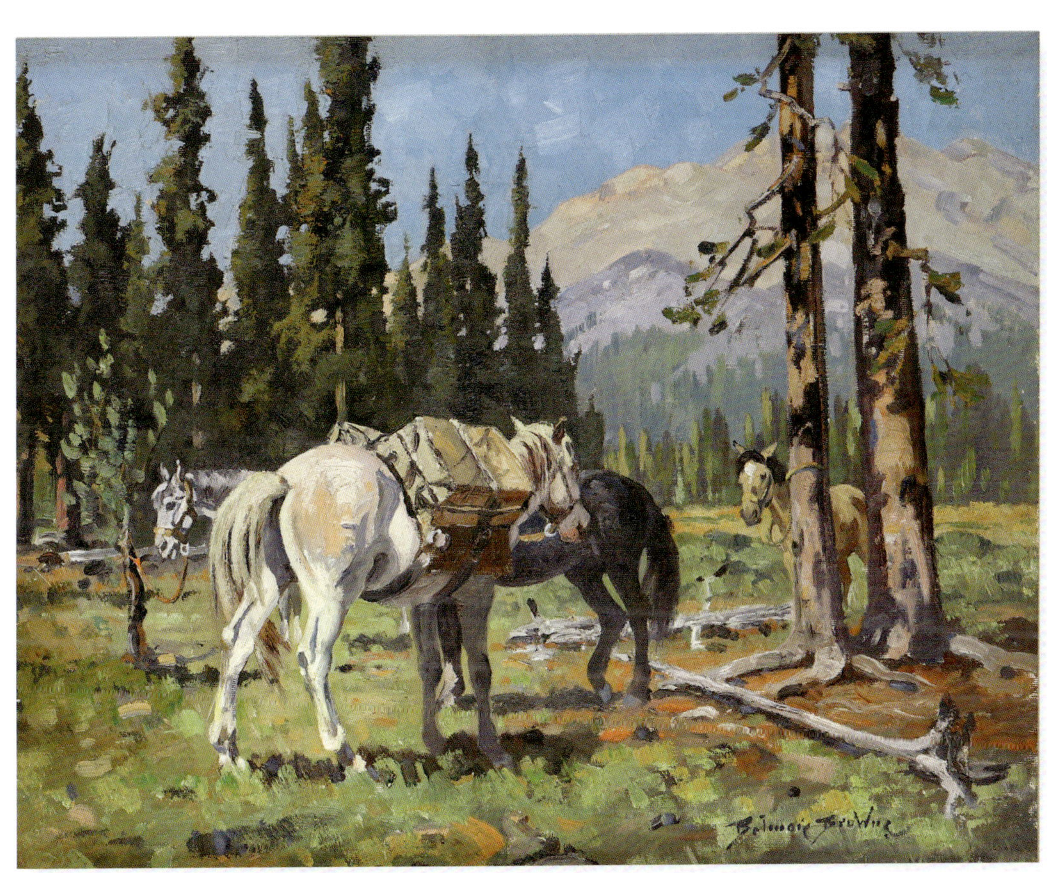

Catharine Whyte

Simpson's Cabin, 1940–1960

Oil on Canvas, 27.0 × 33.0 cm
Collection of the Whyte Museum of the Canadian Rockies

Jimmy Simpson built this octagonal cabin, the Ram Pasture, as part of his first permanent camp at Bow Lake. The view from the front door encompasses the magnificent Bow Glacier lying between the Onion on the left and Portal Peak on the right. Twin falls drain the glacier, as the ice has receded above the headwall. Catharine, typically, includes a dramatic sky in her sketch: enormous dark clouds pile up behind the Onion while a white cloud drifts behind Portal Peak. Sunshine creates shadows in the foreground creek, gently flowing toward the lake. The somber tones of the distant mountains are in contrast to the vibrant greens of the meadow and the warm brown of the log cabin. After Num-Ti-Jah Lodge was completed, Jimmy and Billie continued to use the Ram Pasture as a retreat. The cabin is preserved today, and sometimes the artists in residence can stay in this historic building.

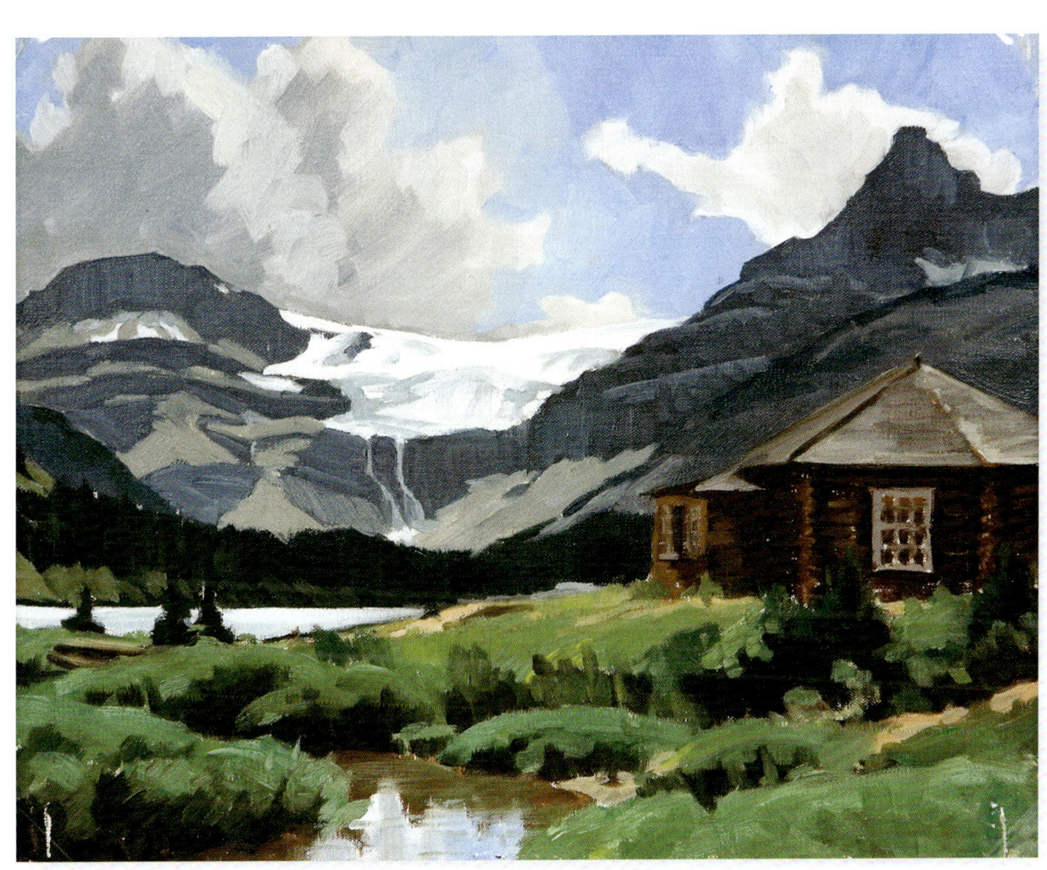

A.C. Leighton

Bow Lake and Mount Thompson, 1965

Watercolour, 27.0 × 33.0 cm
Collection of the Whyte Museum of the Canadian Rockies

A.C. Leighton's impressive view of Mount Thompson and Portal Peak, just left of centre, emphasizes their height as they rise from the north end of Bow Lake. One has the sense of the untamed wilderness far from the haunts of man – the landscape that Leighton sought on his expeditions into the backcountry. The date of his watercolour indicates, however, that Num-Ti-Jah Lodge stands near Leighton's vantage point. Despite the proximity of man's habitation, Leighton chooses to emphasize the towering summits overhead, with three-quarters of the painting taken up by mountain and sky. Leighton's soft, natural colours and subtle differences in value capture the mountains' majestic presence. The summit of Portal Peak in the distance seems to be shrouded in mist. The darkest colours are reserved for the evergreens in the foreground, standing firmly beside the lake, leading the eye up to the peaks.

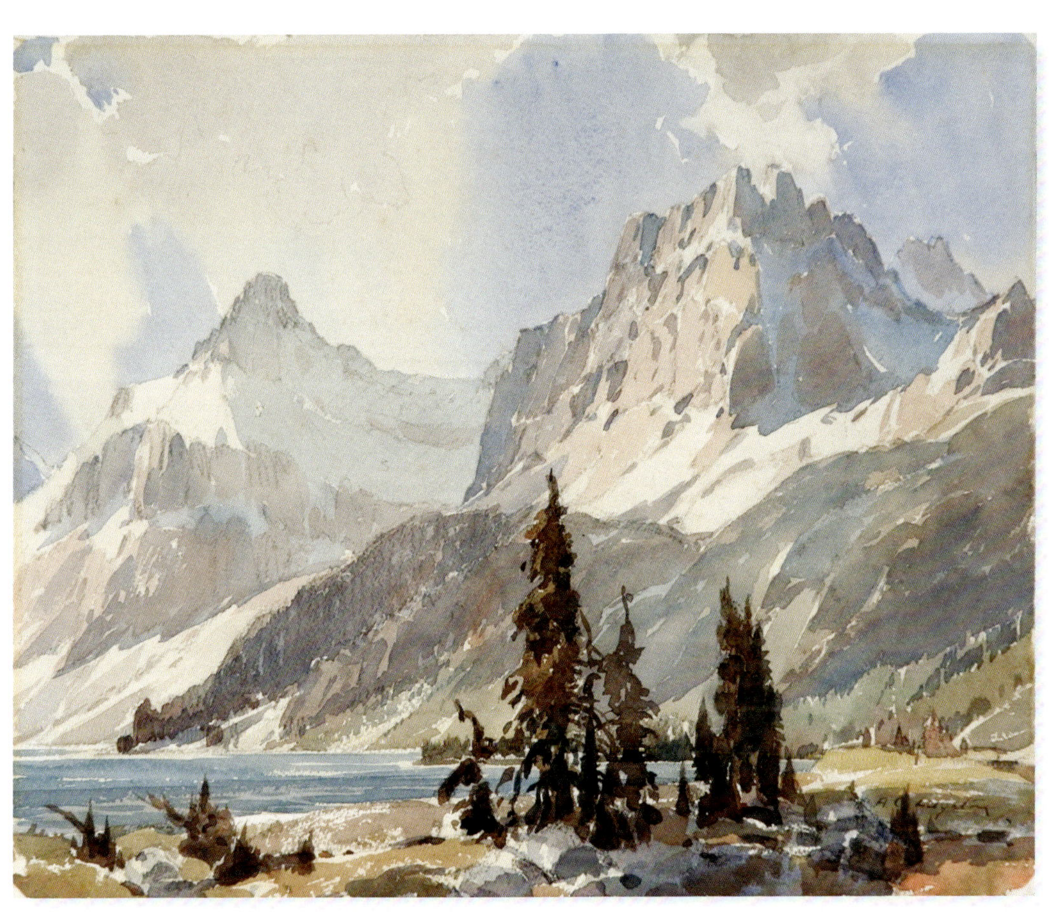

Erica Neumann

Blondie, 1986–2004, 2005

Oil on Canvas, 50.0 × 50.0 cm
Collection of Num-Ti-Jah Lodge

Erica Neumann, an accomplished painter of bears, was asked to commemorate the life of a grizzly named Blondie for the *Art of History* show at Num-Ti-Jah Lodge in May 2005. Blondie was known for her beautiful, light-coloured fur and her calm co-existence with humans in the vicinity of the lodge. Roy Andersen remembers a close encounter with Blondie when he was leading a photography workshop near Bow Lake: the bear was in excellent condition, a good size, with magnificent fur, and she simply took note of the interlopers in her territory and carried on without any aggression. Blondie was also renowned for her success in raising cubs. Erica's portrait shows a noble, handsome grizzly. Her eyes have a steady, confident gaze and the light brings out the warm tones of yellow and orange in her fur. Blondie died suddenly when she was hit on the Trans-Canada Highway near Lake Wapta, many kilometres from Bow Lake. She is remembered with great affection.

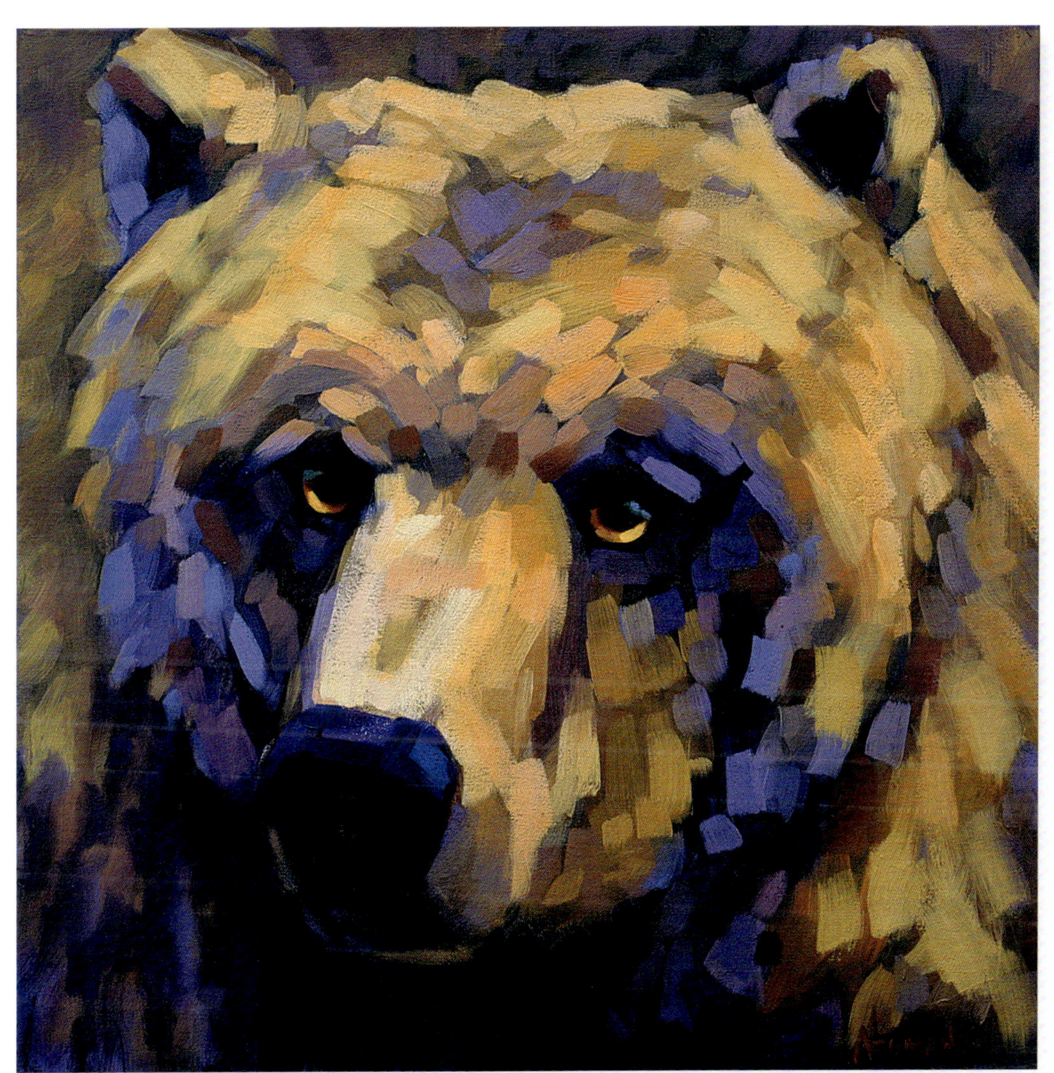

Notes

1 James Hector, "Journal," August 3 to October 7, 1858, in *Exploration–British North America: The Journals, Detailed Reports, and Observations ... by Captain Palliser . . . During the Years 1857, 1858, 1859, and 1860.* (London: Printed by G.E. Eyre and W. Spottiswoode, for H.M. Stationery Office, 1863), 98–116.

2 Hector, "Journal," in Palliser, 107.

3 Ernie Lakusta, *The Intrepid Explorer*[:] *James Hector's Explorations in the Canadian Rockies* (Calgary: Fifth House, 2007), 99.

4 Hector, "Journal," in *Palliser*, 109.

5 Lakusta, *The Intrepid Explorer*, 103.

6 Hector, "Journal," in *Palliser*, 109.

7 Nicky Brink and Stephen R. Bown, *Forgotten Highways*[:] *Wilderness Journeys Down the Historic Trails of the Canadian Rockies* (Edmonton: Brindle & Glass, 2007), 22.

8 Lakusta, *The Intrepid Explorer*, 104.

9 E.J. Hart, *Diamond Hitch*[:] *The Pioneer Guides and Outfitters of Banff and Jasper* (Banff: EJH Literary Enterprises, 2001), 15, 18–19.

10 Hart, *Diamond Hitch*, 27–28.

11 Hart, *Diamond Hitch*, 29.

12 Hart, *Diamond Hitch*, 29.

13 Philip S. Abbot, "The First Ascent of Mount Hector, Canadian Rockies, *Appalachia*, VIII (1896–1898), 2.

14 Abbot, "First Ascent," 3.

15 Abbot, "First Ascent," 8.

16 Abbot, "First Ascent," 8.

17 Abbot, "First Ascent," 14.

18 Abbot, "First Ascent," 16.

19 Hart, *Diamond Hitch*, 49.

20 Walter D. Wilcox, *The Rockies of Canada,* a revised and enlarged edition of *Camping in the Canadian Rockies.* (New York and London: The Knickerbocker Press, 1900), 140.

21 Wilcox, *Rockies* (1900), iv.

22 Wilcox, *Rockies* (1900), 139.

23 Wilcox, *Rockies* (1900), 140.

24 Wilcox, *Rockies* (1900), 149.

25 Wilcox, *Rockies* (1900), 141.

26 Wilcox, *Rockies* (1900), 142.

27 Wilcox, *Rockies* (1900), 144.

28 Walter D. Wilcox, *The Rockies of Canada*, a revised and enlarged edition of *Camping in the Canadian Rockies*, 3rd ed. (New York and London: G.P. Putnam's Sons, 1909), 143.

29 Wilcox, *Rockies* (1909), 275.

30 Wilcox, *Rockies* (1900), 147.

31 Wilcox, *Rockies* (1900), 147–48.

32 Hugh E.M. Stutfield and J. Norman Collie, *Climbs & Exploration in the Canadian Rockies* (Calgary: Rocky Mountain Books, 2008; first published London: Longmans, Green, 1903), 12.

33 Stutfield and Collie, *Climbs & Exploration*, 14.

34 Charles S. Thompson, "At the Headwaters of the Bow," *Appalachia*, VIII (1896–1898), 321.

35 Harold B. Dixon, "The Ascent of Mount Lefroy and Other Climbs in the Rocky Mountains," *The Alpine Journal*, XIX (1898–1899), 107.

36 Stutfield and Collie, *Climbs & Exploration*, 15.

37 Charles E. Fay, "Old Times in the Canadian Alps," *Canadian Alpine Journal*, XII (1922), 100.

38 Thompson, "Headwaters," 323.

39 Thompson, "Headwaters," 323.

40 Dixon, "Ascent of Mount Lefroy," 108.

41 Thompson, "Headwaters," 324.

42 Thompson, "Headwaters," 324–25.

43 Stutfield and Collie, *Climbs & Exploration*, 16–18.

44 Dixon, "Ascent of Mount Lefroy," 111.

45 Fay, "Old Times," 100–101.

46 Thompson, "Headwaters," 326.

47 Thompson, "Headwaters," 327.

48 Stutfield and Collie, *Climbs & Exploration*, 22.

49 Stutfield and Collie, *Climbs & Exploration*, 24.

50 Stutfield and Collie, *Climbs & Exploration*, 30.

51 George M. Weed, "Pipestone Creek and a New Pass to the Upper Bow," *Appalachia*, IX (1899–1901), 10–11.

52 Stutfield and Collie, *Climbs & Exploration*, 60.

53 Stutfield and Collie, *Climbs & Exploration*, 80–81.

54 Stutfield and Collie, *Climbs & Exploration*, 82–83.

55 Ralph Edwards, *The Trail to the Charmed Land* (Saskatoon: H.R. Larson, 1950), 8.

56 Fay, "Old Times," 101.

57 Weed, "Pipestone Creek," 17.

58 Edwards, *Charmed Land*, 56.

59 Edwards, *Charmed Land*, 63.

60 Edwards, *Charmed Land*, 67.

61 Charles L. Noyes, "Mount Balfour and the Waputehk Snow-field," *Appalachia*, IX, 1 (1899–1901), 20.

62 Noyes, "Mount Balfour," 24.

63 Noyes, "Mount Balfour," 25.

64 Edwards, *Charmed Land*, 78.

65 Noyes, "Mount Balfour," 25.

66 Noyes, "Mount Balfour," 30–31.

67 James Simpson, "Days Remembered," *American Alpine Journal*, XIX, 1 (1974), 44.

68 Noyes, "Mount Balfour," 31.

69 E.J. Hart, *Jimmy Simpson*[:] *Legend of the Rockies*, 2nd ed. (Banff: Altitude, 1999), 25.

70 Stutfield and Collie, *Climbs & Exploration*, 135.

71 Hart, *Jimmy Simpson*, 25–26.

72 Letter from Bill Beach to Jimmy Simpson, June 7, 1921. (Banff: Archives of the Whyte Museum of the Canadian Rockies, M78/26).

73 Simpson, "Days Remembered," 54.

74 Simpson, "Days Remembered," 44.

75 Hart, *Jimmy Simpson*, 23.

76 Hart, *Jimmy Simpson*, 24–25.

77 Simpson, "Days Remembered," 46.

78 James Outram, *In the Heart of the Canadian Rockies* (London and New York: Macmillan, 1923), 269–71.

79 Hart, *Jimmy Simpson*, 34–35.

80 Hart, *Jimmy Simpson*, 31–32.

81 Simpson, "Days Remembered," 48.

82 Hart, *Jimmy Simpson*, 37.

83 Outram, *Heart of the Canadian Rockies*, 276.

84 Outram, *Heart of the Canadian Rockies*, 277–78.

85 Outram, *Heart of the Canadian Rockies*, 290.

86 E.J. Hart, *Yahe-Weha – Mountain Woman*[:] *The Life and Travels of Mary Schäffer Warren, 1861-1939.* Introduction to *A Hunter of Peace: Mary T.S. Schäffer's Old Indian Trails of the Canadian Rockies... with Photographs by the Author [et al.]*, edited by E.J. Hart (Banff: The Whyte Foundation, 1980), 5–6.

87 Hart, *Yahe-Weha – Mountain Woman*, 6.

88 Hart, *Yahe-Weha – Mountain Woman*, 9–10.

89 Schäffer, *Old Indian Trails*, 18.

90 Schäffer, *Old Indian Trails*, 23.

91 Schäffer, *Old Indian Trails*, 24.

92 Stewardson Brown, *Alpine Flora of the Canadian Rocky Mountains* (New York and London: G.P. Putnam's Sons, 1907), 44.

93 "Report of 1910 Camp," *Canadian Alpine Journal*, III (1911), 189.

94 Hart, *Jimmy Simpson*, 44.

95 E.F.M. MacCarthy and A.M. Barfleet, "Two Englishmen in the Yoho Valley," *Canadian Alpine Journal*, II, 2 (1910), 145.

96 "Bow Valley and Yoho Expedition," *Canadian Alpine Journal*, III (1911), 194. In the same volume, see B.S. Darling, "Up the Bow and Down the Yoho," 157–71, for an entertaining account of the trip.

97 Hart, *Jimmy Simpson*, 24.

98 Hart, *Jimmy Simpson*, 39–40.

99 Schäffer, *Old Indian Trails*, 51.

100 Simpson, "Days Remembered," 54.

101 Jon Whyte, "The Packer and the Painter[:] Jimmy Simpson and Carl Rungius," Jon Whyte Fonds (Banff: Archives of the Whyte Museum of the Canadian Rockies, M88/62), 4.

102 *Wary Game*, 1908, by Carl Rungius, is reproduced in *Carl Rungius[:] Artist and Sportsman* (Toronto: Warwick Publishing Inc., 2001), 73.

103 Simpson, "Days Remembered," 53.

104 Hart, *Jimmy Simpson*, 66–67.

105 William J. Schaldach, *Carl Rungius Big Game Painter[:] Fifty Years with Brush and Rifle* (West Hartford, Vt.: The Countryman Press, 1945), 82.

106 *The Old Billy* is reproduced in *Carl Rungius[:] Artist and Sportsman*, 6, 94. In the same volume, a further testament to the friendship of Carl Rungius and Jimmy Simpson is illustrated in the sketch for *The Mountaineer*, 131, with Jimmy posing on his horse. See page 159 for a reproduction of the finished painting.

107 Simpson, Letter to Thorington, May 22, 1969 (Banff: Archives of the Whyte Museum of the Canadian Rockies, M106/171), 18.

108 Schaldach, *Carl Rungius, Big Game Painter*, 84.

109 Philip Goodwin, *Pack Train Coming to Stream, Lead Rider Looking Back*, n.d. (Glenbow, 59.15.3) and Carl Rungius, *Crossing the Stream*, c.1920 are so similar in subject that Elizabeth Dear, guest curator, surmises that the men were on the same trip. Information about the Jimmy Simpson Collection supplied by email from Quyen Hoang, July 18, 2007.

110 Letter to Jim Simpson from Philip Goodwin, December 4, 1911 (Banff: Archives of the Whyte Museum of the Canadian Rockies, M78/2).

111 Letters to Mr. Simpson from Louis Fuertes, March 3 to May 12, 1921 (Banff: Archives of the Whyte Museum of the Canadian Rockies, M78/25, M78/26).

112 Whyte, "The Packer and the Painter," 3.

113 Letter to Mr. Simpson from Philip E. Dennison, March 31, 1920 (Banff: Archives of the Whyte Museum of the Canadian Rockies, M78/21).

114 Letter to Mr. Simpson from A. Thorburn, December 11, 1920 (Banff: Archives of the Whyte Museum of the Canadian Rockies, M78/24).

115 Receipt from A. Thorburn (Banff: Archives of the Whyte Museum of the Canadian Rockies, M78/25).

116 Joseph McAleenan, *Hunting with Rifle and Camera in the Canadian Rockies* (Privately printed diary of 20 copies, 1916), 2. Quoted by E.J. Hart, *The Place of Bows[:] Exploring the Heritage of the Banff-Bow Valley, Part I to 1930* (Banff: EJH Literary Enterprises, 1999), 318.

117 Hart, *Jimmy Simpson*, 94.

118 Hart, *Jimmy Simpson*, 96.

119 Hart, *Jimmy Simpson*, 96–97.

120 Letters from Allan Brooks to Jimmy Simpson, 1922, 1924, 1944 (Banff: Archives of the Whyte Museum of the Canadian Rockies, M78/31, 35, 36, 96).

121 Letter from E. Richardson, Calgary Exhibition and Stampede, to Jimmy Simpson, March 20, 1928 (Banff: Archives of the Whyte Museum of the Canadian Rockies, M78/50).

122 Letter from Carl Rungius to Jimmy Simpson, April 22, 1928 (Banff: Archives of the Whyte Museum of the Canadian Rockies, M78/50).

123 Hart, *Jimmy Simpson*, 158.

124 Hart, *Jimmy Simpson*, 176–77.

125 Hart, *Jimmy Simpson*, 201.

126 Hart, *Jimmy Simpson*, 201–2.

127 Typescript of Jimmy's letter to "Doc" Thorington, January 23, 1969 (Banff: Archives of the Whyte Museum of the Canadian Rockies, M106/171), 14.

128 Hart, *Jimmy Simpson*, 202.

129 Hart, *Jimmy Simpson*, 158.

130 See Jane Lytton Gooch, *Mount Assiniboine[:] Images in Art* (Calgary: Rocky Mountain Books, 2007), 126–29.

131 In a letter to Jimmy, December 13, 1945, Ian McTaggart Cowan thanks him for sending the painting, which recreates so well a scene familiar to them both after their trip together (Banff: Archives of the Whyte Museum of the Canadian Rockies, M78/98).

132 Letter to Jimmy from J. Smart, Controller, Canada Department of Mines & Resources, January 6, 1945 (Banff: Archives of the Whyte Museum of the Canadian Rockies, M78/98).

133 Hart, *Jimmy Simpson*, 200–201.

134 *Bulletin of the Trail Riders and Skyline Hikers of the Canadian Rockies*, No. 6 (Winter 1967), [15].

135 Hart, *Jimmy Simpson*, 155.

136 Letters from Carl Rungius to Jimmy Simpson, January to June 1922 (Banff: Archives of the Whyte Museum of the Canadian Rockies, M78/29, 30).

137 Schaldach, *Carl Rungius, Big Game Painter*, 2.

138 Jon Whyte and E.J. Hart, *Carl Rungius[:] Painter of the Western Wilderness* (Vancouver: Douglas & McIntyre, 1985), 12–14.

139 Whyte and Hart, *Rungius*, 41.

140 Eva Smithwick, "The Development of an Artist," *Glenbow* (Nov/Dec 1985), 7.

141 Whyte and Hart, *Rungius*, 14.

142 Whyte and Hart, *Rungius*, 16.

143 Whyte and Hart, *Rungius*, 22.

144 Schaldach, *Carl Rungius, Big Game Painter*, 81–82.

145 Whyte, "The Packer and the Painter," 15.

146 Whyte and Hart, *Rungius*, 104.

147 Whyte, "The Packer and the Painter," 20.

148 Herschel C. Parker, "Conquering Mt. McKinley. The Parker–Browne Expedition of 1912," *Canadian Alpine Journal*, V (1913), 17.

149 Belmore Browne, "Paintbrush on the Heights," *American Alpine Journal*, IV, 2 (1941), 196–99.

150 Browne, "Paintbrush," 197.

151 Walter D. Wilcox, "Early Days in the Canadian Rockies," *American Alpine Journal*, IV, 2 (1941), 185.

152 Agnes Browne's Diary (Banff: Archives of the Whyte

Museum of the Canadian Rockies, M473/9). Original diaries held by Special Collections Division of the Baker Library of Dartmouth College in Hanover, New Hampshire.

153 Hart, *Jimmy Simpson*, 128.

154 Agnes Browne's Diary (Banff: Archives of the Whyte Museum of the Canadian Rockies, M473/10).

155 Agnes Browne's Diary (Banff: Archives of the Whyte Museum of the Canadian Rockies, M473/11).

156 Frank Panabaker, *Reflected Lights* (Toronto: Ryerson Press, 1957), 50.

157 Francis Schwenger provided details about her parents' trip to the Rockies, July to September 1929, from her mother's diaries, by email May 30, 2008.

158 E.N. Davis, "The Official Trail Rides and Pow-Wow," *Bulletin of the Trail Riders of the Canadian Rockies*, No. 8 (May 26, 1926), 4–5.

159 Schaldach, *Carl Rungius, Big Game Painter*, 100.

160 "Proposed Ride to Bow Lake," *Bulletin of the Trail Riders of the Canadian Rockies*, No. 32 (June 1933), 7–9.

161 Terry Fenton, *A.C. Leighton and the Canadian Rockies* (Banff: Whyte Museum of the Canadian Rockies, 1989), 7.

162 David Leighton, "Cowboy with a Palette," *Artists, Builders and Dreamers: Fifty Years at the Banff School* (Toronto: McClelland & Stewart, 1982), 30.

163 Fenton, *Leighton and the Canadian Rockies*, 10.

164 Leighton, "Cowboy with a Palette," 29.

165 Lorne E. Render, *A.C. Leighton* (Glenbow–Alberta Institute, 1971), 7–8.

166 Fenton, *Leighton and the Canadian Rockies*, 10.

167 Leighton, "Cowboy with a Palette," 29–30.

168 Fenton, *Leighton and the Canadian Rockies*, 12, 15.

169 Walter J. Phillips writing about A.C. Leighton, Unidentified Clipping, Crabb Collection. Quoted in Douglas Cole and Maria Tippet, eds., *Phillips in Print[:] The Selected Writings of Walter J. Phillips on Canadian Nature and Art*, Vol. 6 (Winnipeg: Manitoba Record Society, 1982), 104.

170 *Phillips in Print*, 18.

171 "Canadian Art," *Phillips in Print*, 66.

172 "Seasons: Companions," *Phillips in Print*, 35.

173 Quoted by Render, *A.C. Leighton*, 114.

174 "Canadian Sketching Grounds: I Like Waterfalls," *Phillips in Print*, 40.

175 "Canadian Sketching Grounds: The Rocky Mountains," *Phillips in Print*, 54.

176 "Seasons: Wild Animals," *Phillips in Print*, 38.

177 Jon Whyte, *Mountain Glory[:] The Art of Peter and Catharine Whyte* (Banff: Whyte Museum of the Canadian Rockies, 1988), 10–11.

178 Jon Whyte, ed. *Pete 'n' Catharine[:] Their Story* (Banff: The Whyte Foundation, 1980), 46.

179 Whyte, *Mountain Glory*, 11, 14.

180 Whyte, *Mountain Glory*, 15.

181 Letter from Catharine Whyte to her mother, June 17, 1937 (Banff: Archives of the Whyte Museum of the Canadian Rockies, M36/102).

182 Letters from Catharine Whyte to her mother, August to September 1954 (Banff: Archives of the Whyte Museum of the Canadian Rockies, M36/135).

183 See Christine Barnes, *Great Lodges of the Canadian Rockies* (Bend, Oregon: W.W. West, 1999), 97–107, for an account of Jimmy Simpson's buildings at Bow Lake.

184 Conversation with Lee O'Donnell at the Pension Tannenhof on Cave Avenue in Banff, May 13, 2008, about the origins, development and successes of the artist-in-residence program at Num-Ti-Jah Lodge.

185 C.J.M. (Max) Elliott, "Lodge offers haven for artists," *The Banff Crag & Canyon*, June 19, 2002, 24.

186 Details about the shows were received by email from Roy Andersen, May 23, 2008.

List of Artists

Carolyn Oldale Adams
April on Bow Lake, 2004
Oil on canvas, 44.5 × 34.3 cm
Private collection of Lee O'Donnell
Photograph: Roy Andersen

Roger D. Arndt (1959–)
Winter Canyon, 2005
Oil on prepared panel, 40.6 × 40.6 cm
Collection of Num-Ti-Jah Lodge
Photograph: Allen Arndt

George Herbert William (Herb) Ashley (1908–2004)
Jimmy Simpson, 1983
Pastel, 65.0 × 50.0 cm
Collection of the Whyte Museum of the Canadian Rockies. AsH.03.01

Glen W. Boles (1934–)
Bow Lake, 2008
Acrylic on canvas, 22.9 × 30.5 cm
Private collection of Maxine Herbert
Photograph: Glen Boles

W.J. Bradley (1958–)
Blue Notes, 2007
Oil on canvas, 40.6 × 50.8 cm
Private collection of Christie Saunders
Photograph: Roy Andersen

Belmore Browne (1880–1954)
Bow Glacier, c.1928
Oil on board, 29.0 × 40.0 cm
Collection of the Whyte Museum of the Canadian Rockies. BwB.02.04

Clouds Over Crowfoot Glacier, no date
Oil on canvas, 63.5 × 76.2 cm
Collection of Glenbow Museum, Calgary, Canada. 58.34.4

Hector Lake, Canadian Rockies, no date
Watercolour on paper, 10.8 × 16.6 cm
Collection of the Whyte Museum of the Canadian Rockies. BwB.05.01

Pack Horses, Bow Lake, no date
Oil on canvas, 40.6 × 50.8 cm
Collection of Glenbow Museum, Calgary, Canada. 59.33.54

Bill Burns (1960–)
Rockies #6, 2003
Oil on board, 24.5 × 30.0 cm
Private collection of Lee O'Donnell
Photograph: Roy Andersen

Horace Champagne (1937–)
Bow Lake, Always Fresh with Nature's Surprises, c.2003
Pastel on paper, 61.0 × 45.7 cm
Private collection
Photograph: Horace Champagne

Saint Nicholas Peak, My Favourite Point of View, c.2003
Pastel on paper, 61.0 × 45.7 cm
Private collection
Photograph: Horace Champagne

C.J.M. (Max) Elliott (1962–)
Iceberg Lake (detail mixed-media collage), 2006
Acrylic on paper, 12.0 × 18.5 cm
Private collection of Emma and Joe Anderson
Photograph: Roy Andersen

May Afternoon, Crowfoot Glacier, 2006
Oil on canvas, 40.6 × 40.6 cm
Private collection of Tim Whyte
Photograph: Roy Andersen

Sarah Kidner (1964–)
Trees at Bow Lake, 2008
Oil on linen board, 45.7 × 61.0 cm
Private collection
Photograph: Sarah Kidner

Alfred Crocker (A.C.) Leighton (1900–1965)
Bow Lake and Mount Thompson, 1965
Watercolour, 27.0 × 33.0 cm
Collection of the Whyte Museum of the Canadian Rockies. LaC.05.27

Bow Pass – Early Morning, no date
Watercolour, 28.5 × 37.5 cm
Collection of the Whyte Museum of the Canadian Rockies. LaC.05.04

Untitled (Bow Lake), no date
Oil on canvas, 45.8 × 56.2 cm
Art Gallery of Alberta Collection
Gift of Archibald H. and Grace A.M. Dickson
Photograph © Art Gallery of Alberta. 94.36

Barbara Mary (Harvey) Leighton (1911–1986)
Evening, Bow Lake, no date
Linocut, 31.0 × 37.2 cm
Collection of the Whyte Museum of the Canadian Rockies. LeB.04.08

Donna Jo Massie (1948–)
Bow Lake, 2006
Watercolour on board, 35.6 × 68.6 cm
Private collection of Bob and Colleene Peterson
Photograph: Richard Berry

David McEown (1963–)
Bow River Headwaters, 2003
Watercolour, 139.7 × 91.6 cm
Private collection of Lee O'Donnell
Photograph: Roy Andersen

Sunrise on Bow Lake, 2009
Watercolour, 38.1 × 55.9 cm
Collection of the artist

Janet (Holly) B. Middleton (1922–)
Fireweed at Bow Lake and Crowfoot Glacier, 1996
Watercolour, 54.6 × 75.6 cm
Private collection
Photograph: Roy Andersen

Dominik J. Modlinski (1970–)
Creation, 2009
Oil on board, 40.6 × 50.8 cm
Collection of the artist
Photograph: Ted Clarke

Zelda Nelson (1943–)
Saint Nicholas Peak, 2005
Oil on canvas, 61.0 × 91.4 cm
Private collection of Nick J. Kuzyk
Photograph: Zelda Nelson

Erica Neumann (1968–)
Blondie, 1986–2004, 2005
Oil on canvas, 50.0 × 50.0 cm
Collection of Num-Ti-Jah Lodge
Photograph: Roy Andersen

Ralph E. Oberg (1950–)
Fall Morning at Bow Lake, 2001
Oil on canvas, 24.1 × 29.2 cm
Collection of Num-Ti-Jah Lodge
Photograph: Roy Andersen

Walter Joseph Phillips (1884–1963)
Mount Nicholas, 1963
Woodcut, 11.0 × 12.5 cm
Collection of the Whyte Museum of the Canadian Rockies. PhW.04.07
© Estate of Walter J. Phillips

Mountain Landscapes (Bow Lake, Early Spring), 1959
Watercolour and pencil on paper, 16.5 × 27.3 cm
Collection of Glenbow Museum, Calgary, Canada. 61.21.33, Purchased 1961
© Estate of Walter J. Phillips

The Source of the Bow, no date
Wood engraving, 16.0 × 10.0 cm
Collection of the Whyte Museum of the Canadian Rockies. PhW.04.14
© Estate of Walter J. Phillips

Carl Clemens Moritz Rungius (1869–1959)
A Camp in the Rockies, c.1925
Oil on canvas, 100.5 × 125.5 cm
Collection of Glenbow Museum, Calgary, Canada. 59.5.1

Bow Lake, no date
Oil on canvas, 27.9 × 33.0 cm
Collection of Glenbow Museum, Calgary, Canada. 59.67.177

Preliminary Sketch for *The Mountaineer*, c.1920
Oil on canvas, 44.2 × 37.4 cm
Collection of Glenbow Museum, Calgary, Canada. 59.7.528

Spreading Glacier Tongues, no date
Oil on canvas, 22.7 × 27.9 cm
Collection of Glenbow Museum, Calgary, Canada. 55.12.21

The Old Billy, 1911
Oil on canvas, 76.7 × 102.2 cm
Collection of Glenbow Museum, Calgary, Canada. 59.15.11

Carl Rungius and Jimmy Simpson,
Untitled (Mountain Sheep), 1918
Watercolour on paper, 22.0 × 29.5 cm
Collection of the Whyte Museum of the Canadian Rockies. RuC.05.01

Alice Saltiel-Marshall (1948–)
Crowfoot Mountain through the Looking-Glass, 1999
Studio oil, 91.4 × 137.2 cm
Private collection
Photograph: Roy Andersen

Saint Nicholas Peak, 1993
Watercolour on paper, 12.7 × 17.8 cm
Private collection of Rick and Lynn Dale
Photograph: Bill Marshall

Justin James McCarthy (Jimmy) Simpson, (1877–1972)
Autumn Evening, 1958
Watercolour, 29.5 × 34.5 cm
Collection of the Whyte Museum of the Canadian Rockies. SiJ.05.60

Bow Lake, 1962
Watercolour, 29.0 × 37.8 cm
Collection of the Whyte Museum of the Canadian Rockies. SiJ.05.59

Crowfoot Glacier, Bow Lake, 1943
Watercolour, 24.0 × 35.0 cm
Collection of the Whyte Museum of the Canadian Rockies. SiJ.05.02

Untitled (Moonlight, Bow Glacier), 1968
Watercolour, 8.9 × 17.8 cm
Collection of the Whyte Museum of the Canadian Rockies. SiJ.05.35

Winter Break-Up, 1957
Watercolour, 26.7 × 34.8 cm
Collection of Glenbow Museum, Calgary, Canada. 58.21.2

Jimmy Simpson and Carl Rungius
Untitled (Mountain Sheep), 1918
Watercolour on paper, 22.0 × 29.5 cm
Collection of the Whyte Museum of the Canadian Rockies. RuC.05.01

Mike Svob (1955–)
Winter, Bow Glacier, 2007
Acrylic on thick canvas wrap with black painted sides, 61.0 × 121.9 cm
Private collection of Kenneth and Heidy MacLeod
Photograph: Mike Svob

Catharine Robb Whyte (1906–1979)
Bow Panorama, no date
Oil on canvas, 14.2 × 35.0 cm
Collection of the Whyte Museum of the Canadian Rockies. WyC.01.039

Crowfoot Glacier, 1940–1960
Oil on canvas, 27.7 × 35.2 cm
Collection of the Whyte Museum of the Canadian Rockies. WyC.01.143

Mount Nicholas, no date
Oil on canvas, 25.1 × 30.0 cm
Collection of the Whyte Museum of the Canadian Rockies. WyC.01.273

Simpson's Cabin, 1940–1960
Oil on canvas, 27.0 × 33.0 cm
Collection of the Whyte Museum of the Canadian Rockies. WyC.01.321

Peter Whyte (1905–1966)
Bow Lake from the Summit, no date
Oil on canvas, 63.5 × 76.5 cm
Collection of the Whyte Museum of the Canadian Rockies. WyP.02.15

Mount Hector, Bow Lake, no date
Oil on canvas, 27.6 × 34.8 cm
Collection of the Whyte Museum of the Canadian Rockies. WyP.01.456

Elizabeth M. Wiltzen (1962–)
Bow Lake, 2003
Studio watercolour, 35.6 × 53.3 cm
Private collection of Tim Wiltzen
Photograph: Elizabeth Wiltzen

Rob Zeer (1956–)
Bow Lake in March, 2005
Acrylic on canvas, 77.4 × 100.0 cm
Collection of Num-Ti-Jah Lodge
Photograph: Roy Andersen

Bibliography

Abbot, Philip S. "The First Ascent of Mount Hector, Canadian Rockies," *Appalachia*, VIII (1896–1898), 1–17.

Alpine Club of Canada. "Report of 1910 Camp," *Canadian Alpine Journal*, III (1911), 189.

Ashley, G.H.W., Letter to W.P. Morgan, Curator, Dunlop Art Gallery, June 15, 1981. Calgary: Glenbow Archives.

Barfleet, A.M., and E.F.M. MacCarthy. "Two Englishmen in the Yoho Valley," *Canadian Alpine Journal*, II, 2 (1910), 143–57.

Barnes, Christine. *Great Lodges of the Canadian Rockies*. Bend, Oregon: W.W. West, 1999.

Beck, Janice Sanford. *No Ordinary Woman*[:] *The Story of Mary Schäffer Warren*. Calgary: Rocky Mountain Books, 2001. Third printing, 2006.

"Bow Valley and Yoho Expedition," *Canadian Alpine Journal*, III (1911), 194.

Brennan, Brian. *Romancing the Rockies*[:] *Mountaineers, Missionaries, Marilyn and More*. Calgary: Fifth House, 2005.

Brink, Nicky L., and Stephen R. Bown. *Forgotten Highways*[:] *Wilderness Journeys Down the Historic Trails of the Canadian Rockies*. Edmonton: Brindle & Glass, 2007.

Brown, Stewardson. *Alpine Flora of the Canadian Rocky Mountains*. Illustrated with water-colour drawings and photographs by Mrs. Charles Schäffer. New York and London: G.P. Putnam's Sons, 1907.

Browne, Agnes. Diaries. Banff: Archives of the Whyte Museum of the Canadian Rockies, M473/9, 10, 11.

Browne, Belmore. "Paintbrush on the Heights," *American Alpine Journal*, IV, 2 (1941), 196–99.

Burpee, Lawrence J. "The Five-Day Ride," *Bulletin of The Trail Riders of the Canadian Rockies*, 11 (Sept. 1, 1926), 2–4.

Carl Rungius[:] *Artist and Sportsman*. Companion to the Exhibit organized by Glenbow Museum, 2000. Toronto: Warwick Publishing, 2001.

Cole, Douglas, and Maria Tippett, eds. *Phillips in Print*[:] *The Selected Writings of Walter J. Phillips on Canadian Nature and Art*. Vol. 6 of The Manitoba Record Society Publications. Winnipeg: Manitoba Record Society, 1982.

Coleman, A.P. *The Canadian Rockies*[:] *New and Old Trails*. Mountain classics collection, 1. Surrey, BC: Rocky Mountain Books, 2006. First published 1911 by H. Frowde.

Coleman, H. Travers. "Carl Rungius: Artist and Trail Hiker," *Skyline Trails Bulletin*, 69 (Summer 1960), 5–6.

Conaty, Gerald T., ed. *The Bow*[:] *Living with a River*. Essays by Gerald T. Conaty, Daryl Betenia and Catharine Mastin. Glenbow Museum. Toronto: Key Porter Books, 2004.

Darling, B.S. "Up the Bow and Down the Yoho," *Canadian Alpine Journal*, III (1911), 157–71.

Davis, E.N. "The Official Trail Rides and Pow-Wow," *Bulletin of the Trail Riders of the Canadian Rockies*, 8 (May 26, 1926), 4–5.

Dixon, Harold B. "The Ascent of Mount Lefroy and Other Climbs in the Rocky Mountains," *The Alpine Journal*, XIX (1898–1899), 97–112.

Dowling, Phil. *The Mountaineers*[:] *Famous Climbers in Canada*. Edmonton: Hurtig, 1979.

East, Alfred. "Mountains from a Painter's Point of View," *The Alpine Journal*, XXIII (1906–1907), 617–23.

Edwards, Ralph. *The Trail to the Charmed Land*. Saskatoon: H.R. Larson, 1950.

Elliott, C.J.M. (Max). "Lodge offers haven for artists," *The Banff Crag & Canyon*, June 19, 2002, 24.

Erasmus, Peter, and Henry Thompson. *Buffalo Days and Nights*. Calgary: Fifth House, 1999. First edition published 1976 by Glenbow–Alberta Institute.

Fay, Charles E. "Old Times in the Canadian Alps," *Canadian Alpine Journal*, XII (1922), 91–103.

Fenton, Terry. *A.C. Leighton and the Canadian Rockies*. Banff: Whyte Museum of the Canadian Rockies, 1989.

Fleming, Sir Sandford. "Memories of the Mountains," *Canadian Alpine Journal*, I, 1 (1907), 10–33.

Gooch, Jane Lytton. *Mount Assiniboine*[:] *Images in Art*. Calgary: Rocky Mountain Books, 2007.

Haig, Bruce. *James Hector, Explorer*. Following Historic Trails. Calgary: Detselig Enterprises, 1983.

Hart, E.J. *Diamond Hitch*[:] *The Pioneer Guides and Outfitters of Banff and Jasper*. Banff: EJH Literary Enterprises, 2001. First published 1979 by Summerthought.

———. *Jimmy Simpson*[:] *Legend of the Rockies*. 2nd ed. Banff: Altitude, 1999. First published 1991. (Republished Calgary: Rocky Mountain Books, 2009).

———. *The Place of Bows*[:] *Exploring the Heritage of the Banff-Bow Valley, Part I, to 1930*. Banff: EJH Literary Enterprises, 1999.

———. *Yahe-Weha – Mountain Woman*[:] *The Life and Travels of Mary Schäffer Warren, 1861–1939*. Introduction to *A Hunter of Peace: Mary T.S. Schäffer's Old Indian Trails of the Canadian Rockies... with Photographs by the Author [et al.]*, edited by E.J. Hart. Banff: The Whyte Foundation, 1980.

Hector, James. "Journal." In *Exploration – British North America: The Journals, Detailed Reports, and Observations Relative to the Exploration, by Captain Palliser, of That Portion of British North America, Which, in Latitude, Lies between the British Boundary Line and the Height of Land or Watershed of the Northern or Frozen Ocean Respectively, and in Longitude, between the Western Shore of Lake Superior and the Pacific Ocean During the Years 1857, 1858, 1859, and 1860.* London: Printed by G.E. Eyre and W. Spottiswoode for H.M. Stationery Office, 1863, 98–116.

"Herb Ashley." Obituary. *The Banff Crag & Canyon*, Oct. 26, 2004.

Hickson, J.W.A. "Notes of a Trip to the Saskatchewan River and Freshfield Glacier," *Canadian Alpine Journal*, IV (1914–1915), 93–98.

"In Memoriam, Arthur Philemon Coleman, 1852–1939," *American Alpine Journal*, IV, 1 (1940), 119–21.

"In Memoriam, Sir James Outram," *Canadian Alpine Journal*, XV (1925), 127–28.

Lakusta, Ernie. *The Intrepid Explorer*[:] *James Hector's Explorations in the Canadian Rockies*. Calgary: Fifth House, 2007.

Leighton, David, and Peggy Leighton. *Artists, Builders and Dreamers: Fifty Years at the Banff School*. Toronto: McClelland & Stewart, 1982.

"List of Members," *Canadian Alpine Journal*, I, 1 (1907), 182–196.

MacCarthy, E.F.M., and A.M. Barfleet. "Two Englishmen in the Yoho Valley," *Canadian Alpine Journal*, II, 2 (1910), 143–57.

McCowan, Dan. *Hill-Top Tales*. Toronto: Macmillan Canada, 1948.

Noyes, Charles L. "Mount Balfour and the Waputehk Snow-field," *Appalachia*, IX, 1 (1899–1901), 20–31.

Outram, James. *In the Heart of the Canadian Rockies*. London and New York: Macmillan, 1923. First published 1905. (Republished Calgary: Rocky Mountain Books, 2007).

Panabaker, Frank Shirley. *Reflected Lights*. Toronto: Ryerson Press, 1957.

Parker, Herschel C. "Conquering Mt. McKinley. The Parker–Browne Expedition of 1912," *Canadian Alpine Journal*, V (1913), 11–19.

Phillips, Walter J. "Art and Artists," *Winnipeg Evening Tribune*, May 13, 1939, 8.

"Proposed Ride to Bow Lake," *Bulletin of The Trail Riders of the Canadian Rockies*, 32 (June 1933), 6–9.

Putnam, William Lowell, Glen W. Boles and Roger W. Laurilla. *Place Names of the Canadian Alps*. Revelstoke, BC: Footprint, 1990. (Revised and updated as *Canadian Mountain Place Names: The Rockies and Columbia Mountains*, Calgary: Rocky Mountain Books, 2006).

Render, Lorne E. *A.C. Leighton*. Calgary: Glenbow–Alberta Institute, 1971.

Sandford, R.W. *The Canadian Alps*[:] *The History of Mountaineering in Canada*. Vol. 1. Banff: Altitude, 1990.

———. *Trail Riders of the Canadian Rockies*[:] *75th Anniversary 1923–1998*. Canmore, Alta.: The Alpine Club of Canada and McAra Printing, 1998.

Schaldach, William J. *Carl Rungius, Big Game Painter*[:] *Fifty Years with Brush and Rifle*. West Hartford, Vt.: The Countryman Press, 1945.

Schäffer, Mary T.S. *Old Indian Trails of the Canadian Rockies*. In *A Hunter of Peace: Mary T.S. Schäffer's Old Indian Trails of the Canadian Rockies … with Photographs by the Author [et al.]*, edited by E.J. Hart. Banff: The Whyte Foundation, 1980. Originally published in 1911 by G.P. Putnam's Sons. (Reprinted Calgary: Rocky Mountain Books, 2007).

———. "Sir James Hector," *Rod and Gun in Canada*, V, 8 (January 1904), 416–18.

Secor, Deborah. "Joie de Vivre," *The Pastel Journal*, 60 (February 2009), 32–39.

Simpson, James. "Days Remembered," *American Alpine Journal*, XIX, 1 (1974), 43–54.

———. Letter to "Doc" Thorington, January 23, 1969. Banff: Archives of the Whyte Museum of the Canadian Rockies, M106/171, 14.

———. Letter to "Doc" Thorington, May 22, 1969. Banff: Archives of the Whyte Museum of the Canadian Rockies, M106/171, 18.

———. Letters to James Simpson. Banff: Archives of the Whyte Museum of the Canadian Rockies, M78/2, 21, 24–26, 29–31, 35, 36, 50, 96, 98.

———. Photograph in *Bulletin of The Trail Riders and Skyline Hikers of the Canadian Rockies*, 6 (Winter 1967), [15].

Skyline Hikers of the Canadian Rockies. *Fifty Years of Trails and Tales*. Edited by Marian Goldstrom and Stephen G. Klatzel. Calgary: Skyline Hikers of the Canadian Rockies, 1982.

Smith, Cyndi. *Off The Beaten Track*[:] *Women Adventurers and Mountaineers in Western Canada*. Canmore, Alta.: Coyote Books, 1989.

Smithwick, Eva. "The Development of an Artist," *Glenbow* (November/December 1985), 4–8.

Snow, John. *These Mountains Are Our Sacred Places*. Calgary: Fifth House, 2005. First published 1977 by Samuel Stevens.

Spry, Irene M. *The Palliser Expedition*[:] *The Dramatic Story of Western Canadian Exploration 1857–1860*.

Calgary: Fifth House, 1995. First published 1963 by Macmillan.

Stutfield, Hugh E.M., and J. Norman Collie. *Climbs & Exploration in the Canadian Rockies*. Mountain Classics Collection no. 4. Calgary: Rocky Mountain Books, 2008. First published 1903 by Longmans, Green & Co., New York and London.

Tetarenko, Lorne, and Kim Tetarenko. *Ken Jones*[:] *Mountain Man*. Calgary: Rocky Mountain Books, 1996.

Thompson, Charles S. "At the Headwaters of the Bow," *Appalachia*, VIII (1896–1898), 320–27.

Walcott, Mary Vaux. *North American Wild Flowers*. 5 vols. Washington, DC: Smithsonian Institution, 1925.

Weed, George M. "Pipestone Creek and a New Pass to the Upper Bow," *Appalachia*, IX (1899–1901), 10–20.

Whyte, Catharine. Letters. Banff: Archives of the Whyte Museum of the Canadian Rockies, M36/102, 135, 136.

Whyte, Jon. *Mountain Glory*[:] *The Art of Peter and Catharine Whyte*. Banff: Whyte Museum of the Canadian Rockies, 1988.

———. "The Packer and the Painter[:] Jimmy Simpson and Carl Rungius," Jon Whyte Fonds. Banff: Archives of the Whyte Museum of the Canadian Rockies, M88/62.

———, ed. *Pete 'n' Catharine*[:] *Their Story*. Banff: The Whyte Foundation, 1980.

Whyte, Jon, and E.J. Hart. *Carl Rungius*[:] *Painter of the Western Wilderness*. Vancouver: Douglas & McIntyre, 1985.

Wilcox, Walter D. "Early Days in the Canadian Rockies," *American Alpine Journal*, IV, 2 (1941), 177–89.

———. *The Rockies of Canada*. A revised and enlarged edition of *Camping in the Canadian Rockies*. 3rd ed. New York and London: G.P. Putnam's Sons, 1909. First published 1900 by The Knickerbocker Press. (Reprinted Calgary: Rocky Mountain Books, 2008).

Williams, M.B. *The Banff Jasper Highway*[:] *Descriptive Guide*. Illustrated by Mabel Bain. Saskatoon: H.R. Larsen Publishing Co., 1948.

Woolley, Hermann. "Six Weeks in the Canadian Rocky Mountains," *The Alpine Journal*, XXI (1902–1903), 364–77.

Zimon, Kathy E. *Alberta Society of Artists*[:] *The First Seventy Years*. Calgary: University of Calgary Press, 2000.

Index

A

Abbot, Philip 19, 21, 25, 30, 34
Adams, Carolyn Oldale 64, 112, 185
Adams, Mollie 41
Alberta College of Art and Design 67, 73. *See also* Provincial Institute of Technology and Art.
Albizzi, Marquis Nicholas degli. *See* Beach-Nicholl, Mary de la
Allen, Samuel 21
Alpine Club of Canada 26, 32, 42
Alpine Flora of the Canadian Rocky Mountains 42
Andersen, Roy 64, 180
Appalachian Club 19, 21, 26, 30, 32, 34, 35, 37, 58
Arndt, Roger D. 65, 164, 185
Arnold, Arthur 24
Art of History, The 64, 68, 180
Ashley, Herb 2, 65, 185
Avenue West 63

B

Baker, George Pierce 25, 31, 35
Ballard, Fred 39
Banff Crag & Canyon, The 64
Banff School of Fine Arts 50, 69
Beach, Bill 38
Beach-Nichol, Mary de la 44
Beatty (Beattie?), Wilfred (Wilfrid?) 36
Black, C. 31
Boles, Duke of Eureka 62
Boles, Glen W. 66, 138, 185
Bradley. W.J. 66, 162, 185
Brearley, Arthur 18
Brewster, Pat 57
Brewster's Icefield Chalet 64
Bronx Zoo 44
Brooks, Allan 49
Browne, Agnes 55, 88, 152
Browne, Belmore 51, 55, 57, 58, 60, 63, 65, 88, 98, 152, 174, 185
Browne, Evelyn 55, 88
Browne, George 55, 88
Brown, Stewardson 41
Brunstermann, Miss 38
Bulletin of the Trail Riders and Skyline Hikers, The 52, 58
Burns, Bill 66, 146, 185

C

Calgary Allied Arts Centre 50
Calgary Stampede 49
Calverley, H.W. 18
Campbell, Bob 32, 33
Camping in the Canadian Rockies 21
Canadian Alpine Journal 43
Canadian Pacific Railway (CPR) 18, 37, 45, 48, 58
Carnegie Prize 54
Champagne, Horace 67, 86, 148, 185
Chateau Lake Louise 58
Coleman, Dr. A.P. 41
Collie, Dr. J. Norman 25, 31, 32, 34, 35, 38, 39
Curtis, Rest F. 32, 33

D

Darling, B.S. 75, 151
Dawson, Dr. G.M. 24
degli Albizzi. *See* Beach-Nicholl, Mary de la
Dennison, Philip E. 47
Dickerson, Captain 25
Dixon, Harold B. 25
Dodge, Ira 54
Dominion Topographic Survey 19, 39
Drewry, W.S. 18
Drummond-Davis, Nora 60, 65

E

Edwards, Ralph 32, 33, 34, 38, 58
Elliott, Max 63, 67, 122, 156, 185
Eureka, Duke of. *See* Boles, Duke of Eureka

F

Fay, Dr. Charles E. 19, 21, 25, 32, 33
Fort Edmonton 18
Freshfield, Douglas 32
Fuertes, Louis Agassiz 47, 50
Fulda, Dr. Clemens 53

G

Gallery of Wild Animals 54
Gibbon, John Murray 57, 59
Glacier House 41
Glenbow Foundation 50
Glenbow Museum 46, 47, 48, 50
Godwin, Fred 53
Goodwin, Philip 47, 50
Gordon, Sir John Campbell Hamilton, Earl of Aberdeen 28
Groll, Albert 48, 50
Group of Seven, The 60, 61, 68

H

Habel, Professor Jean 33
Harmon, Byron 43, 57, 96
Harvey, Barbara. *See* Leighton, Barbara (Harvey)
Harvie, Eric 50
Haukaness, Lars 49, 59
Heart of the Canadian Rockies. See *In The Heart of the Canadian Rockies.*
Hector, Dr. James 15, 31, 40, 41
Hibbard, Aldro T. 61
Hiland, Mr. 19
Hornaday, William 53

I

Illahee Lodge 55, 57
In The Heart of the Canadian Rockies 39

K

Kaufmann, Christian 39, 43
Kidner, Sarah 68, 126, 185
Kootenay 17

L

Laggan 18, 19, 21, 26, 31, 32, 34, 38, 42, 171
Lake Louise Chalet 21
Lang, Harry 21, 46
Laut, Agnes 38
Leighton, A.C. 58, 59, 78, 102, 178, 185
Leighton, Barbara (Harvey) 59, 136, 185
Longstaff, Dr. Thomas G. 43
Longstaff, Katherine 43
Lusk, Tom 24

M

MacDonald, J.E.H. 61
Massie, Donna Jo 68, 120, 185
McAleenan, Joseph 48
McArthur, J.J. 18
McEown, David 67, 69, 108, 168, 185
McNichol, Frank 38
McTaggart Cowan, Ian 52
Michael, Arthur 26
Middleton, Holly 68, 69, 118, 185
Modlinski, Dominik 65, 66, 67, 70, 106, 185
Morant, Nicholas 23

N

Nashan-esen (Jimmy Simpson) 44

National Academy of Design, New York 54
Nelson, Zelda 70, 140, 185
Neumann, Erica 70, 180, 185
New York Zoological Society 44, 53
New York Zoological Society Bulletin. See *Zoological Society Bulletin*
Nichols, Harry P. 32, 34
Nimrod 16
Noble, Mr. 49
North American Wild Flowers 43
Noyes, Charles L. 26, 32, 34, 37
Num-Ti-Jah Lodge 37, 38, 49, 51, 63, 65, 66, 68, 70, 71, 110, 114, 120, 122, 126, 132, 176, 178, 180

O

Oberg, Ralph E. 71, 134, 186
O'Donnell, Lee 63, 65, 67, 70
Old Billy, The 46
Old Indian Trails 44
Otto Brothers 43
Outram, Reverend James 39, 43, 94

P

Paintbox 50, 52
Palliser, Captain John 15
Panabaker, Frank 57
Parker, Herschel 26, 55
Parker & Twyford expedition 38, 44
Pearson, General Fred 25
Peyto, Bill 21, 25, 31, 32, 39
Phillips, Walter J. 59, 69, 114, 131, 142, 166, 186
Provincial Institute of Technology and Art 49, 59, 69. *See also* Alberta College of Art and Design.

R

Ram Pasture, The 38, 51, 56, 104, 132, 146, 152, 176
Reid, Williamina (Billie) Ross. *See* Simpson, Billie
Richardson, L. 31
Rockies of Canada, The 21, 25
Rogers, Major A.B. 18
Ross, James 22
Rungius, Carl 43, 45, 46, 47, 49, 50, 51, 52, 53, 57, 58, 61, 63, 65, 71, 92, 132, 172, 186
Rungius, Louise 45, 52, 57
Russell, Charles 47, 48, 50

S

Salmagundi Club 47, 48, 57
Saltiel-Marshall, Alice 71, 128, 144, 186
Sarbach, Peter 25, 31
Schäffer, Dr. Charles 41
Schäffer, Mary (Warren) 38, 41, 44, 57
Schaldach, William 54
School of the Museum of Fine Arts, Boston 61
Scott, Duncan Campbell 60
Simpson, Billie 52, 62
Simpson, Jimmy 2, 37, 39, 42, 43, 46, 47, 49, 50, 51, 52, 53, 54, 56, 57, 61, 62, 63, 82, 100, 104, 116, 152, 160, 170, 171, 172, 176, 186
Smart, Mr. J. 52
Smithsonian Institution 47
Source, The 64, 68
Stephens, Fred 24
Stoney 15, 44, 63
Stutfield, Hugh E.M. 32, 38
Svob, Mike 65, 66, 68, 72, 158, 186

T

Tabuteau, Jim 38
Thompson, Charles S. 19, 21, 25, 32, 33, 34
Thompson, David 17
Thorburn, Archibald 47, 50
Thorington, Dr. J. Monroe 37, 50, 171
Trail Riders of the Canadian Rockies, The 57, 59
Trail to the Charmed Land, The 33

U

Unwin, Sid 42

V

Vaux, Mary (Walcott) 43

W

Walcott, Mary Vaux 43
Walling brothers 38
Warren, Billy 41
Wary Game 44
Weed, George M. 32, 34
Wheeler, A.O. 39, 43
Whyte, Catharine Robb 51, 60, 63, 80, 94, 154, 176, 186
Whyte Museum 51, 68, 71
Whyte, Peter 51, 60, 61, 63, 65, 76, 84, 186
Whyte, Tim 63, 67, 70
Wilcox, Walter 21, 31, 41, 55, 74, 91, 94, 97, 130
Wilson, Tom 18, 19, 21, 31, 32, 37, 41
Wiltzen, Elizabeth 72, 124, 186
Woolley, Herman 32, 38

Z

Zeer, Rob 73, 110, 186
Zoological Society Bulletin 44, 54

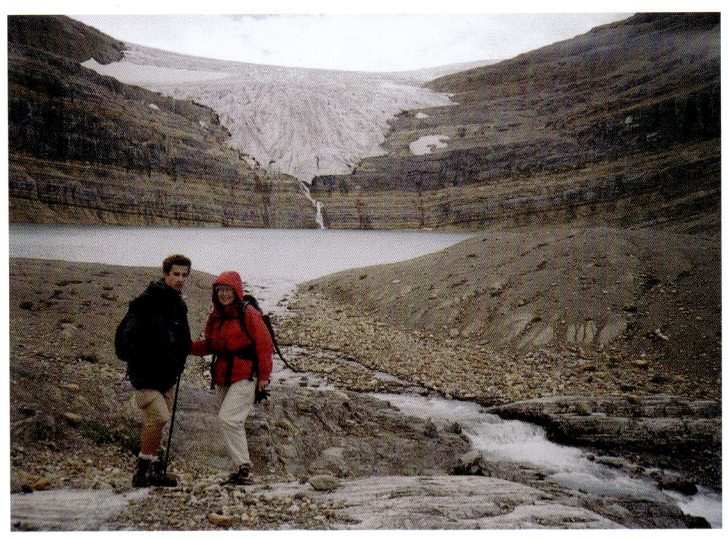

About the Author

This photograph of Jane Gooch and her son Robert was taken at Iceberg Lake, just above Bow Falls, on a hike guided by Max Elliott. Bow Lake has become a favourite destination over the years, with many happy hours hiking the trails. Most recently, in August 2008, in the meadows near Helen Lake, Jane and Robert had the good fortune to encounter, in a non-threatening way, a grizzly and her cub, possibly descendants of Blondie. Summer excursions to the Rockies from her home in Vancouver allow Jane to see the landscape that has inspired so many artists. During the winters, she teaches Renaissance literature at the University of British Columbia. Her interest in arts and letters, combined with her love of the mountains, has led to three books on the art of special places in the Rockies: *Artists of the Rockies: Inspiration of Lake O'Hara* (The Rockies Network and Alpine Club of Canada, 2003); *Mount Assiniboine: Images in Art* (Rocky Mountain Books, 2007) and now *Bow Lake: Wellspring of Art* (Rocky Mountain Books, 2010).